HISTORY COMICS

T0022884

WORLD WAR II
FIGHT ON THE HOME FRONT

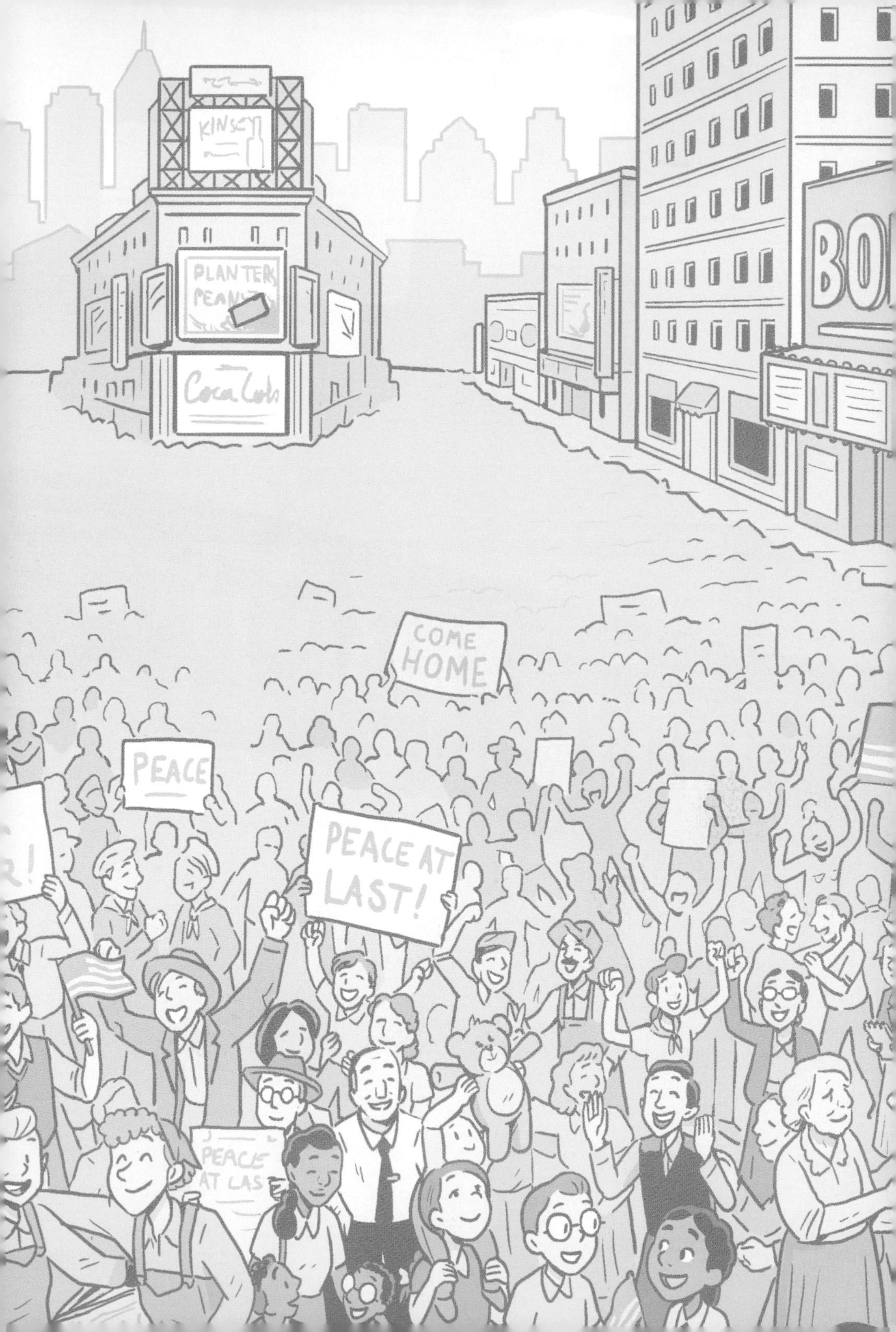
KINSEY
PLANTERS PEANUTS
Coca-Cola
COME HOME
PEACE
PEACE AT LAST!
PEACE AT LAS

HISTORY COMICS

WORLD WAR II
FIGHT ON THE HOME FRONT

written by
Kate Hannigan
art by
Josh Rosen

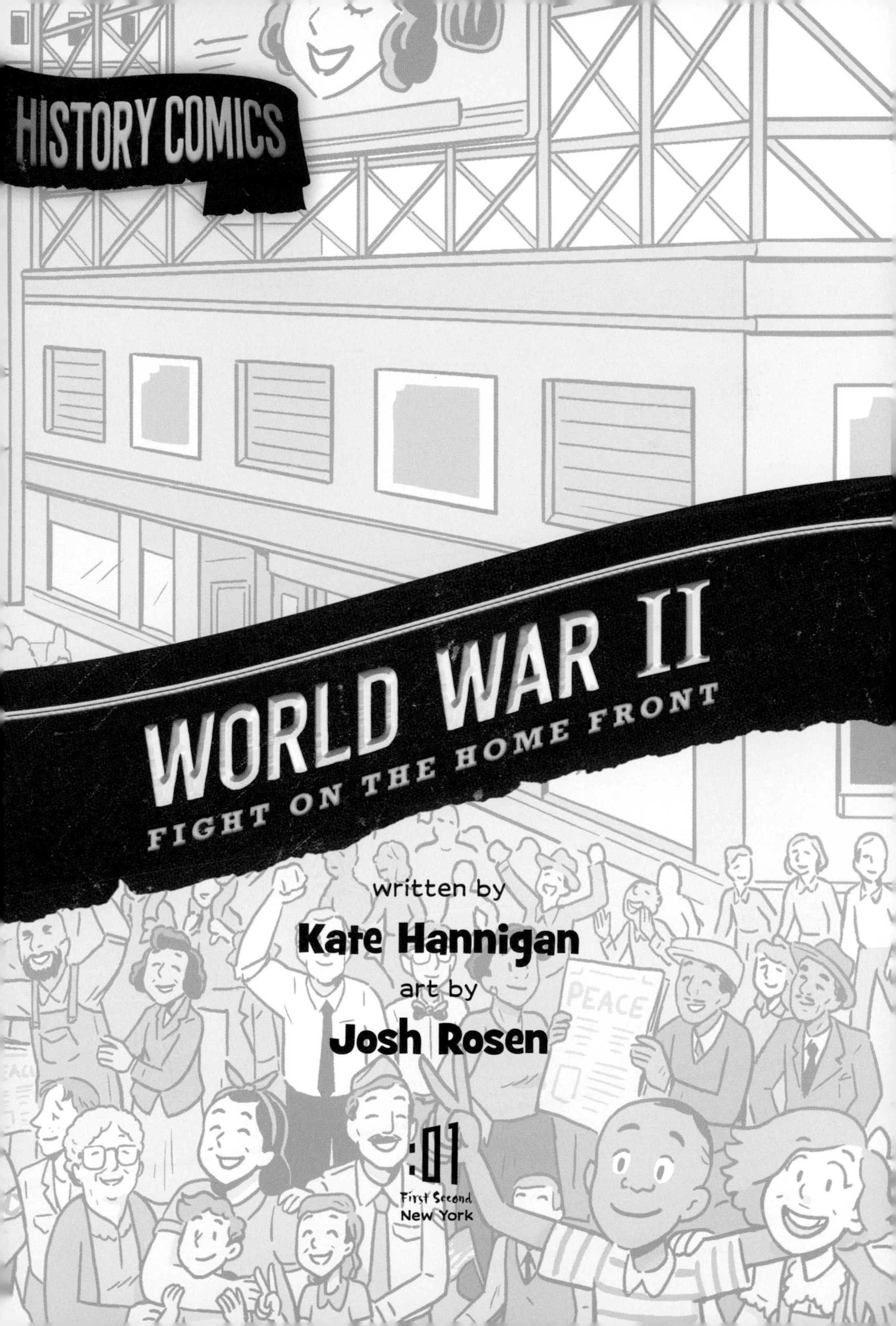

PEACE

:01
First Second
New York

First Second

Published by First Second
First Second is an imprint of Roaring Brook Press,
a division of Holtzbrinck Publishing Holdings Limited Partnership
120 Broadway, New York, NY 10271
firstsecondbooks.com
mackids.com

Library of Congress Control Number: 2022920426

Our books may be purchased in bulk for promotional, educational, or business use.
Please contact your local bookseller or the Macmillan Corporate and Premium Sales Department
at (800) 221-7945 ext. 5442 or by email at MacmillanSpecialMarkets@macmillan.com.

FIRST

EDITION

First edition, 2023
Edited by Dave Roman and Benjamin A. Wilgus
Cover design by Yan L. Moy
Interior book design by Yan L. Moy and Casper Manning
Flatting by Adam Aylard
Production editing by Avia Perez
WWII consultants: James J. Kimble and Kerris Dillon

Drawn and colored in Adobe Photoshop, using a Wacom Cintiq drawing tablet. Layouts and word balloons
produced in Clip Studio Paint. Lettered with the Soliloquous font from Comicraft.

Printed in China by Toppan Leefung Printing Ltd., Dongguan City, Guangdong Province

ISBN 978-1-250-79334-8 (paperback)
10 9 8 7 6 5 4 3 2 1

ISBN 978-1-250-79333-1 (hardcover)
10 9 8 7 6 5 4 3 2 1

It's easy to make a list of American heroes from World War II. Many historians would list public leaders like President Franklin D. Roosevelt and First Lady Eleanor Roosevelt. Others would point to military planners, like General Dwight D. Eisenhower, or those who fought valiantly on the front lines, such as Audie Murphy—who won so many awards for bravery on the battlefield that there were no more left to win. And then there were the millions of Rosie the Riveters, women who rolled up their sleeves and took over the wartime factories to ensure that the troops could fight. All of them were heroes that we still remember today.

But how many remember the ordinary heroes like Mary Norsworthy and Betty Fraiser? The two schoolgirls were twelve years old in the summer of 1942, only six months after the surprise attack at Pearl Harbor pulled the United States into war. After hearing that the steel factories desperately needed old scrap metal to melt down for more weapons production, Mary and Betty began to comb their neighborhood in tiny Gothenburg, Nebraska, for even the smallest metal objects.

When they knocked on the door of an elderly woman on 10th Street, she had a surprise for them. There was an antique cast-iron stove in the basement, she said. Knowing that the old metal was needed for the war effort, she was glad to donate it for scrap. But there was a problem. The stove weighed more than the two youngsters combined!

The girls decided that they would try to move it themselves. Working together, they gradually pushed the stove up the basement stairs. After a brief rest, they then slowly moved it down the sidewalk, aiming for the big community scrap metal pile several blocks away. The stove seemed to get heavier and heavier as they went. But they were determined. The two young girls heaved their prize across town, inch by inch. The journey took them all afternoon.

Mary's and Betty's adventure with the stove reveals a great deal about the American experience during World War II. Every single person on the vast home front—about 130 million people in all—was called to contribute in every way that they could. It would be nice to be able to say that all of them did their part cheerfully and without grumbling. But that would be untrue. In reality, many of those in the wartime generation struggled and despaired and wished for it all to end. Living through the war was not at all like a pleasant picnic. It was a time of worry and shortages and hard work.

Under such conditions, it would have been easy to give up. But most home-front citizens didn't give up. Instead, they were like Mary and Betty, stepping up to do what they could even when it wasn't fun or convenient or easy. When I interviewed Mary in 2007 for a documentary movie project (by this time, she was using her married name, Mary Ostergard, and she was seventy-seven years old), she remembered with great clarity how *difficult* it had been to haul that cast-iron stove across town. Her pride in facing the challenge, even looking back some sixty-five years later, was remarkable. But she and Betty were like most wartime Americans—they felt it was their duty to contribute to the war effort, despite the difficulties. *That's* why their contributions were heroic. This also is why it's important that those of us in younger generations remember the story of the war that they lived through.

Of course, one might say that the story of World War II is too big to understand. After all, thousands of books have been written about it. But as the book you're reading right now shows, that big story is really a great many small stories. Yes, many of those stories are about the Roosevelts and the generals and the soldiers and the Rosies. But it is easy to forget that it's also the story of children like Mary and Betty, who even at the age of twelve believed that it was their civic duty to heave a rusting potbelly stove across their small town, inch by inch.

Many of the stories in this book will inspire you, because they are about people much like those two girls. These stories teach us that wartime, as awful as it can be, sometimes brings out the best in people. They teach us the importance of sacrificing for others in our families and communities. And they teach us that despite their all-too-human flaws, heroes can emerge from the most unlikely places—no matter their race, personal beliefs, neighborhood, or family history.

Indeed, the heroes of the World War II home front included senior citizens, middle-aged laborers, men serving as air-raid wardens for their block, women working in factories and driving buses, and even children gathering scrap metal and collecting paper to recycle. Some of that recycled paper, by the way, came from the kids' own superhero comic books, which they willingly gave up to support the war effort. You see, they knew that the United States didn't really need those superheroes to win the war. It had plenty of everyday heroes already, right here on the home front.

—**James J. Kimble,** author of *Prairie Forge:*
The Extraordinary Story of the Nebraska Scrap Metal Drive of World War II

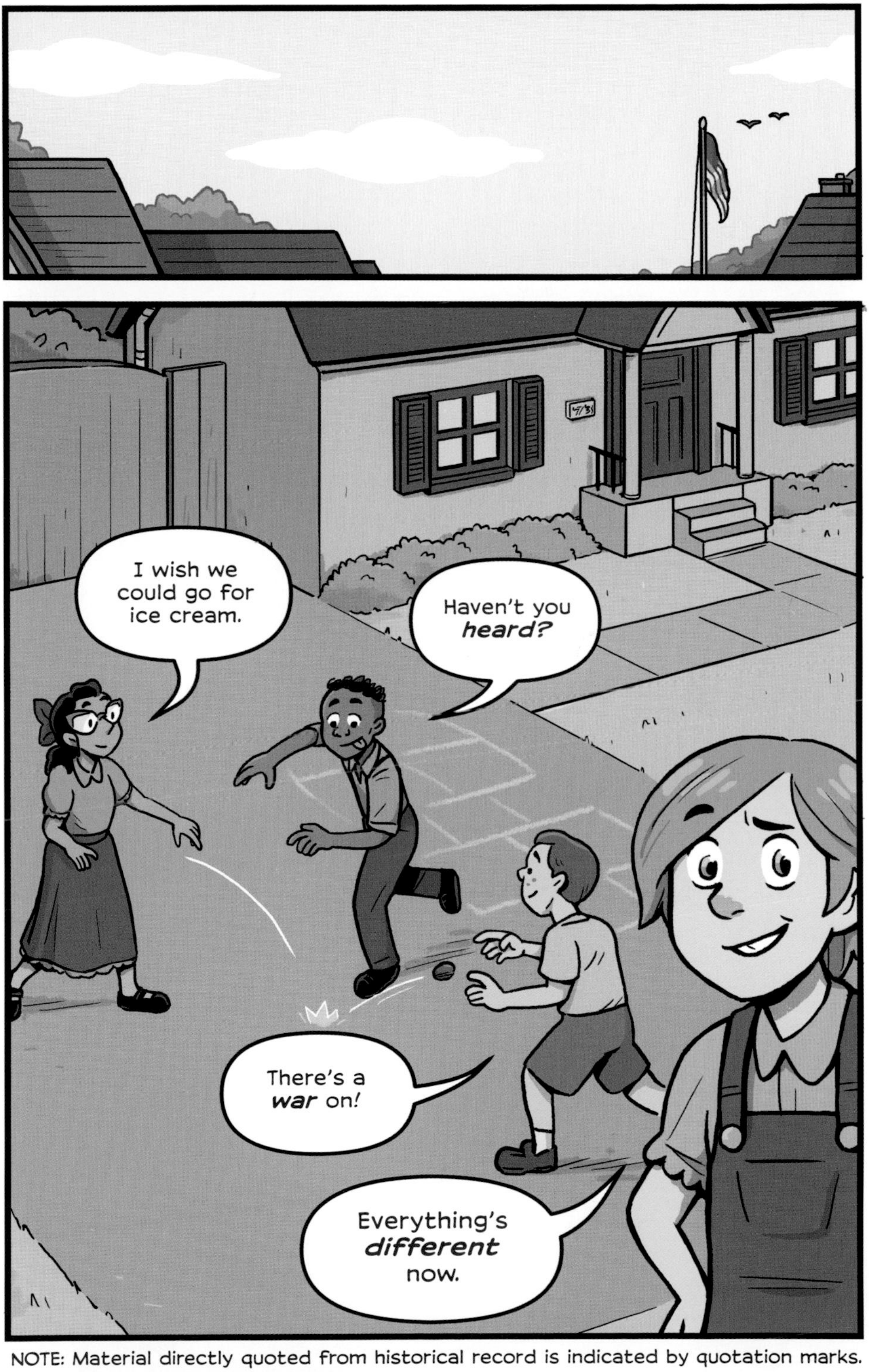
I wish we could go for ice cream.
Haven't you *heard?*
There's a *war* on!
Everything's *different* now.

NOTE: Material directly quoted from historical record is indicated by quotation marks.

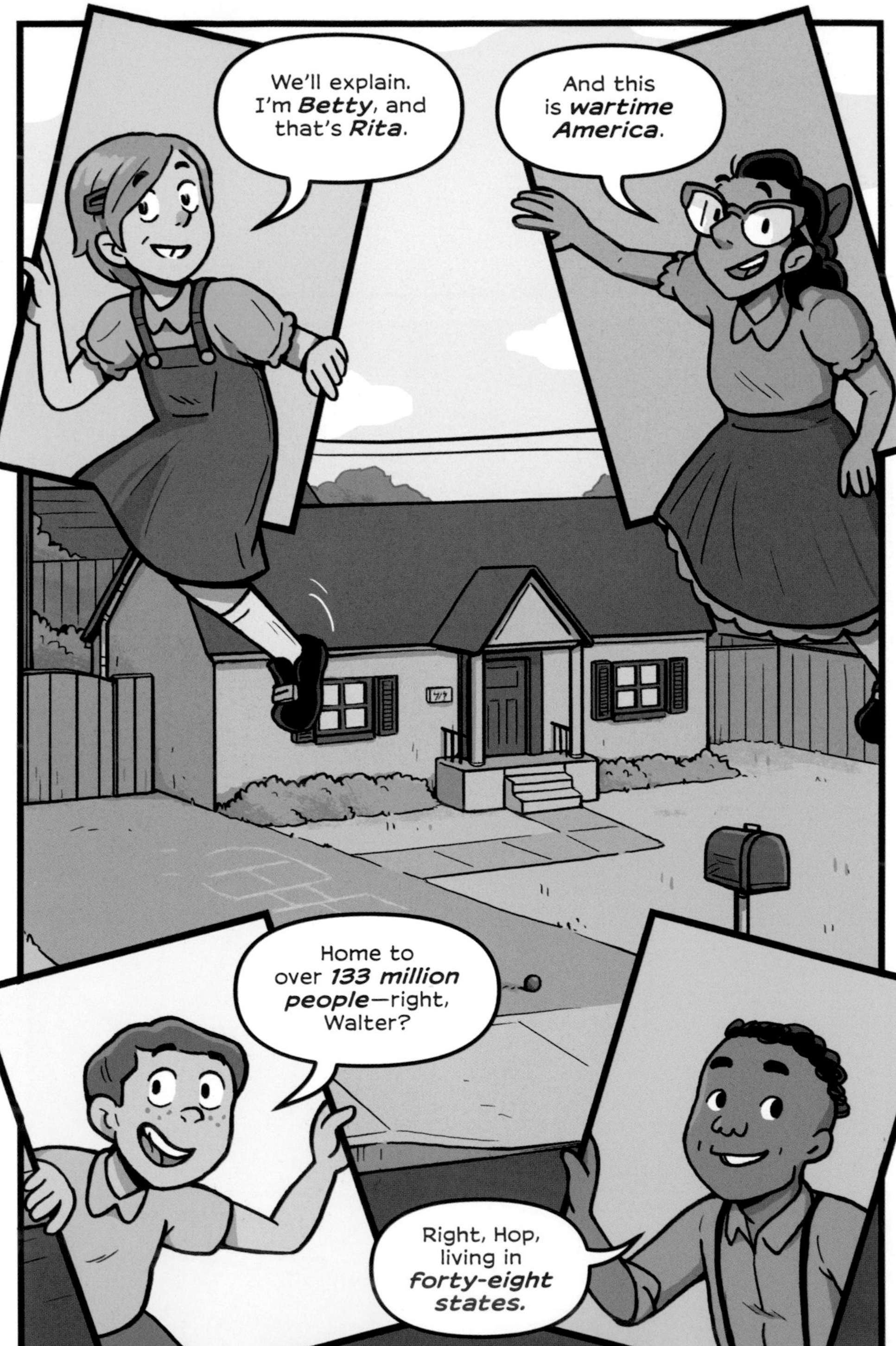
We'll explain. I'm *Betty*, and that's *Rita*.
And this is *wartime America*.
Home to over *133 million people*—right, Walter?
Right, Hop, living in *forty-eight states.*

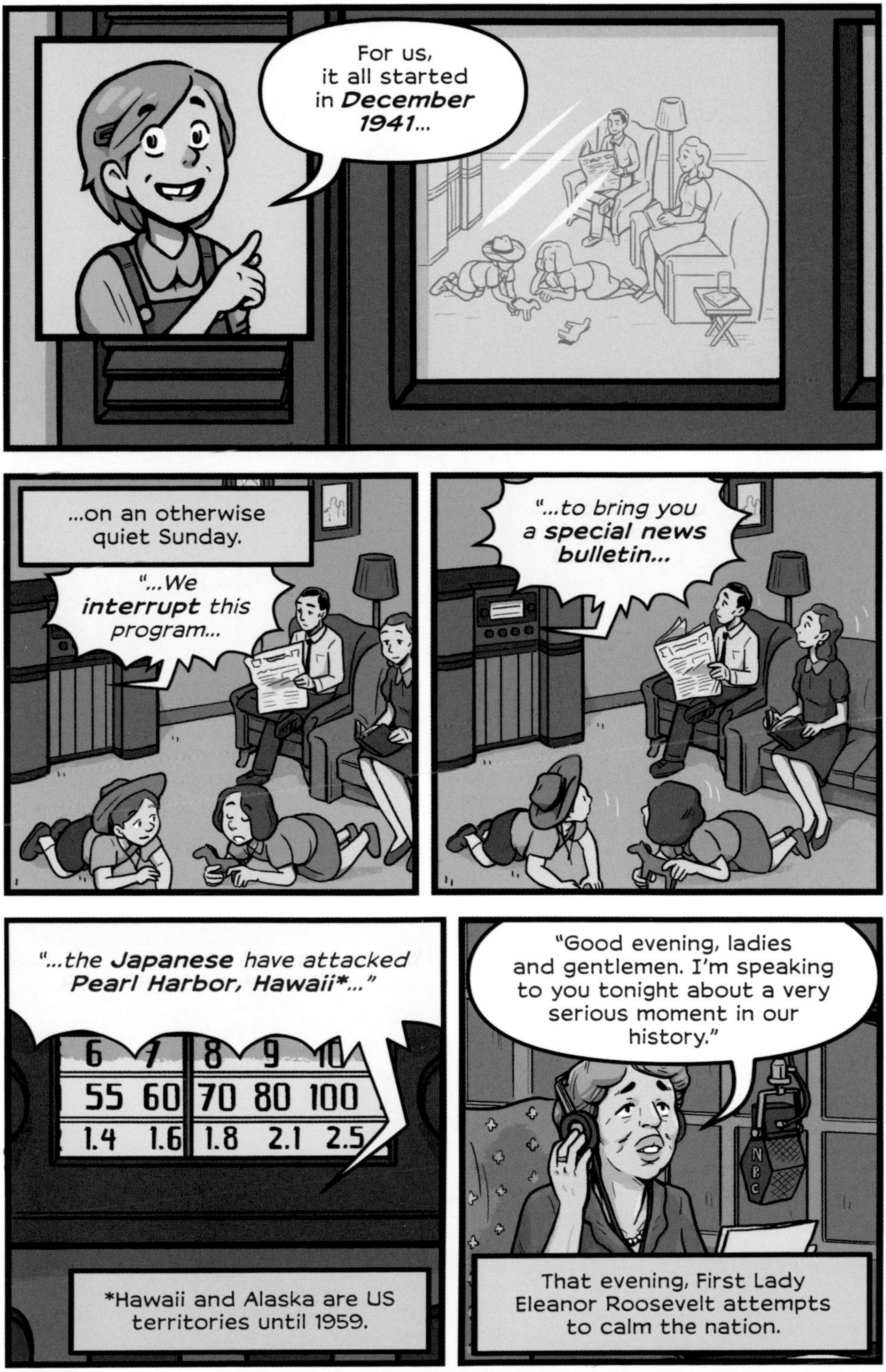
For us, it all started in ***December 1941...***
...on an otherwise quiet Sunday.
"...We ***interrupt*** this program...
"...to bring you a ***special news bulletin...***
"...the ***Japanese*** have attacked ***Pearl Harbor, Hawaii*...***"
6 7 8 9 10
55 60 70 80 100
1.4 1.6 1.8 2.1 2.5
*Hawaii and Alaska are US territories until 1959.
"Good evening, ladies and gentlemen. I'm speaking to you tonight about a very serious moment in our history."
NBC
That evening, First Lady Eleanor Roosevelt attempts to calm the nation.

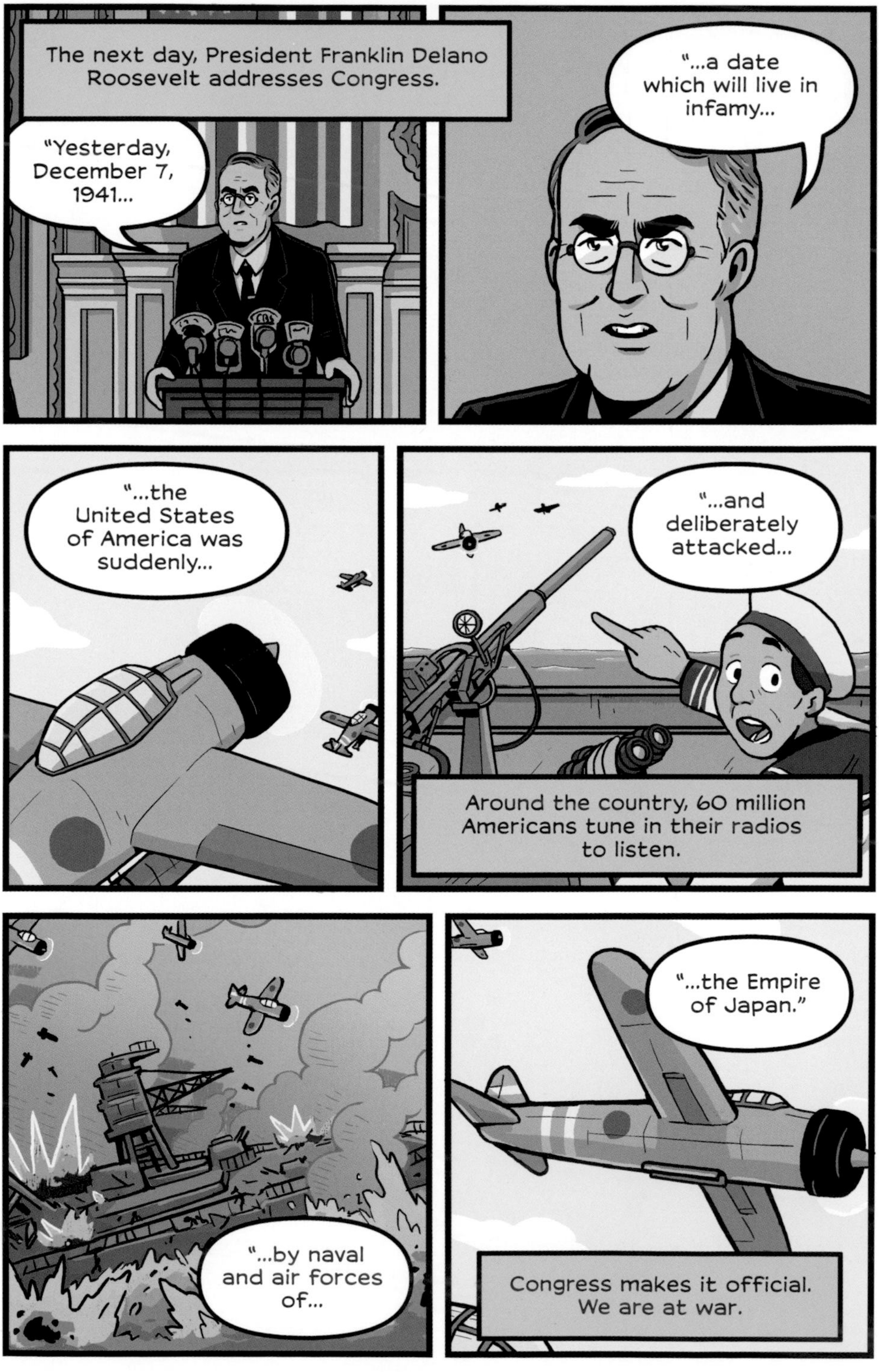
The next day, President Franklin Delano Roosevelt addresses Congress.
"Yesterday, December 7, 1941...
"...a date which will live in infamy...
"...the United States of America was suddenly...
"...and deliberately attacked...
Around the country, 60 million Americans tune in their radios to listen.
"...by naval and air forces of...
"...the Empire of Japan."
Congress makes it official. We are at war.

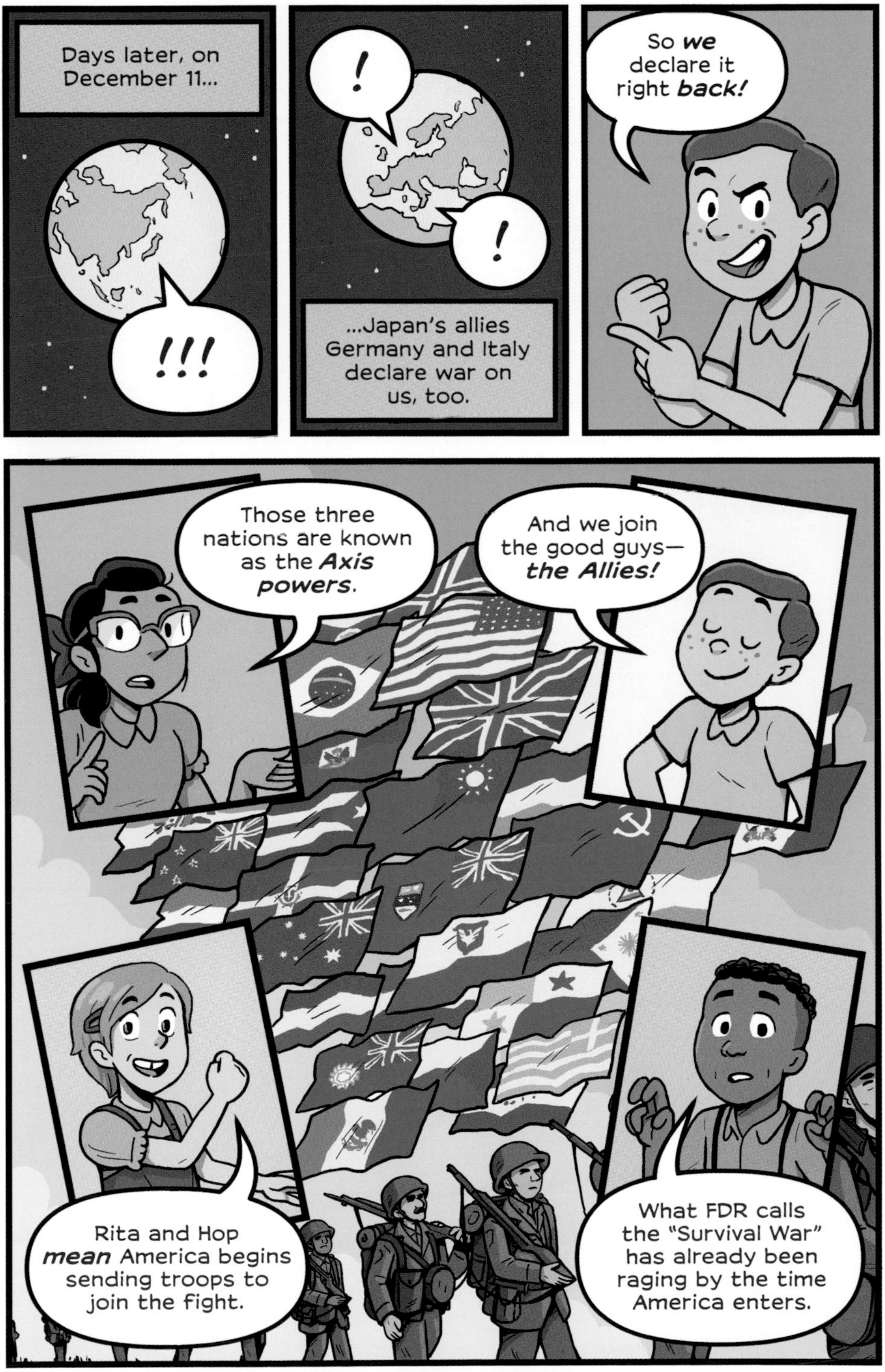

Days later, on December 11...
!!!
!
!
...Japan's allies Germany and Italy declare war on us, too.
So *we* declare it right *back!*
Those three nations are known as the ***Axis powers***.
And we join the good guys—***the Allies!***
Rita and Hop ***mean*** America begins sending troops to join the fight.
What FDR calls the "Survival War" has already been raging by the time America enters.

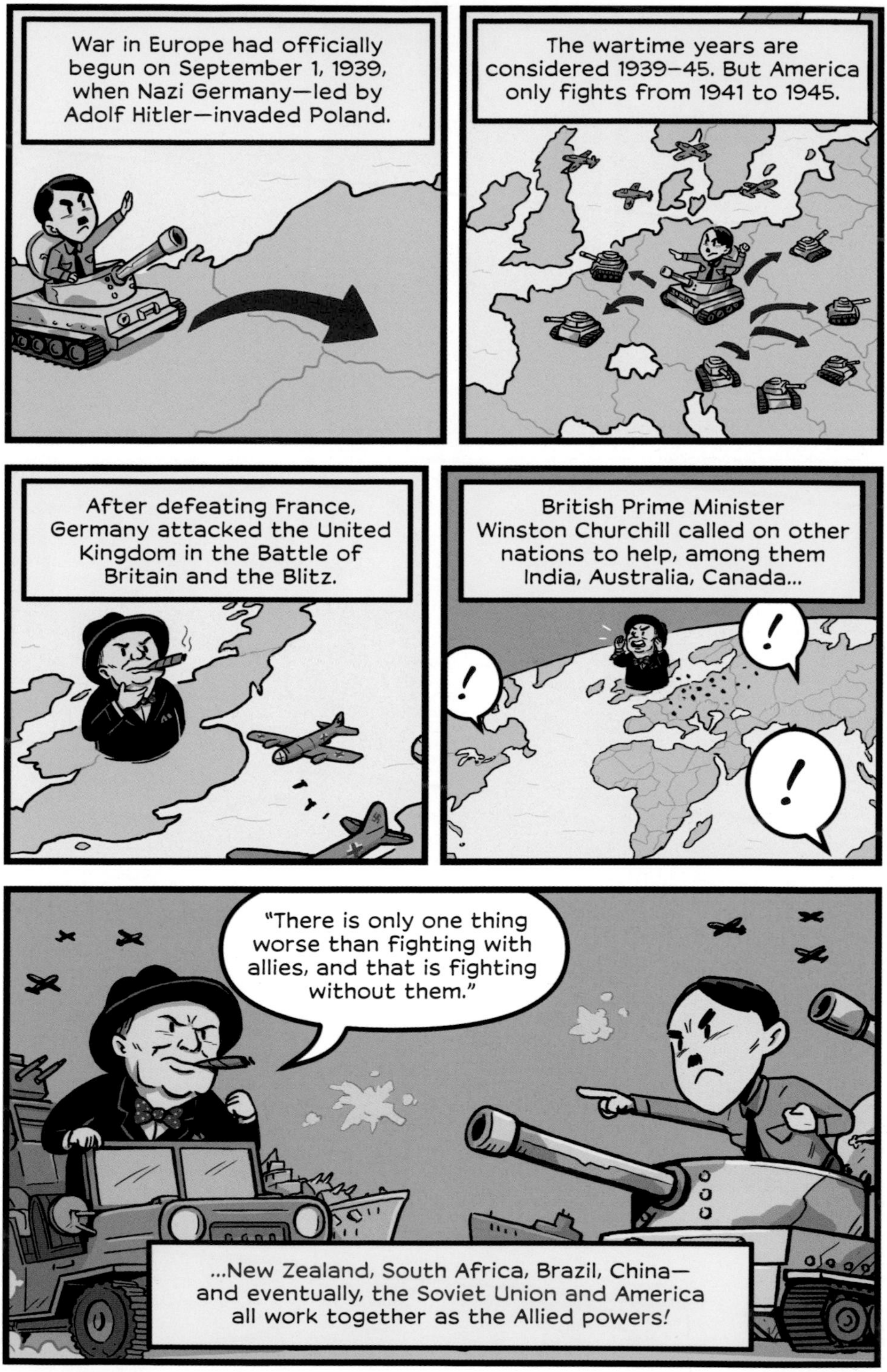
War in Europe had officially begun on September 1, 1939, when Nazi Germany—led by Adolf Hitler—invaded Poland.
The wartime years are considered 1939–45. But America only fights from 1941 to 1945.
After defeating France, Germany attacked the United Kingdom in the Battle of Britain and the Blitz.
British Prime Minister Winston Churchill called on other nations to help, among them India, Australia, Canada...
!
!
!
"There is only one thing worse than fighting with allies, and that is fighting without them."
...New Zealand, South Africa, Brazil, China—and eventually, the Soviet Union and America all work together as the Allied powers!

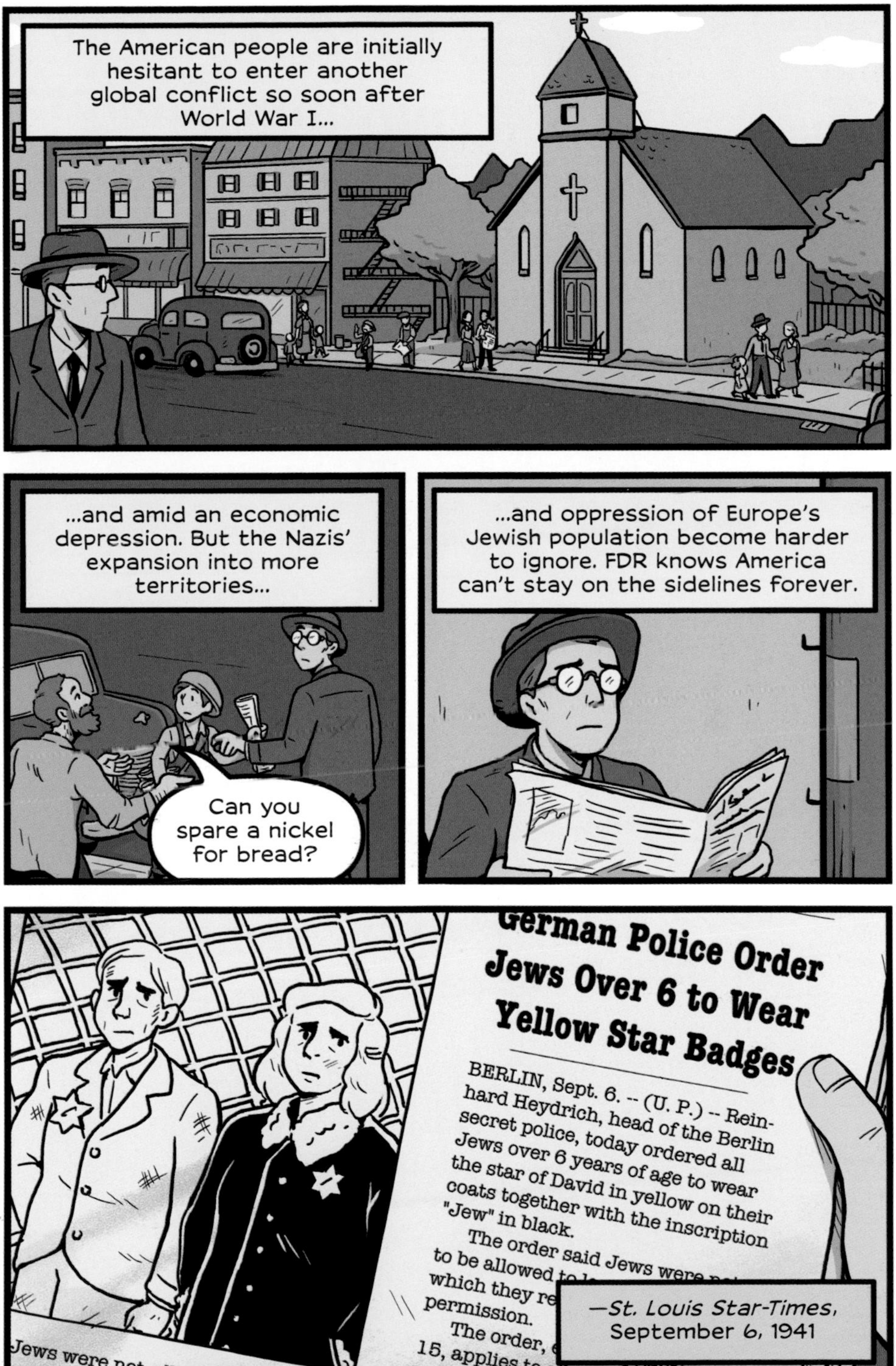
The American people are initially hesitant to enter another global conflict so soon after World War I...
...and amid an economic depression. But the Nazis' expansion into more territories...
Can you spare a nickel for bread?
...and oppression of Europe's Jewish population become harder to ignore. FDR knows America can't stay on the sidelines forever.
German Police Order Jews Over 6 to Wear Yellow Star Badges
BERLIN, Sept. 6. -- (U. P.) -- Reinhard Heydrich, head of the Berlin secret police, today ordered all Jews over 6 years of age to wear the star of David in yellow on their coats together with the inscription "Jew" in black.
The order said Jews were
to be allowed
which they
permission.
The order,
15, applies to all
Jews were not
—St. Louis Star-Times, September 6, 1941

Hope that Russia will thr[...]
greatest force against t[...]
[...]i invaders was expresse[...]
[...]e last night by Chinese C[...]
[...]era[...] with [...]
[...]e sp[...]
[...]z v[...]
[...]h[...]
[...]ro[...]
[...]G[...]

Nazis Herd Jews Into Concentration Camps; [Forei]gn Press Warned

Hitler Gangs Smash Shops, Synagogues

Disturbances Worst Since Fuehrer Came Into Power

BERLIN, Nov. 10—Nazi Germany today indulged in its greatest wave of anti-Jewish violence since Adolf Hitler came to power in 1933.

[1]

Vienna [...]
number co[...]
despair as [...]
[...]ged 21 syn[...]
As a natio[...]
[...]r the e[...]

[...]dment
[...] Loser
[...] Voting

[...] Approved Pro-
to 816 as Offi-
[...]nvas Made

[...]allots cast in Tues-

[2]

Says Treatment of Those in Germany will Depend on Actions of Those Outside

BERLIN, Nov. 11 — (AP) — Ger-many's sudden nation-wide out-burst of anti-Semitism developed tonight into a series of secret polic[e] raids upon Jews of the upper class[...] amid reports that the Ghetto of the middle ages was to be re-estab[...]

NAZIS TAKE ON RUSSIA

Jew Refugees On Way Back

MIAMI, Fla., June 7 (AP) — Their aimless odyssey apparently ended, 907 Jewish refugees were reported on their way back to Germany today aboard the liner *St. Louis*, which [...]dered along the Florida coast for [...]ile welfare agencies [...]ion for them

[3]

Nazi Troops Ready From Rumania To Finland For Fight

By The Associated Press

New York, Sunday, June 22—Adolf Hitler hurled his German armies against Soviet Russia in one of the greatest turn-abouts in history today, declaring all-out war against the erstwhile friend whom he called a liar, double-crosser and secret [a]lly of Great Britain.

Supporting the Germans, declared Hitler, were the vengeance-hungry forces from Fin-[...] both eager to regain ter-

[4]

Nazis Open New Anti-Jewish Drive And Oust Thousands From Homes

by United Press

[5]

BERLIN, Oct. 21—The severest anti-Jewish drive in almost three years appeared to be in progress in Germany and the Bohemia-Mo-ravia protectorate Tuesday [...] thousands being dis[...] notice to Poland or e[...] thier Berlin homes in[...] hutments on the city[...]

Police have stepped [...] checkups on Jews in [...] pamphlets have been [...] thousands of Berlino[...] urging Germans.

Newspapers and dates:

[1] *Harrisburg Telegraph*, Harrisburg, Pennsylvania, November 10, 1938
[2] *Mobile Register*, Mobile, Alabama, November 12, 1938
[3] *Reno Evening Gazette*, Reno, Nevada, June 7, 1939
[4] *Santa Cruz Sentinel*, Santa Cruz, California, June 22, 1941
[5] *Miami Herald*, Miami, Florida, October 22, 1941

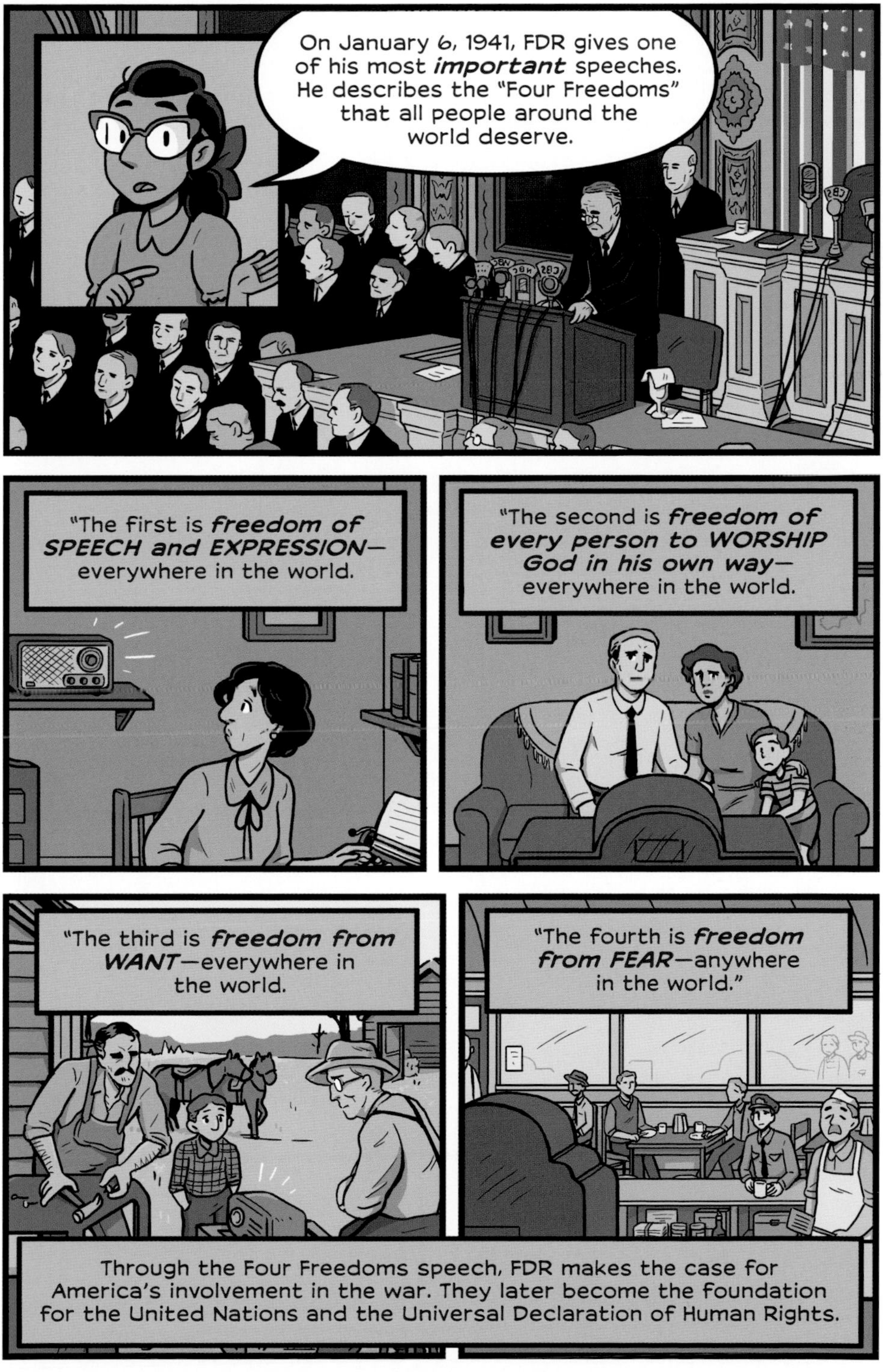
On January 6, 1941, FDR gives one of his most *important* speeches. He describes the "Four Freedoms" that all people around the world deserve.
"The first is ***freedom of SPEECH and EXPRESSION***—everywhere in the world.
"The second is ***freedom of every person to WORSHIP God in his own way***—everywhere in the world.
"The third is ***freedom from WANT***—everywhere in the world.
"The fourth is ***freedom from FEAR***—anywhere in the world."
Through the Four Freedoms speech, FDR makes the case for America's involvement in the war. They later become the foundation for the United Nations and the Universal Declaration of Human Rights.

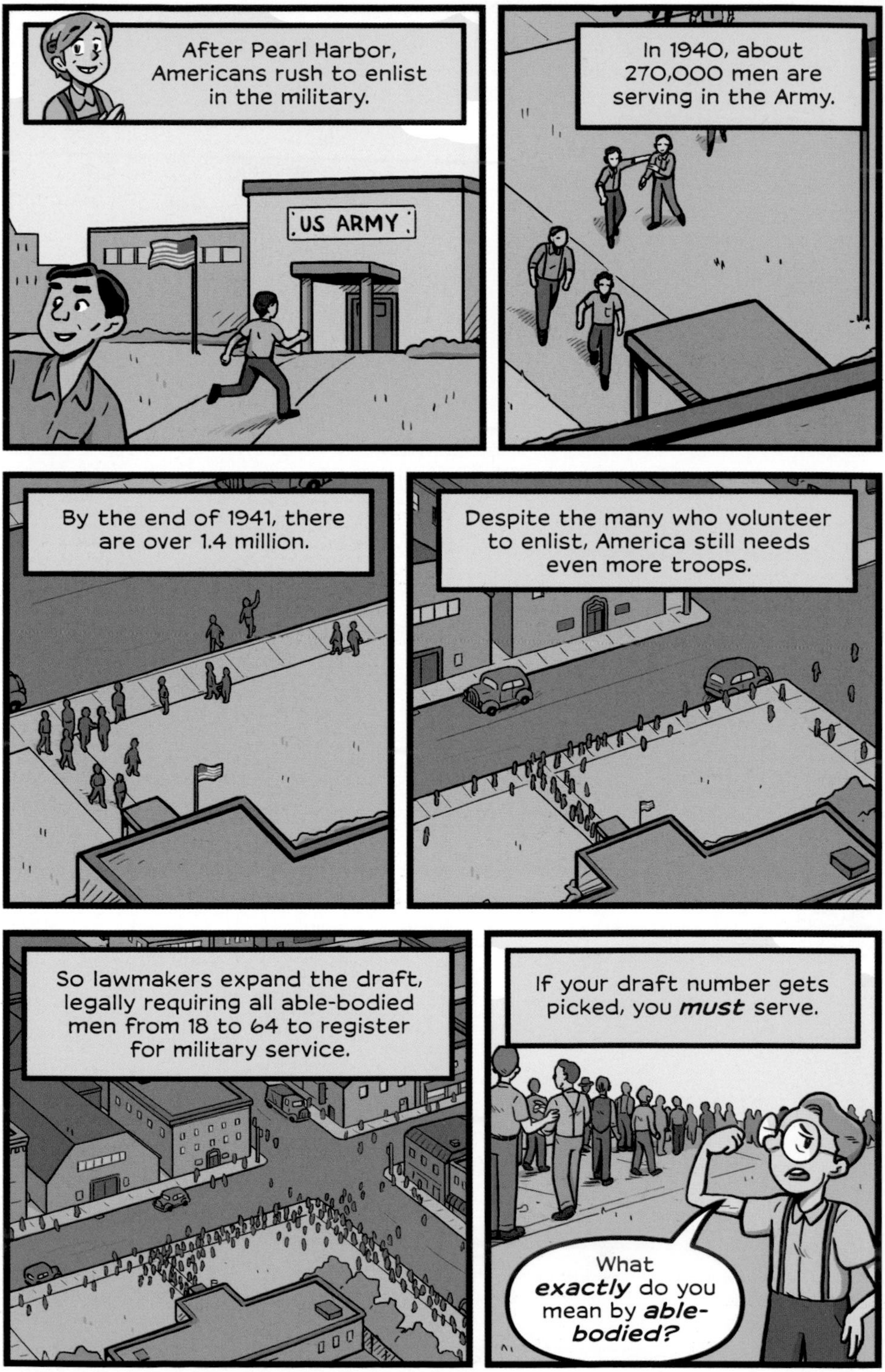
After Pearl Harbor, Americans rush to enlist in the military.
US ARMY
In 1940, about 270,000 men are serving in the Army.
By the end of 1941, there are over 1.4 million.
Despite the many who volunteer to enlist, America still needs even more troops.
So lawmakers expand the draft, legally requiring all able-bodied men from 18 to 64 to register for military service.
If your draft number gets picked, you **must** serve.
What **exactly** do you mean by **able-bodied?**

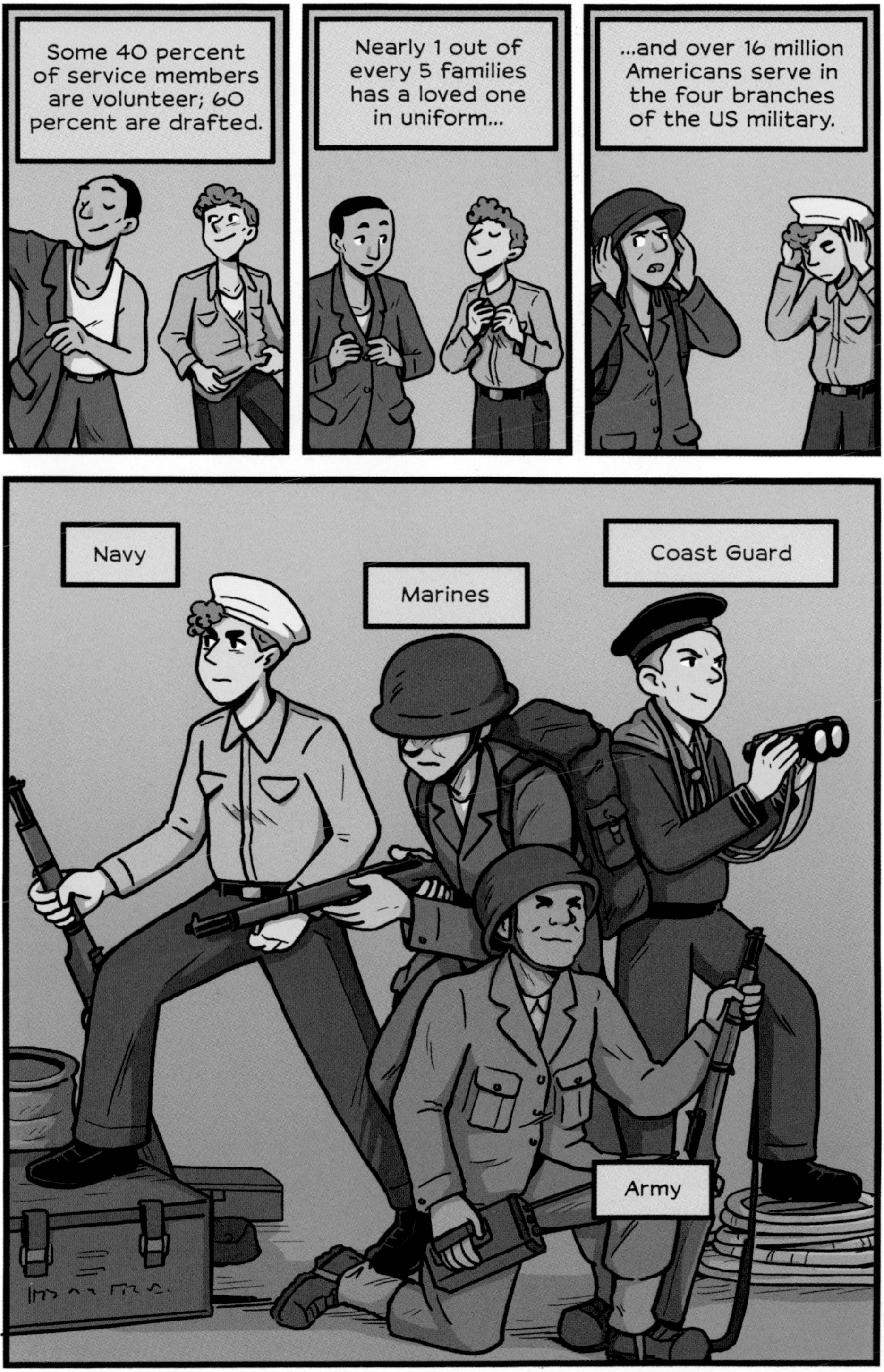
Some 40 percent of service members are volunteer; 60 percent are drafted.
Nearly 1 out of every 5 families has a loved one in uniform...
...and over 16 million Americans serve in the four branches of the US military.
Navy
Marines
Coast Guard
Army

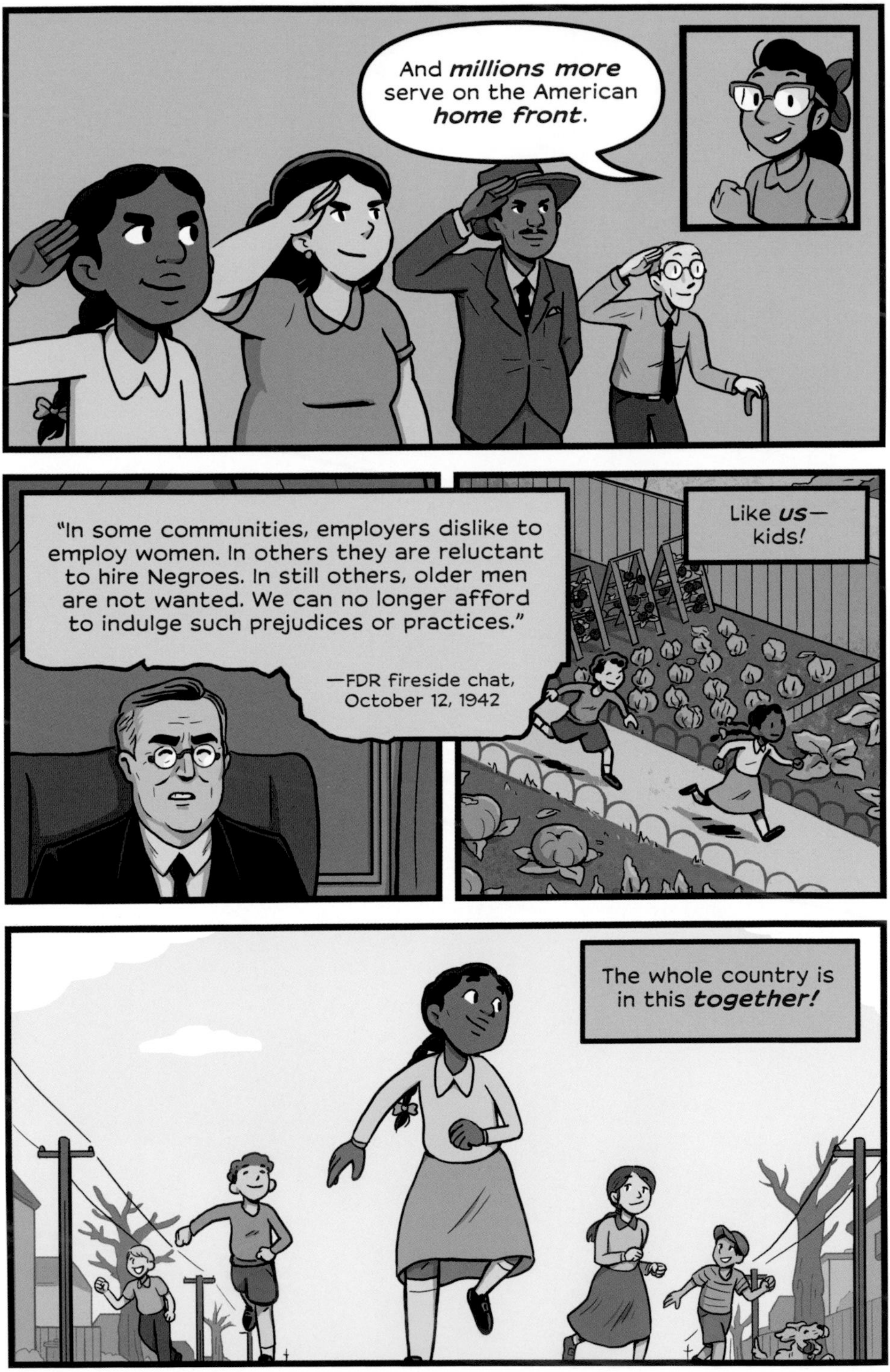
And *millions more* serve on the American *home front*.
"In some communities, employers dislike to employ women. In others they are reluctant to hire Negroes. In still others, older men are not wanted. We can no longer afford to indulge such prejudices or practices."
—FDR fireside chat, October 12, 1942
Like *us*—kids!
The whole country is in this *together!*

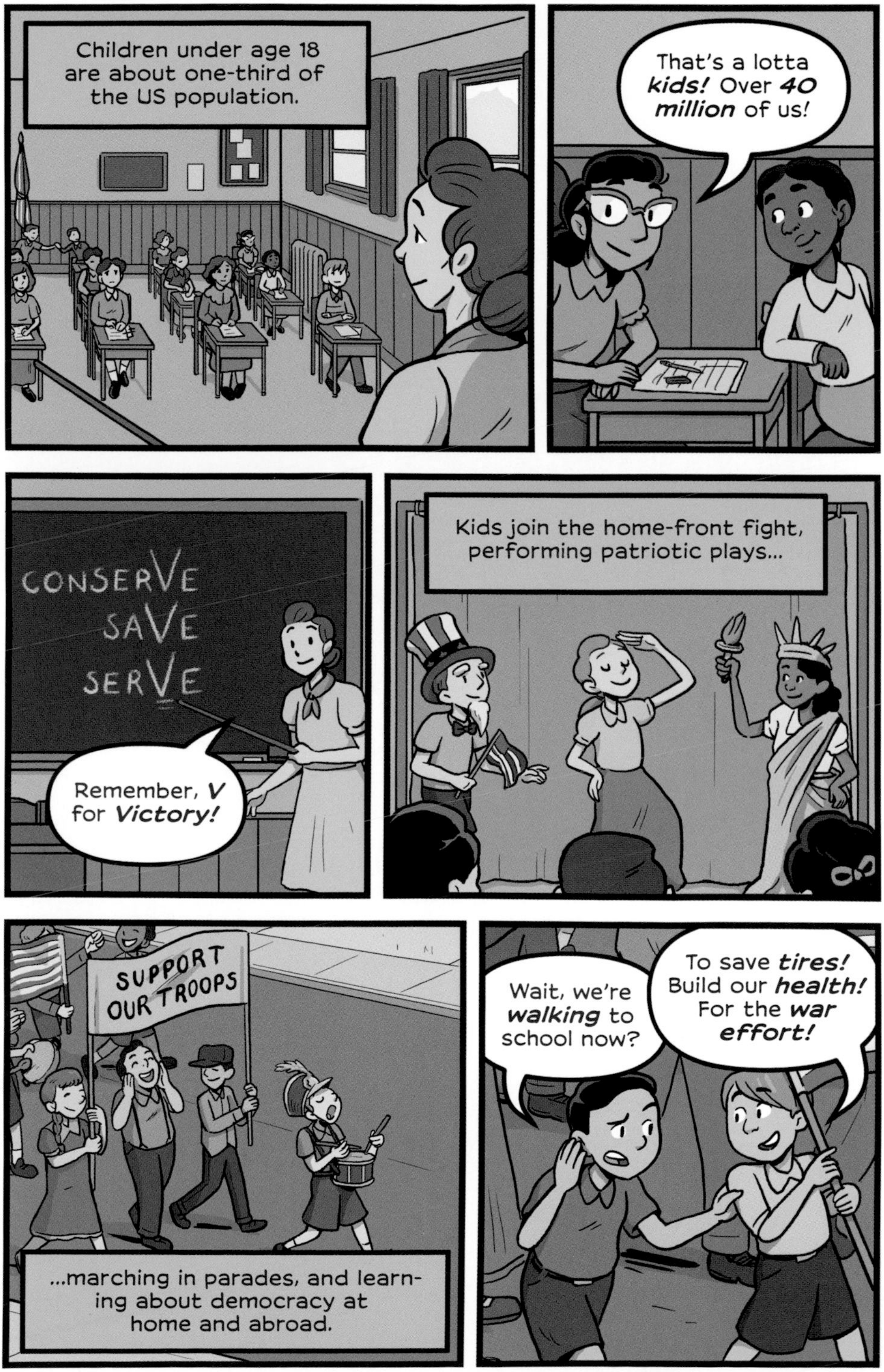
Children under age 18 are about one-third of the US population.
That's a lotta kids! Over 40 million of us!
CONSERVE
SAVE
SERVE
Remember, V for Victory!
Kids join the home-front fight, performing patriotic plays...
SUPPORT OUR TROOPS
...marching in parades, and learning about democracy at home and abroad.
Wait, we're walking to school now?
To save tires! Build our health! For the war effort!

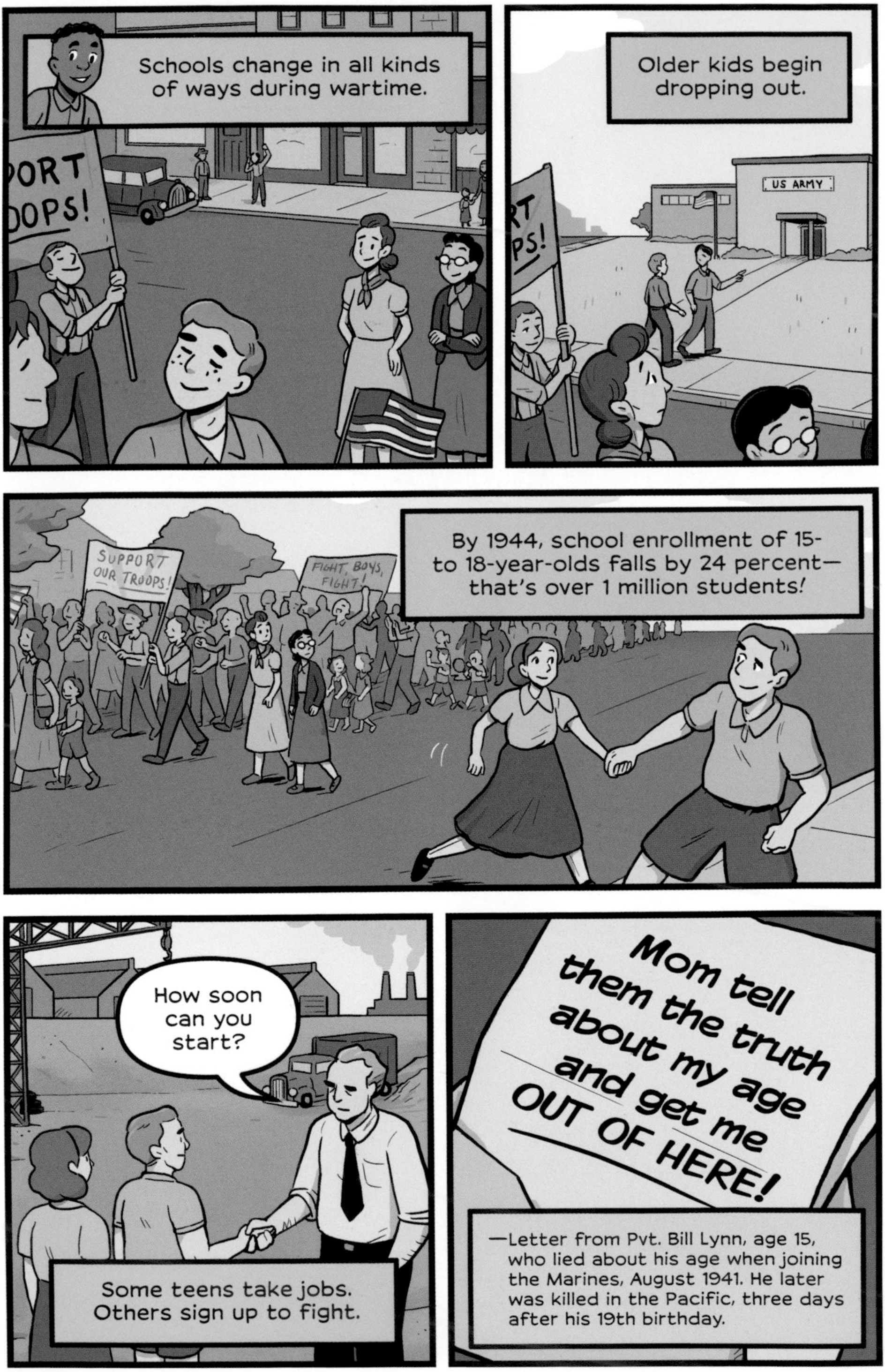
Schools change in all kinds of ways during wartime.
PORT
OOPS!
Older kids begin dropping out.
US ARMY
SUPPORT OUR TROOPS!
FIGHT, BOYS, FIGHT!
By 1944, school enrollment of 15- to 18-year-olds falls by 24 percent—that's over 1 million students!
How soon can you start?
Some teens take jobs. Others sign up to fight.
Mom tell them the truth about my age and get me OUT OF HERE!
—Letter from Pvt. Bill Lynn, age 15, who lied about his age when joining the Marines, August 1941. He later was killed in the Pacific, three days after his 19th birthday.

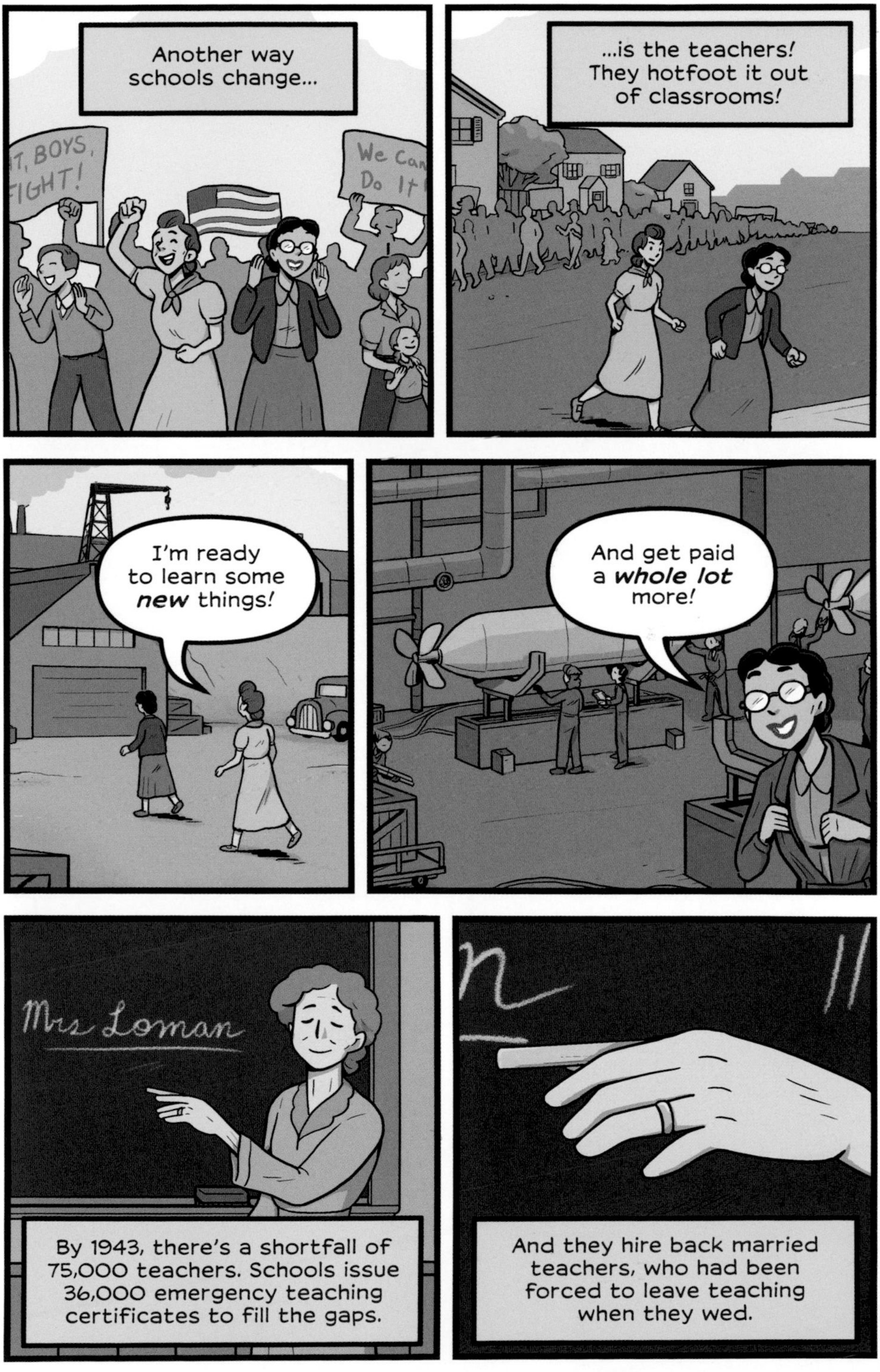

Another way schools change...
...is the teachers! They hotfoot it out of classrooms!
I'm ready to learn some *new* things!
And get paid a ***whole lot*** more!
By 1943, there's a shortfall of 75,000 teachers. Schools issue 36,000 emergency teaching certificates to fill the gaps.
And they hire back married teachers, who had been forced to leave teaching when they wed.

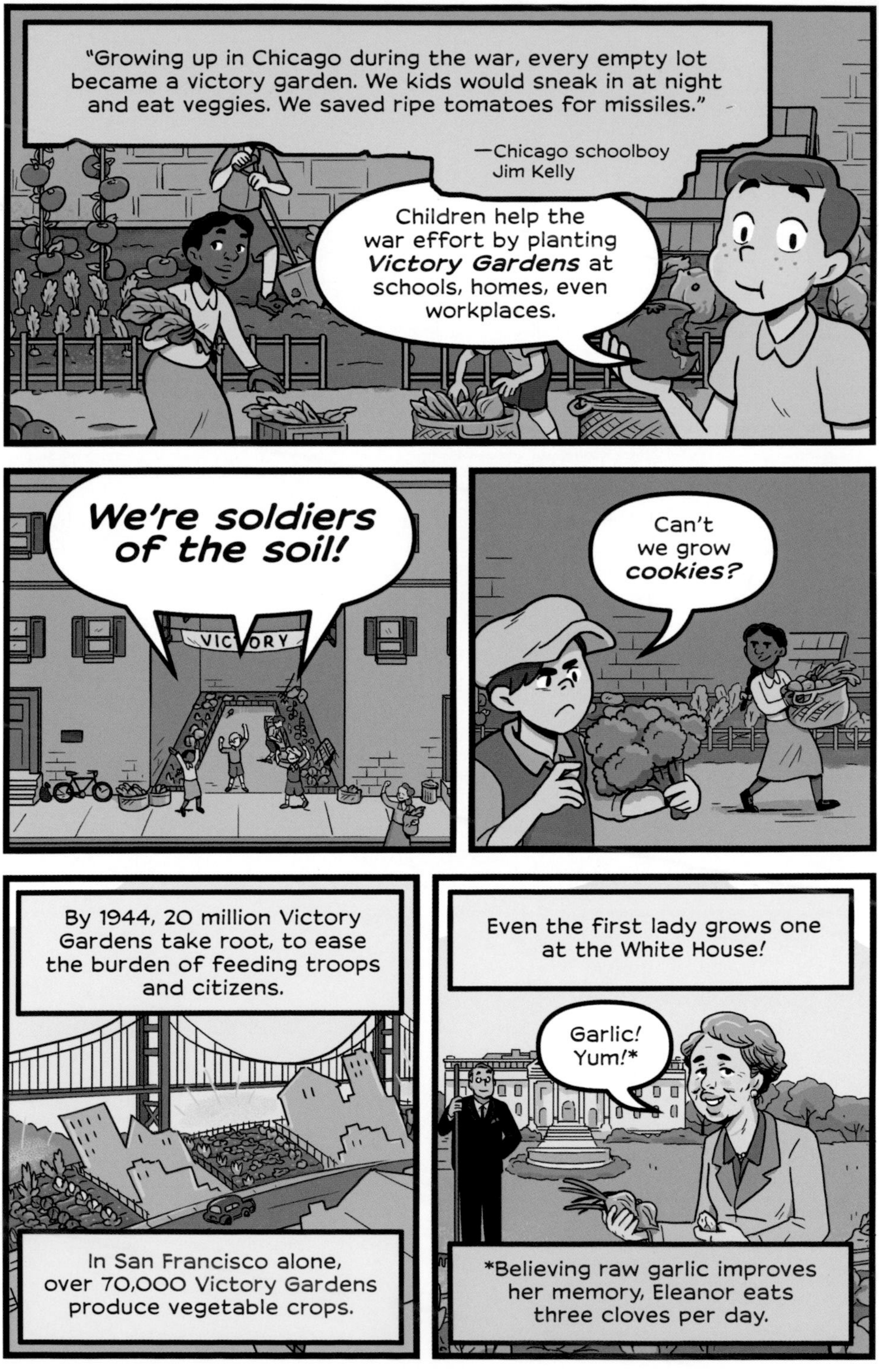
"Growing up in Chicago during the war, every empty lot became a victory garden. We kids would sneak in at night and eat veggies. We saved ripe tomatoes for missiles."
—Chicago schoolboy Jim Kelly
Children help the war effort by planting *Victory Gardens* at schools, homes, even workplaces.
We're soldiers of the soil!
VICTORY
Can't we grow *cookies?*
By 1944, 20 million Victory Gardens take root, to ease the burden of feeding troops and citizens.
In San Francisco alone, over 70,000 Victory Gardens produce vegetable crops.
Even the first lady grows one at the White House!
Garlic! Yum!*
*Believing raw garlic improves her memory, Eleanor eats three cloves per day.

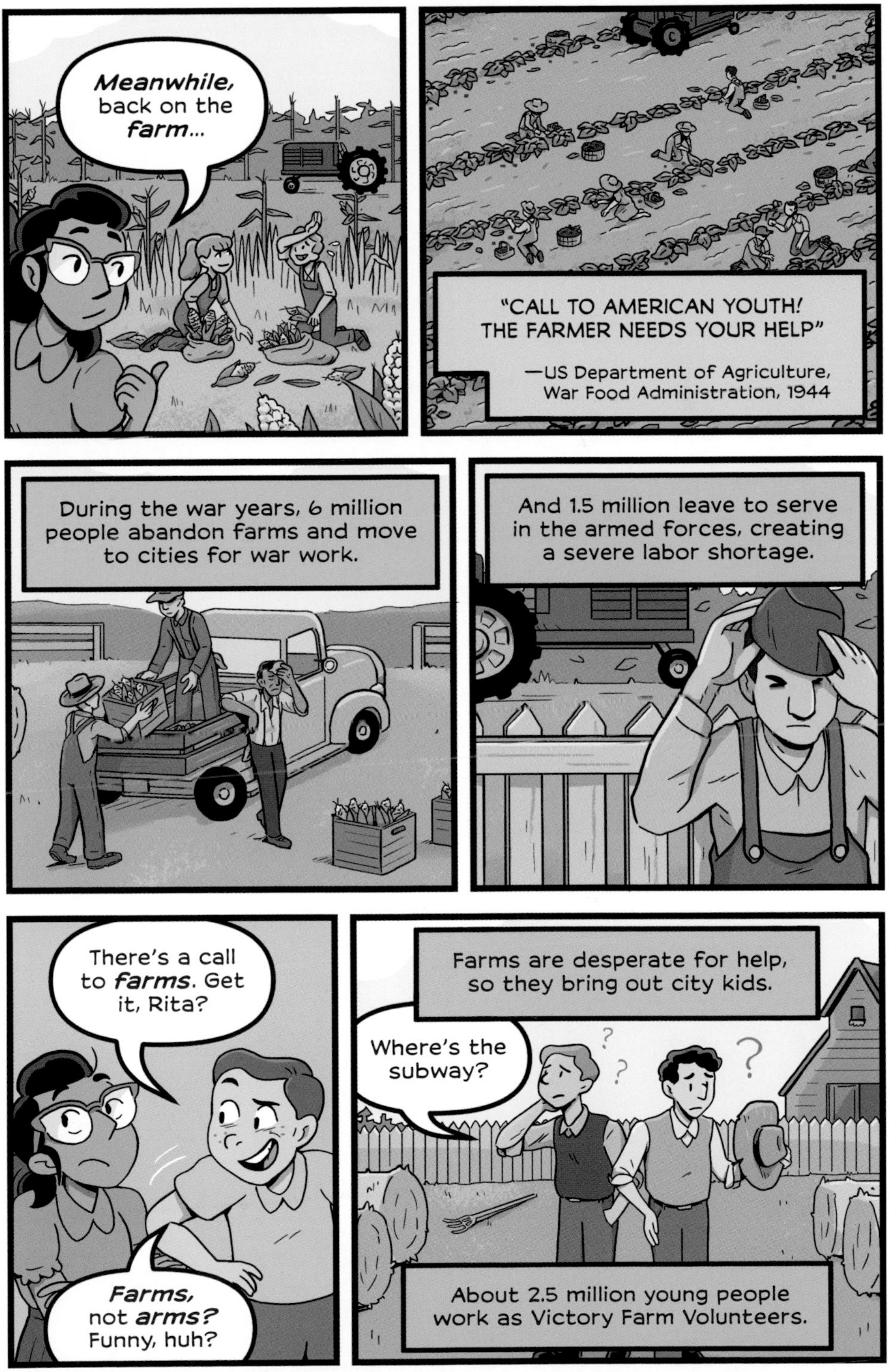

Meanwhile, back on the *farm*...
"CALL TO AMERICAN YOUTH! THE FARMER NEEDS YOUR HELP"
—US Department of Agriculture, War Food Administration, 1944
During the war years, 6 million people abandon farms and move to cities for war work.
And 1.5 million leave to serve in the armed forces, creating a severe labor shortage.
There's a call to *farms*. Get it, Rita?
Farms, not *arms?* Funny, huh?
Farms are desperate for help, so they bring out city kids.
Where's the subway?
About 2.5 million young people work as Victory Farm Volunteers.

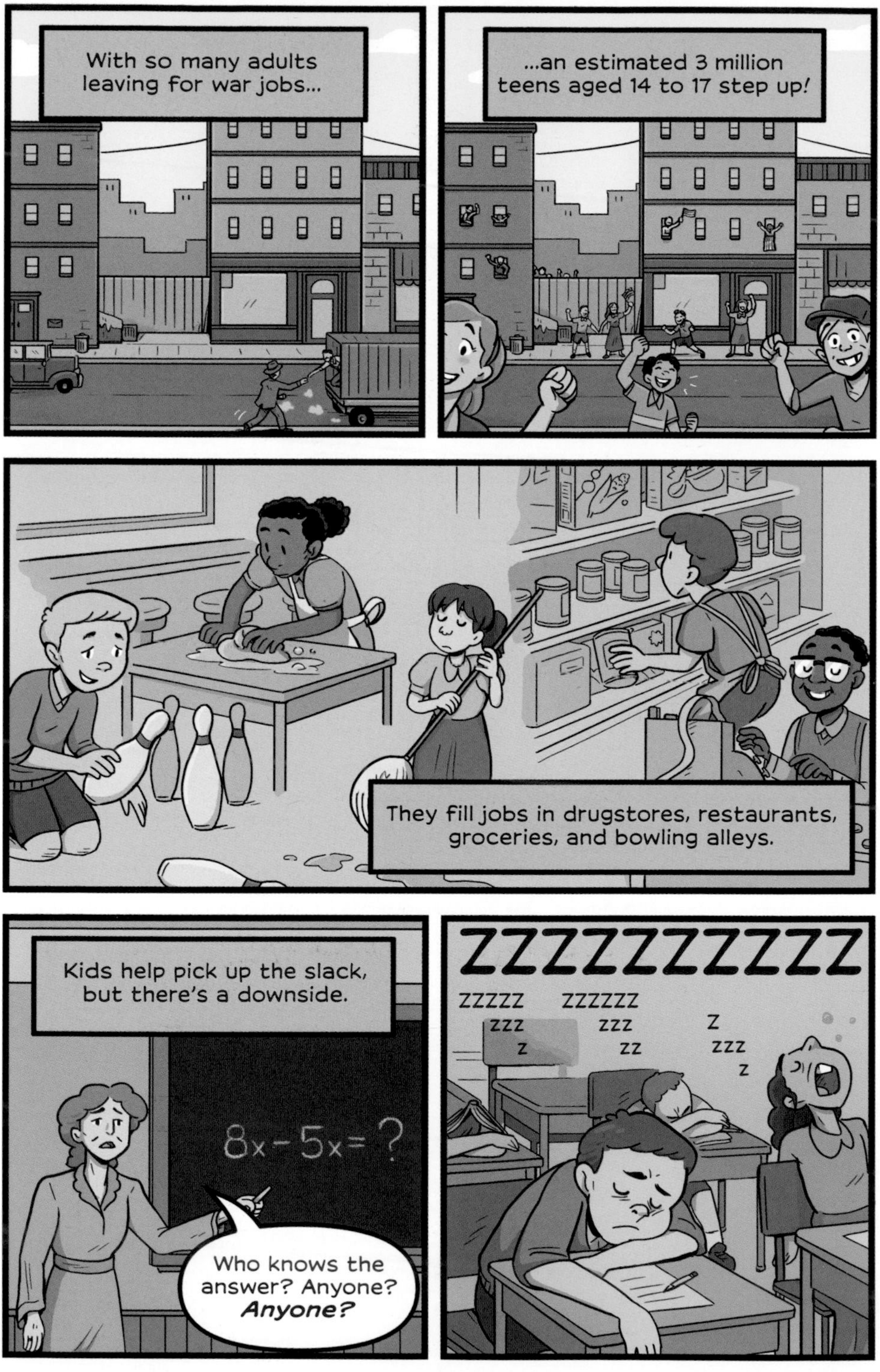

With so many adults leaving for war jobs...
...an estimated 3 million teens aged 14 to 17 step up!
They fill jobs in drugstores, restaurants, groceries, and bowling alleys.
Kids help pick up the slack, but there's a downside.
8x-5x=?
Who knows the answer? Anyone? ***Anyone?***
ZZZZZZZZZZZ
ZZZZZ ZZZ Z
ZZZZZZ ZZZ ZZ
Z ZZZ Z

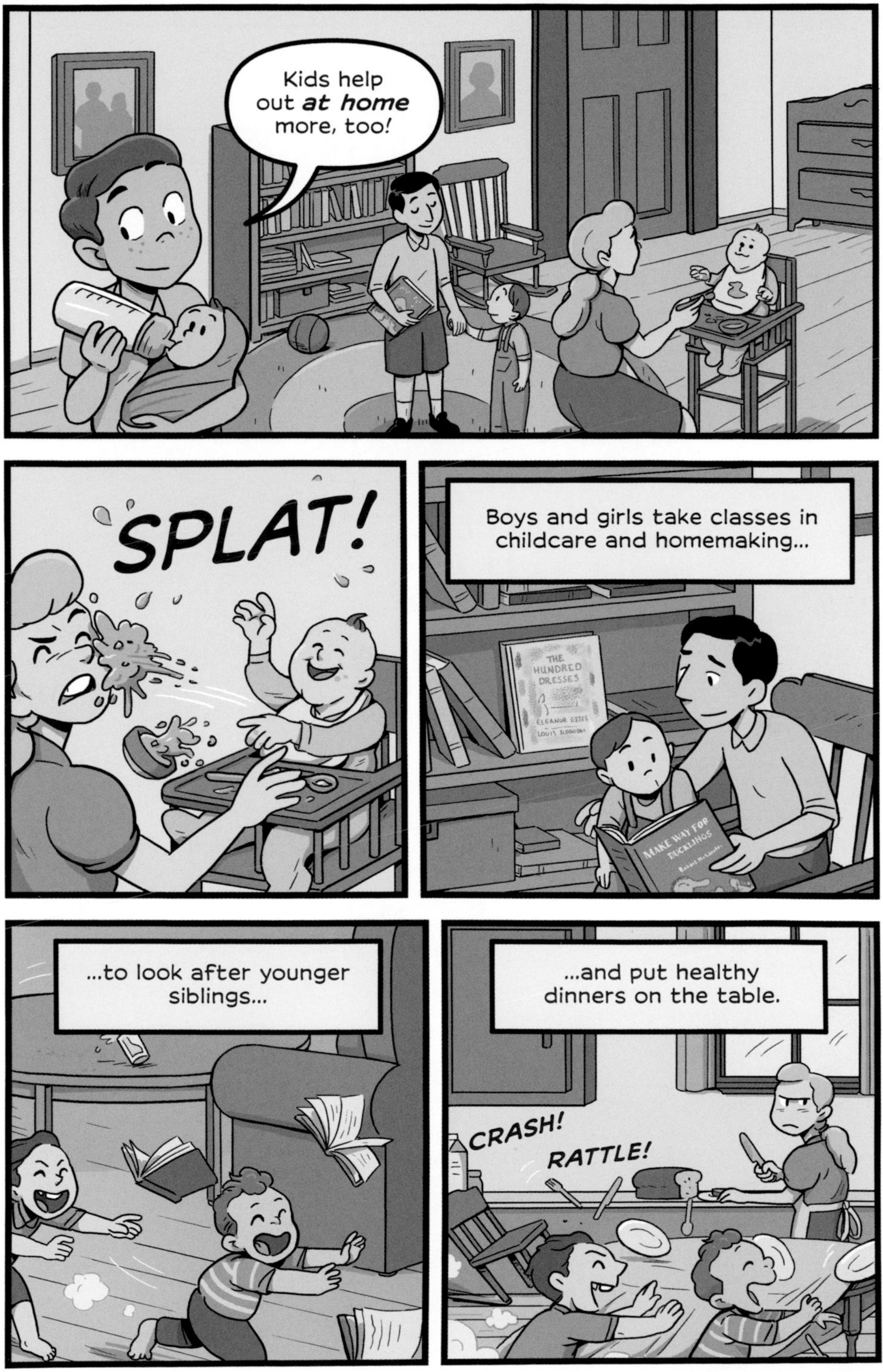
Kids help out *at home* more, too!
SPLAT!
Boys and girls take classes in childcare and homemaking...
THE HUNDRED DRESSES
ELEANOR ESTES
LOUIS SLOBODKIN
MAKE WAY FOR DUCKLINGS
...to look after younger siblings...
...and put healthy dinners on the table.
CRASH!
RATTLE!

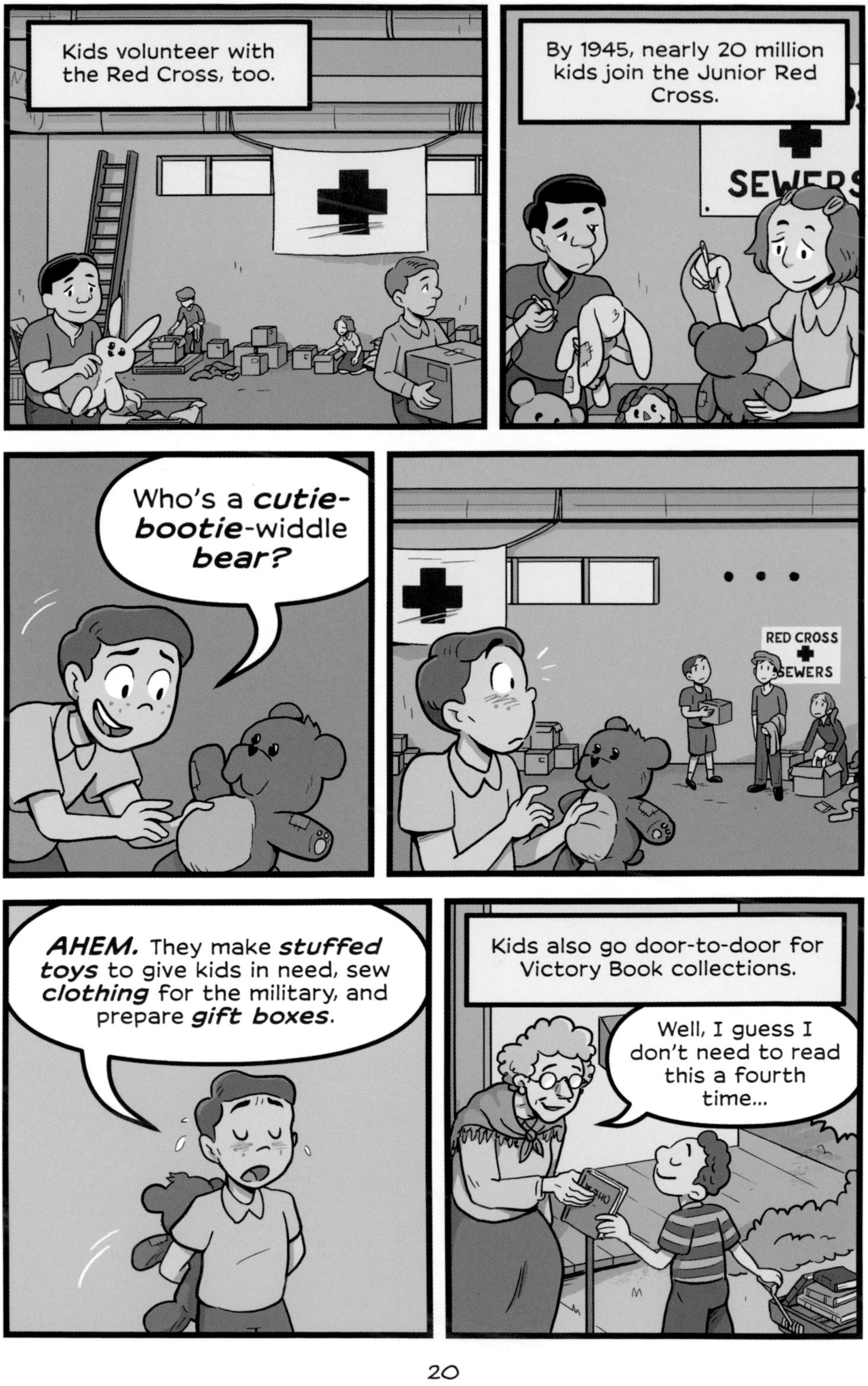
Kids volunteer with the Red Cross, too.
By 1945, nearly 20 million kids join the Junior Red Cross.
SEWERS
Who's a ***cutie-bootie***-widdle ***bear?***
RED CROSS SEWERS
. . .
AHEM. They make ***stuffed toys*** to give kids in need, sew ***clothing*** for the military, and prepare ***gift boxes***.
Kids also go door-to-door for Victory Book collections.
Well, I guess I don't need to read this a fourth time...

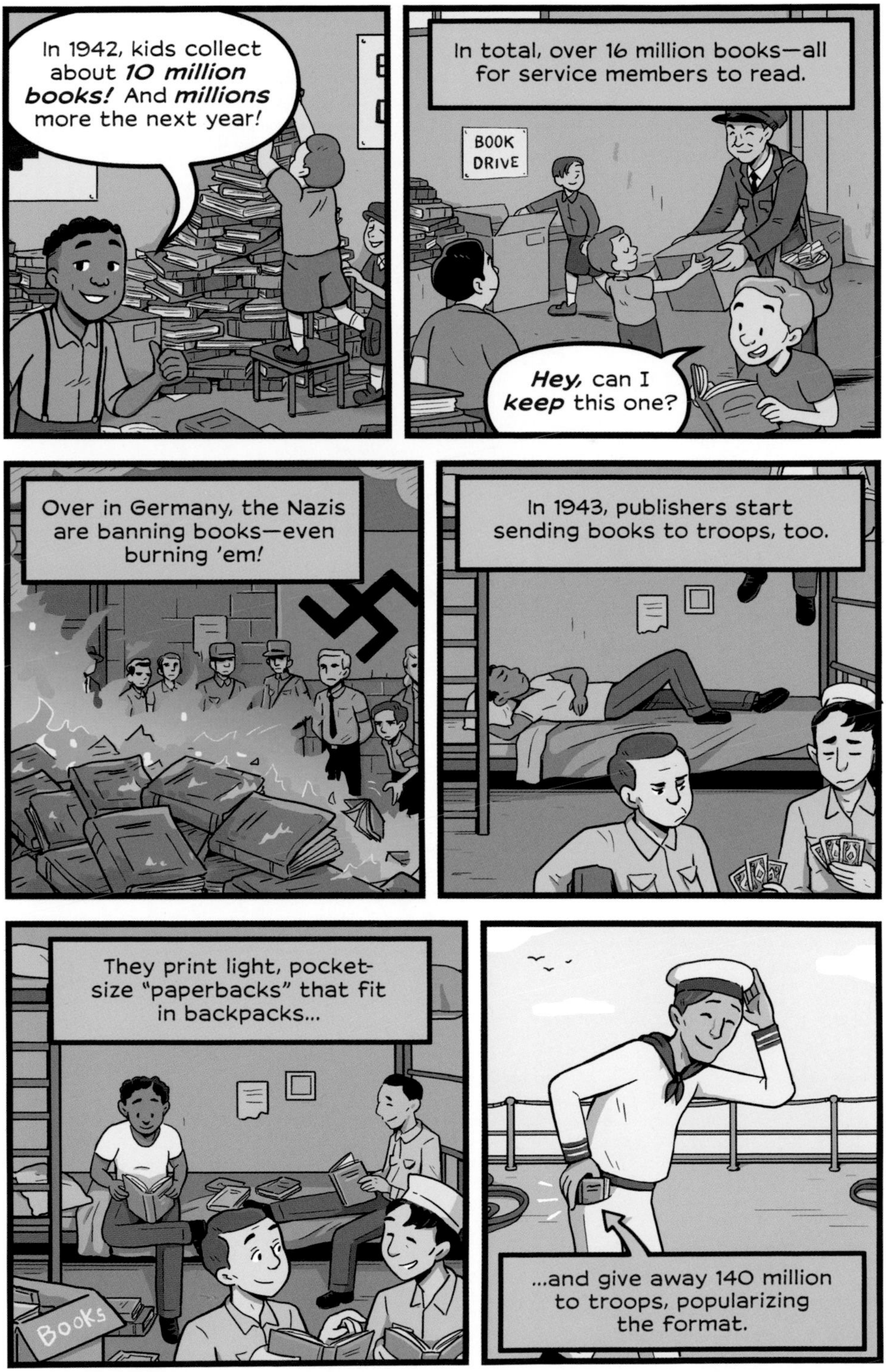
In 1942, kids collect about *10 million books!* And *millions* more the next year!
In total, over 16 million books—all for service members to read.
BOOK DRIVE
Hey, can I *keep* this one?
Over in Germany, the Nazis are banning books—even burning 'em!
In 1943, publishers start sending books to troops, too.
They print light, pocket-size "paperbacks" that fit in backpacks...
BOOKS
...and give away 140 million to troops, popularizing the format.

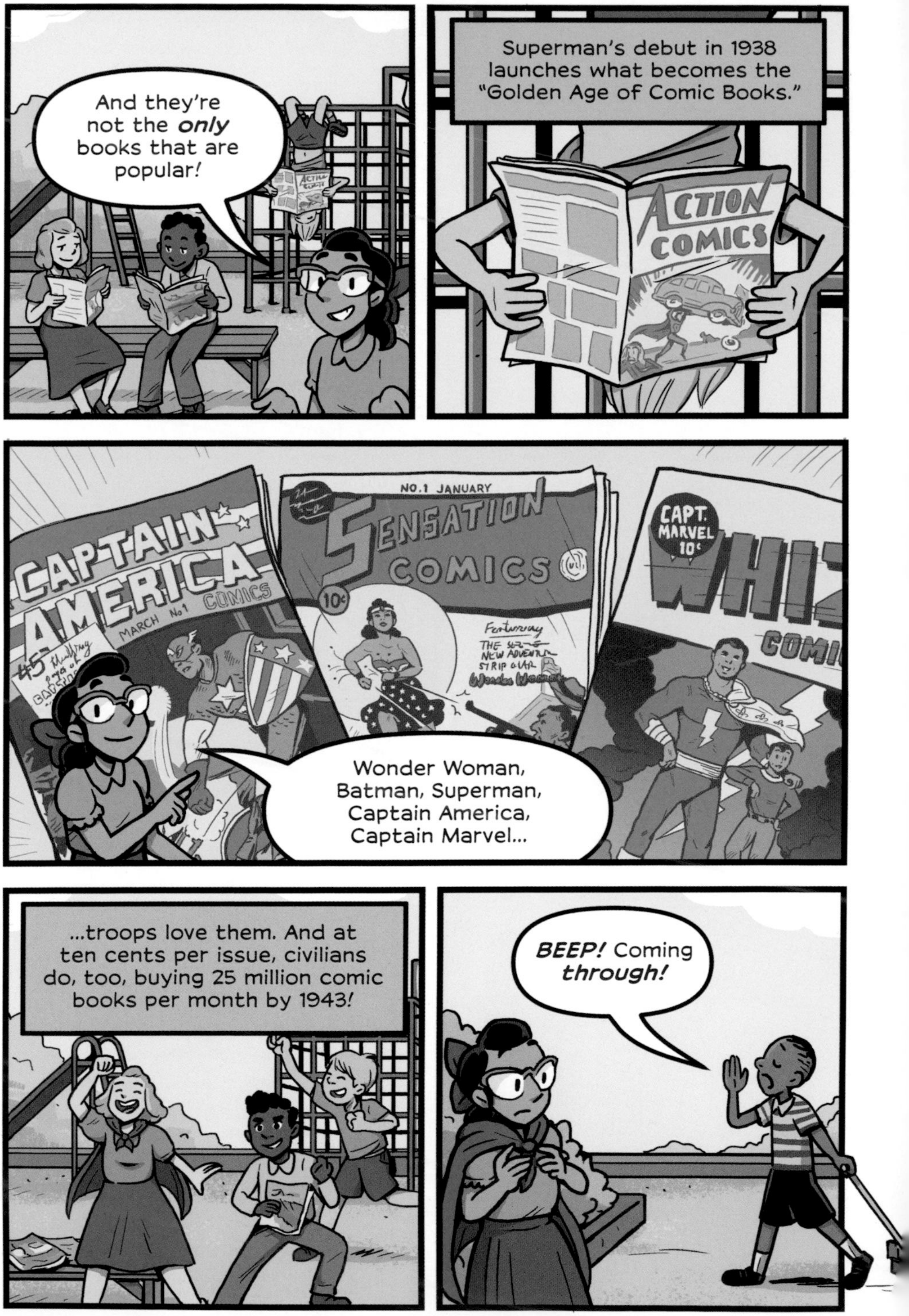

And they're not the *only* books that are popular!
Superman's debut in 1938 launches what becomes the "Golden Age of Comic Books."
ACTION COMICS
CAPTAIN AMERICA COMICS
MARCH No1
NO.1 JANUARY
SENSATION COMICS
10¢
CAPT. MARVEL 10¢
Wonder Woman, Batman, Superman, Captain America, Captain Marvel...
...troops love them. And at ten cents per issue, civilians do, too, buying 25 million comic books per month by 1943!
BEEP! Coming *through!*

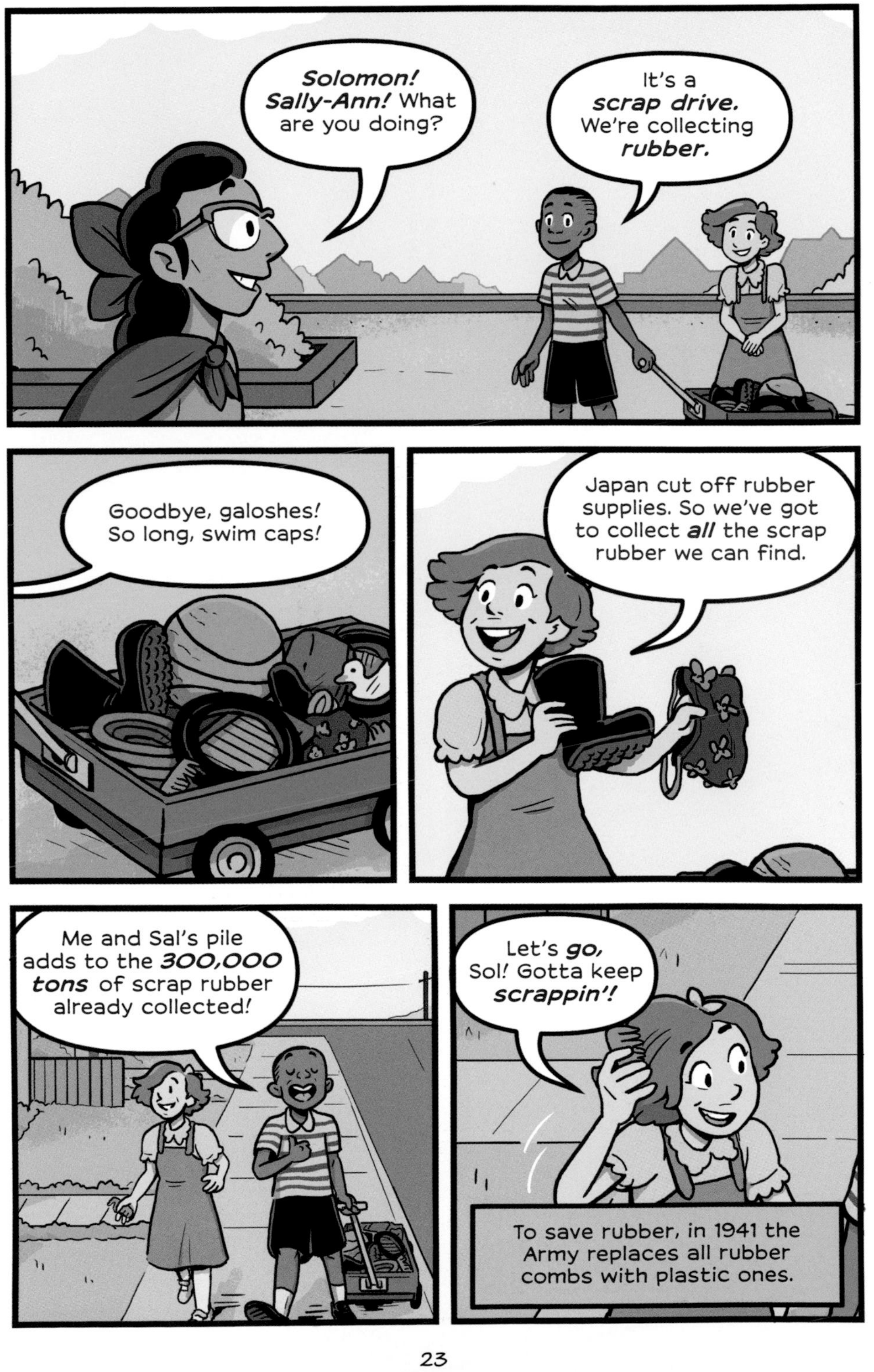

Solomon! Sally-Ann! What are you doing?
It's a scrap drive. We're collecting rubber.
Goodbye, galoshes! So long, swim caps!
Japan cut off rubber supplies. So we've got to collect all the scrap rubber we can find.
Me and Sal's pile adds to the 300,000 tons of scrap rubber already collected!
Let's go, Sol! Gotta keep scrappin'!
To save rubber, in 1941 the Army replaces all rubber combs with plastic ones.

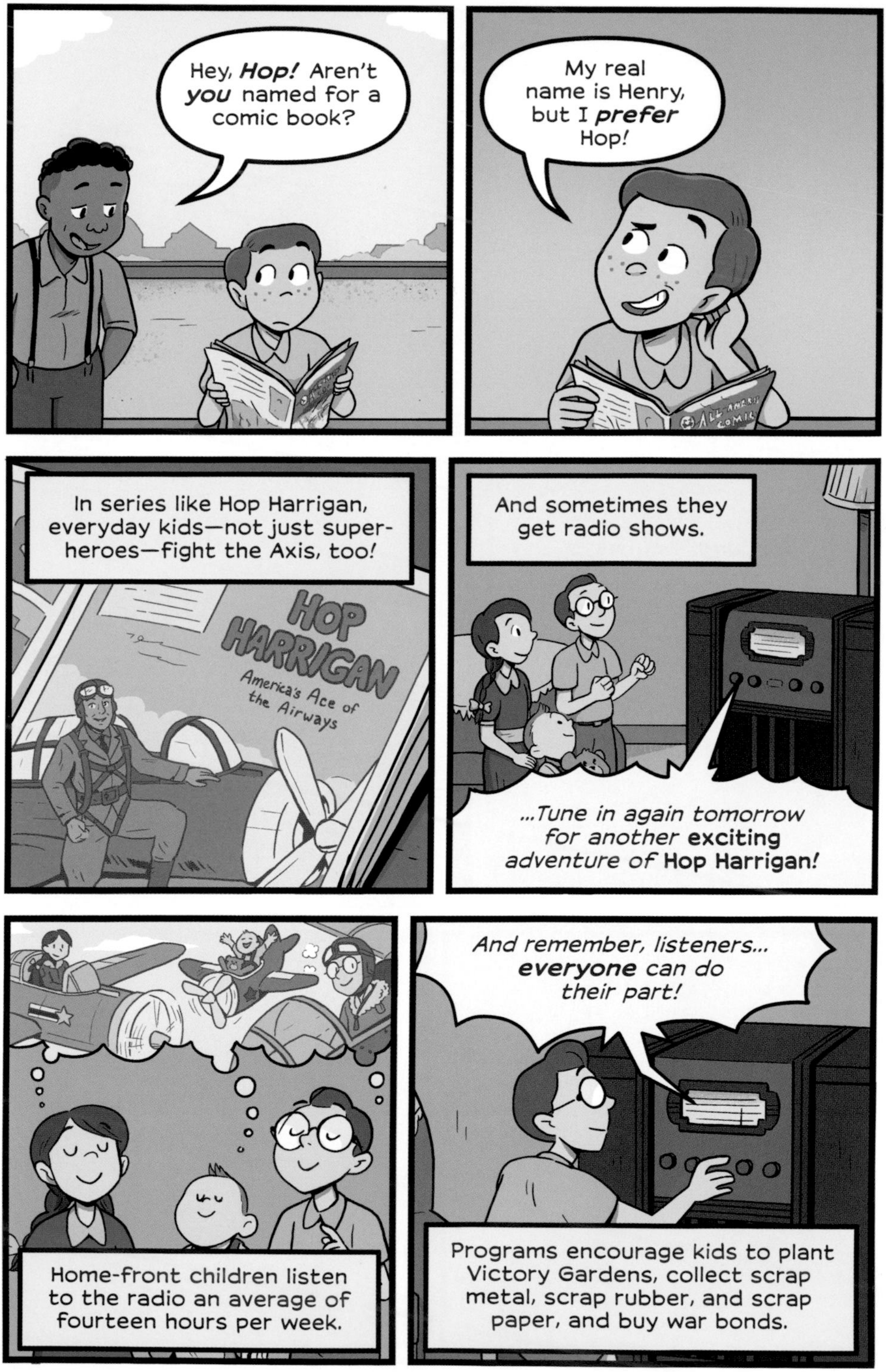
Hey, Hop! Aren't you named for a comic book?
My real name is Henry, but I prefer Hop!
In series like Hop Harrigan, everyday kids—not just super-heroes—fight the Axis, too!
HOP HARRIGAN
America's Ace of the Airways
And sometimes they get radio shows.
...Tune in again tomorrow for another exciting adventure of Hop Harrigan!
Home-front children listen to the radio an average of fourteen hours per week.
And remember, listeners... everyone can do their part!
Programs encourage kids to plant Victory Gardens, collect scrap metal, scrap rubber, and scrap paper, and buy war bonds.

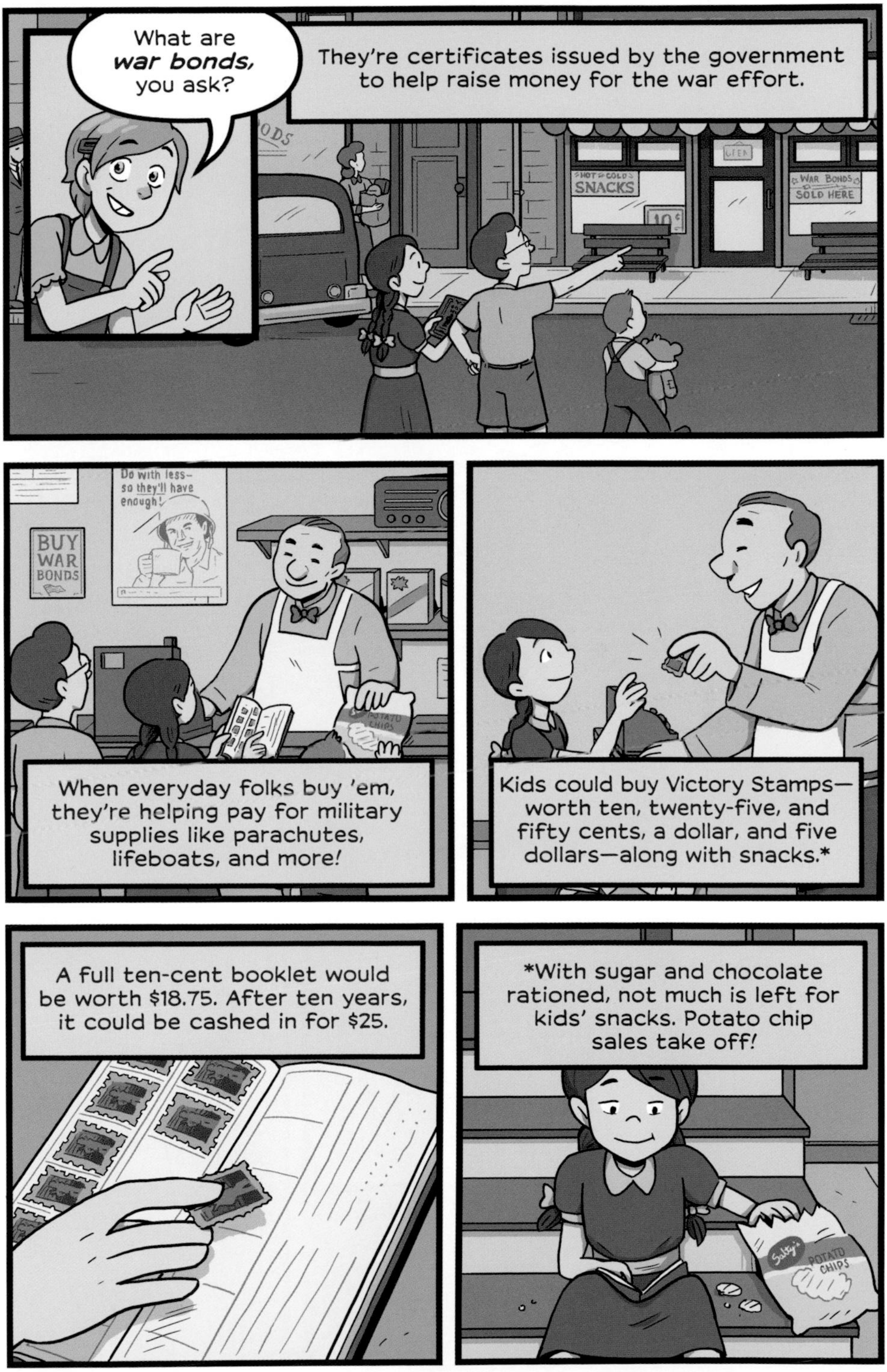
What are *war bonds,* you ask?
They're certificates issued by the government to help raise money for the war effort.
HOT COLD SNACKS
WAR BONDS SOLD HERE
Do with less—so they'll have enough!
BUY WAR BONDS
POTATO CHIPS
When everyday folks buy 'em, they're helping pay for military supplies like parachutes, lifeboats, and more!
Kids could buy Victory Stamps—worth ten, twenty-five, and fifty cents, a dollar, and five dollars—along with snacks.*
A full ten-cent booklet would be worth $18.75. After ten years, it could be cashed in for $25.
*With sugar and chocolate rationed, not much is left for kids' snacks. Potato chip sales take off!
POTATO CHIPS

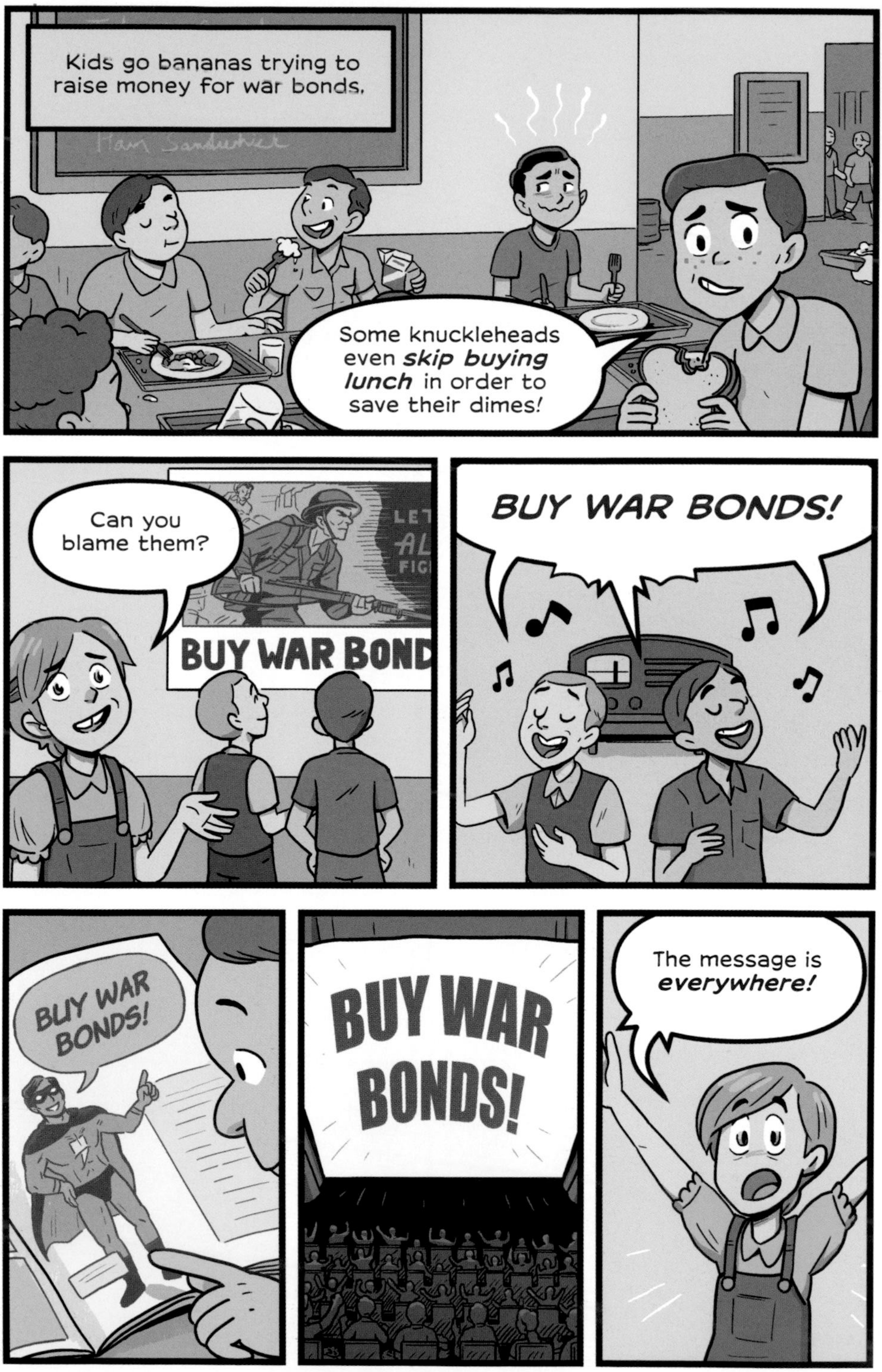
Kids go bananas trying to raise money for war bonds.
Some knuckleheads even ***skip buying lunch*** in order to save their dimes!
Can you blame them?
BUY WAR BOND
BUY WAR BONDS!
BUY WAR BONDS!
BUY WAR BONDS!
The message is ***everywhere!***

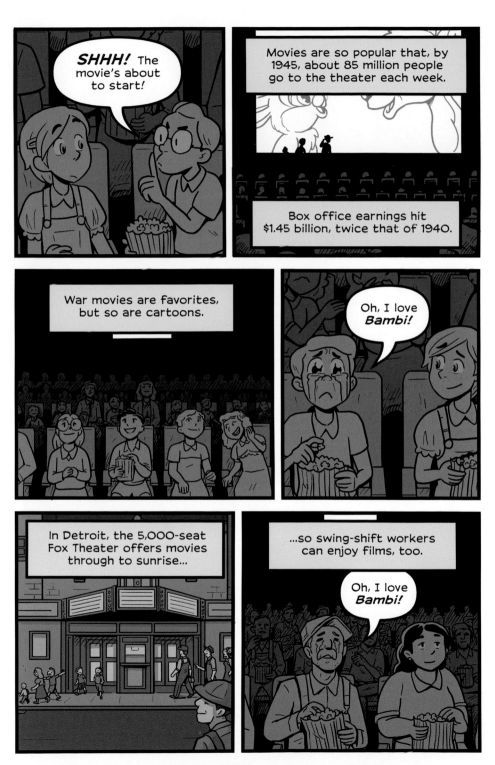

SHHH! The movie's about to start!

Movies are so popular that, by 1945, about 85 million people go to the theater each week.

Box office earnings hit $1.45 billion, twice that of 1940.

War movies are favorites, but so are cartoons.

Oh, I love *Bambi!*

In Detroit, the 5,000-seat Fox Theater offers movies through to sunrise...

...so swing-shift workers can enjoy films, too.

Oh, I love *Bambi!*

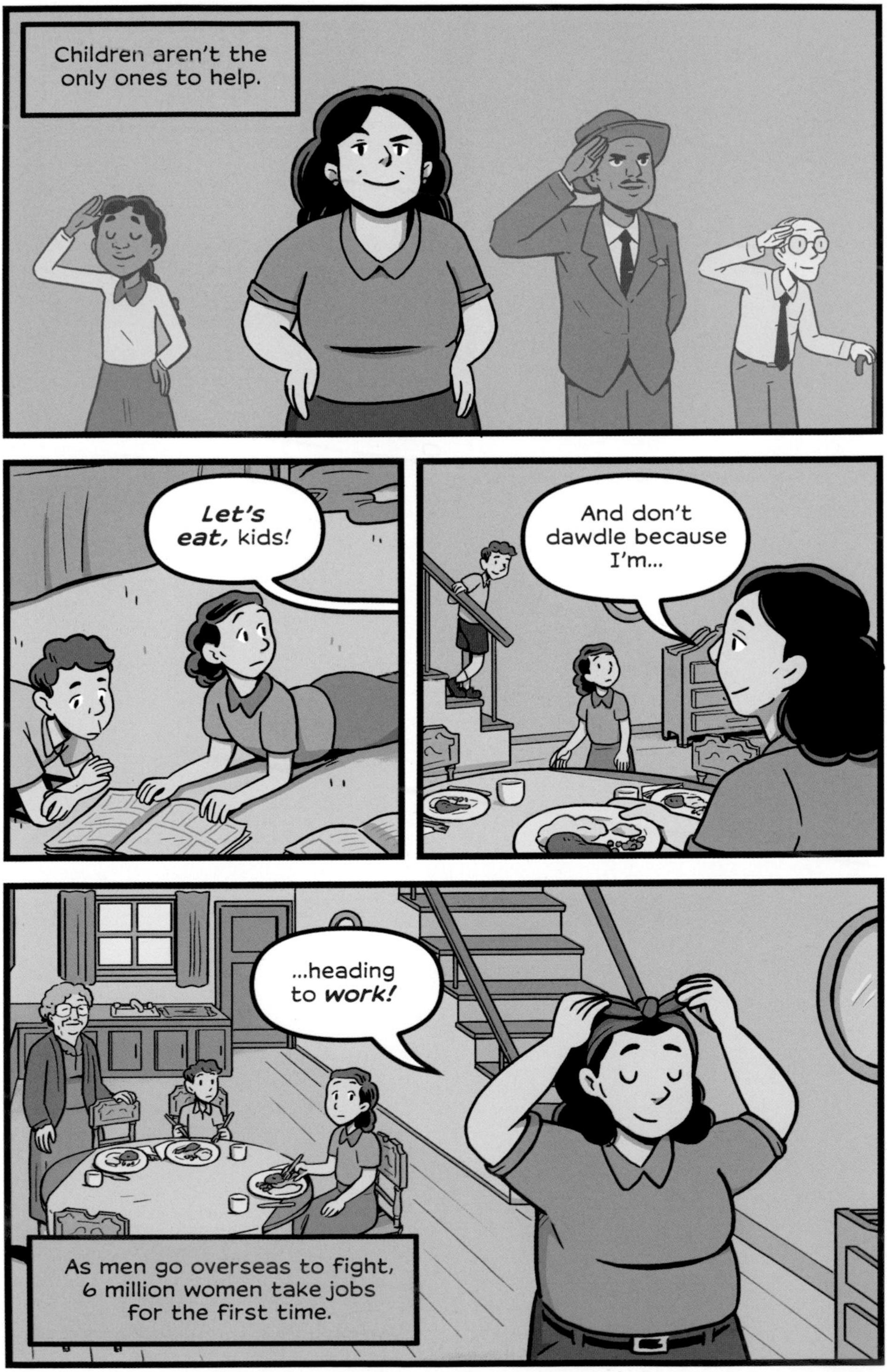
Children aren't the only ones to help.
Let's eat, kids!
And don't dawdle because I'm...
...heading to ***work!***
As men go overseas to fight, 6 million women take jobs for the first time.

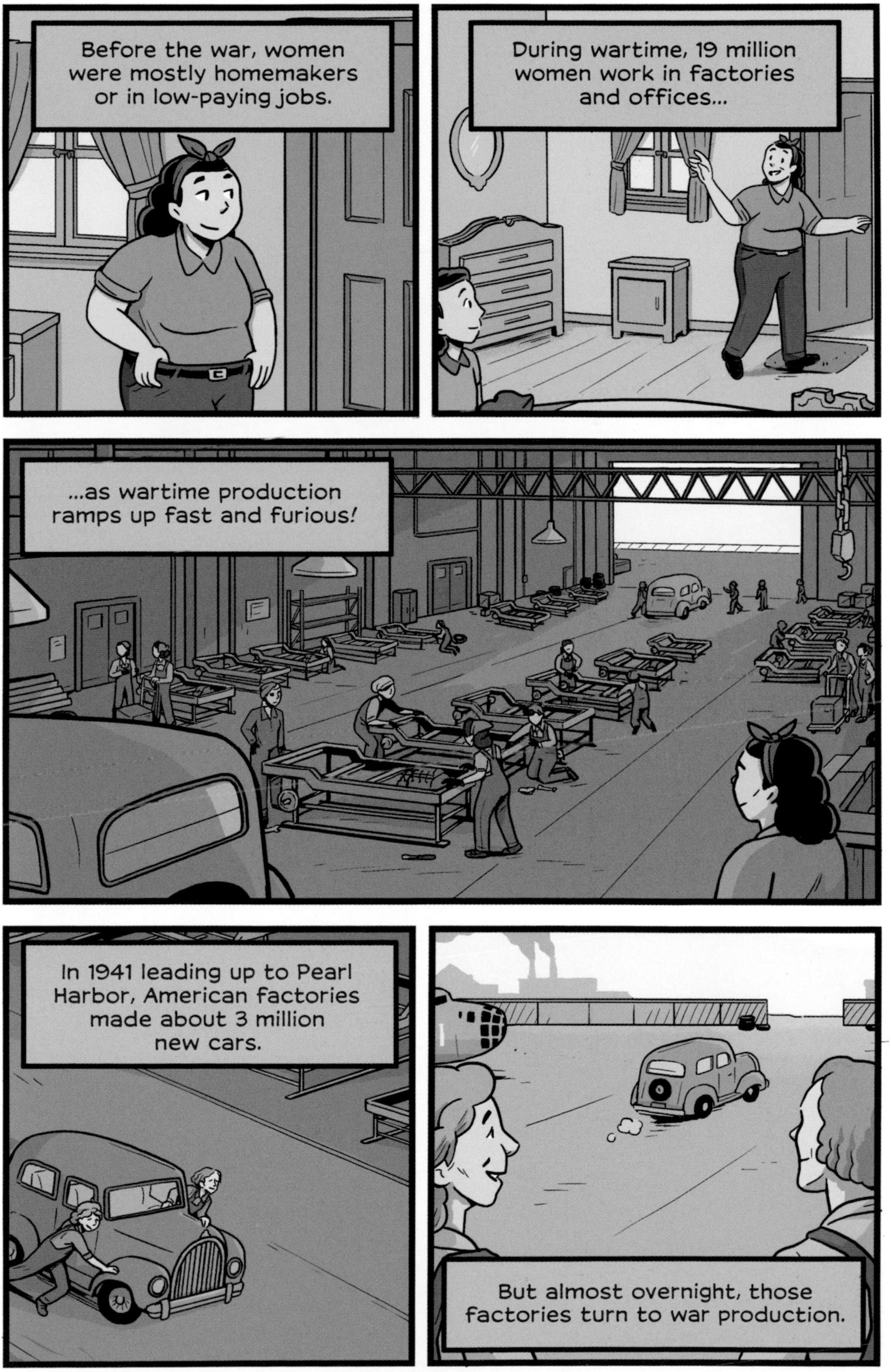
Before the war, women were mostly homemakers or in low-paying jobs.
During wartime, 19 million women work in factories and offices...
...as wartime production ramps up fast and furious!
In 1941 leading up to Pearl Harbor, American factories made about 3 million new cars.
But almost overnight, those factories turn to war production.

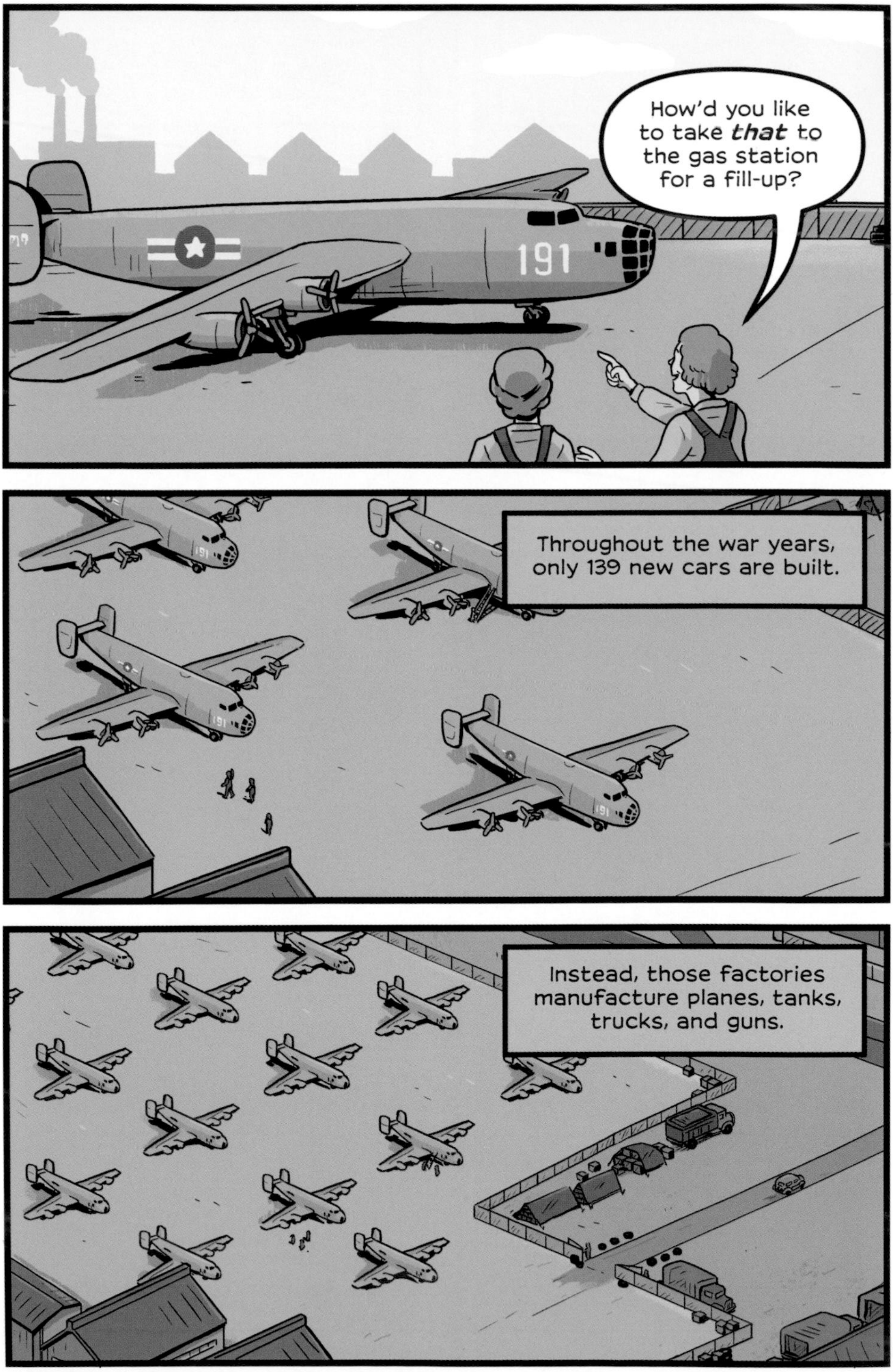
How'd you like to take ***that*** to the gas station for a fill-up?
191
Throughout the war years, only 139 new cars are built.
Instead, those factories manufacture planes, tanks, trucks, and guns.

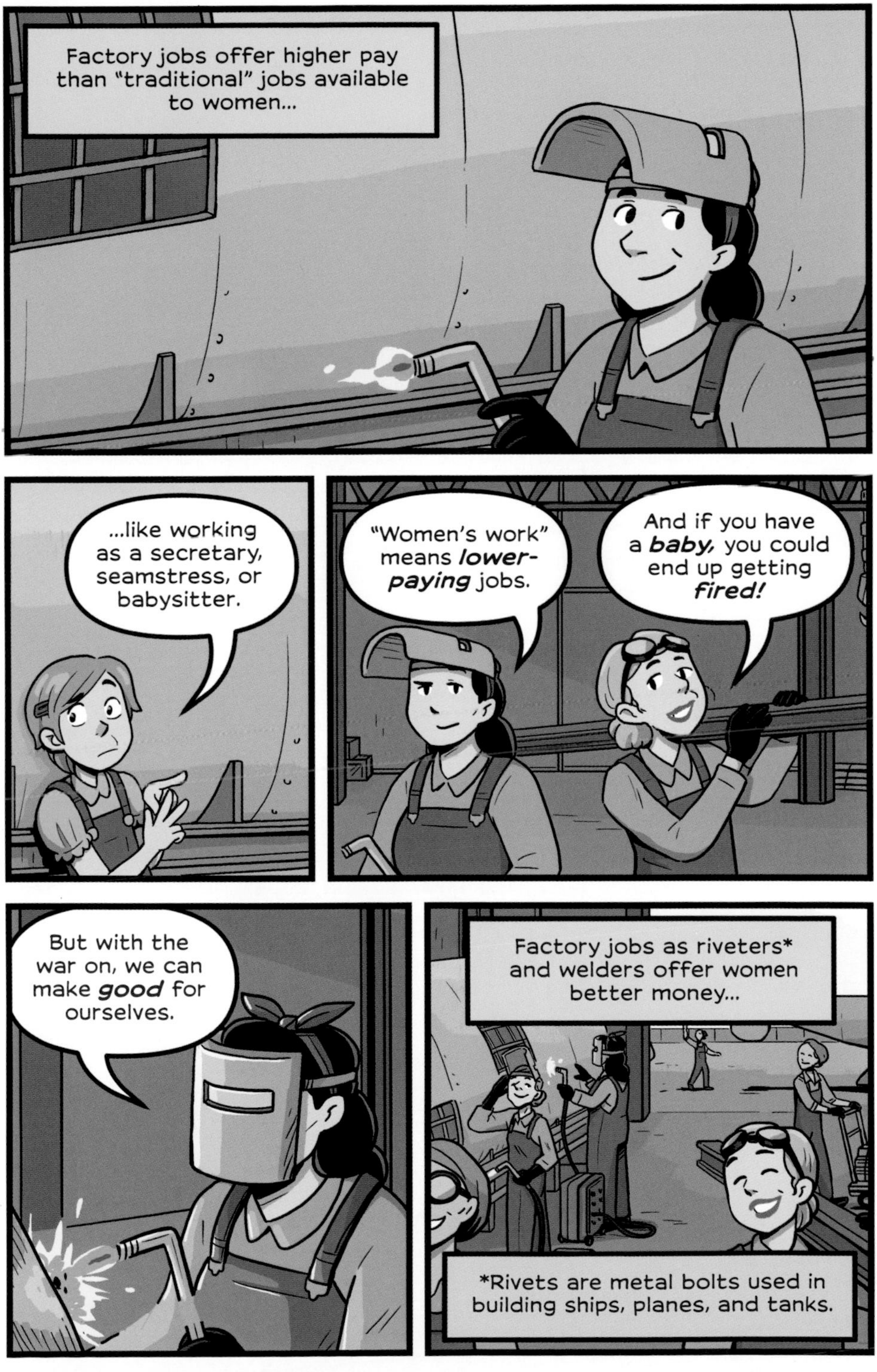
Factory jobs offer higher pay than "traditional" jobs available to women...
...like working as a secretary, seamstress, or babysitter.
"Women's work" means *lower-paying* jobs.
And if you have a *baby,* you could end up getting *fired!*
But with the war on, we can make *good* for ourselves.
Factory jobs as riveters* and welders offer women better money...
*Rivets are metal bolts used in building ships, planes, and tanks.

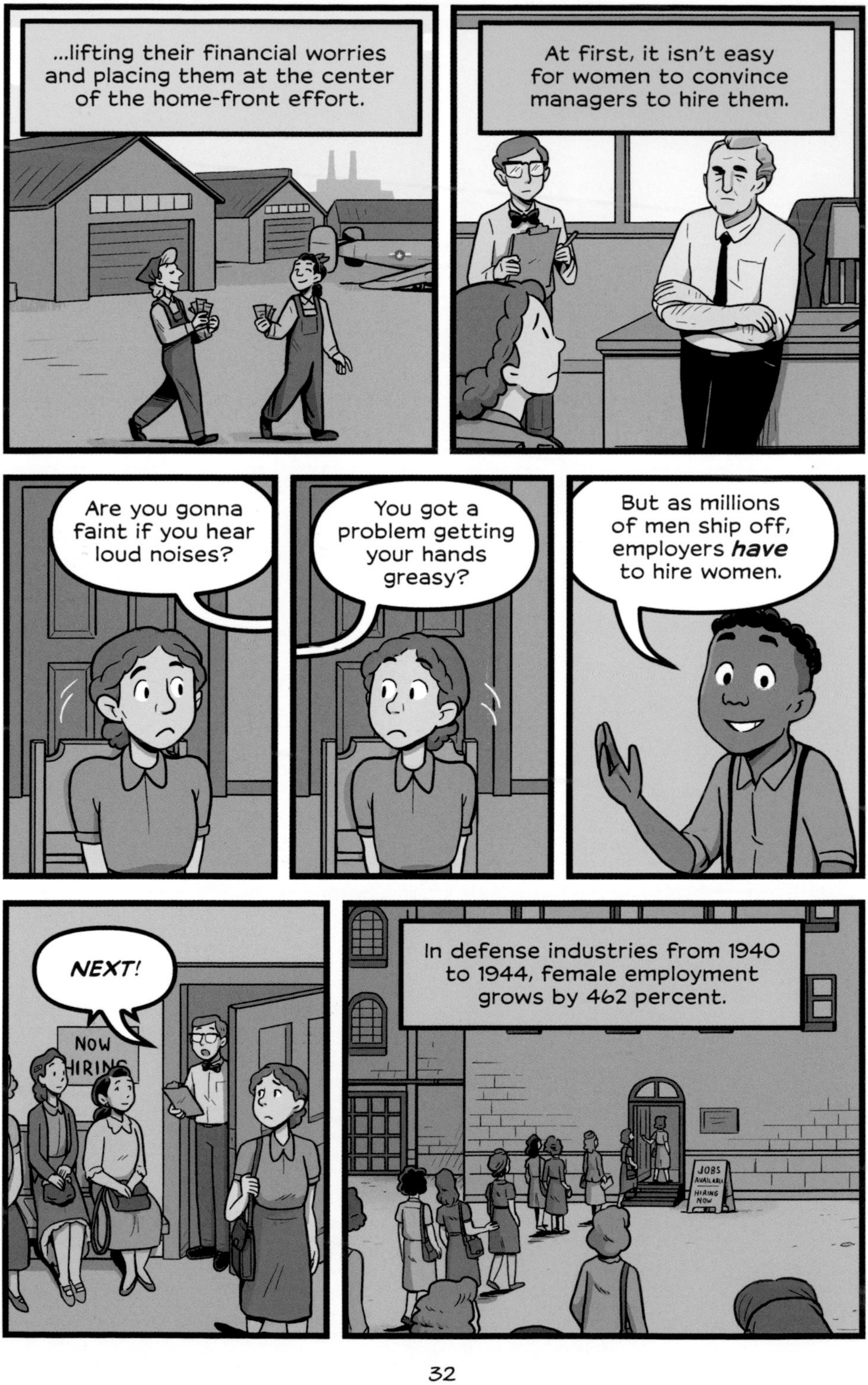
...lifting their financial worries and placing them at the center of the home-front effort.
At first, it isn't easy for women to convince managers to hire them.
Are you gonna faint if you hear loud noises?
You got a problem getting your hands greasy?
But as millions of men ship off, employers ***have*** to hire women.
NEXT!
NOW HIRIN
In defense industries from 1940 to 1944, female employment grows by 462 percent.
JOBS AVAILABLE
HIRING NOW

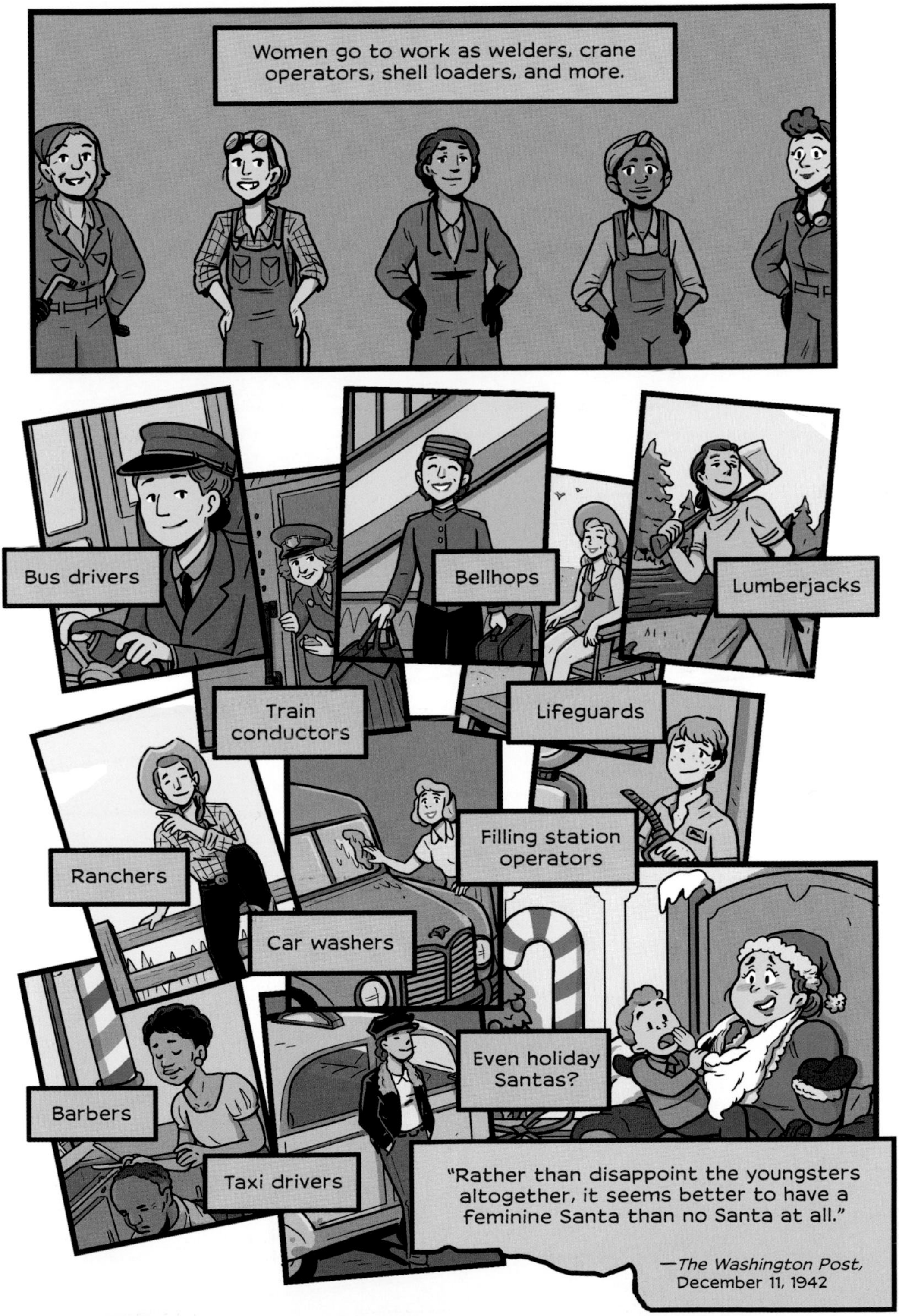

Women go to work as welders, crane operators, shell loaders, and more.
Bus drivers
Train conductors
Bellhops
Lifeguards
Lumberjacks
Ranchers
Car washers
Filling station operators
Barbers
Taxi drivers
Even holiday Santas?
"Rather than disappoint the youngsters altogether, it seems better to have a feminine Santa than no Santa at all."
—*The Washington Post*, December 11, 1942

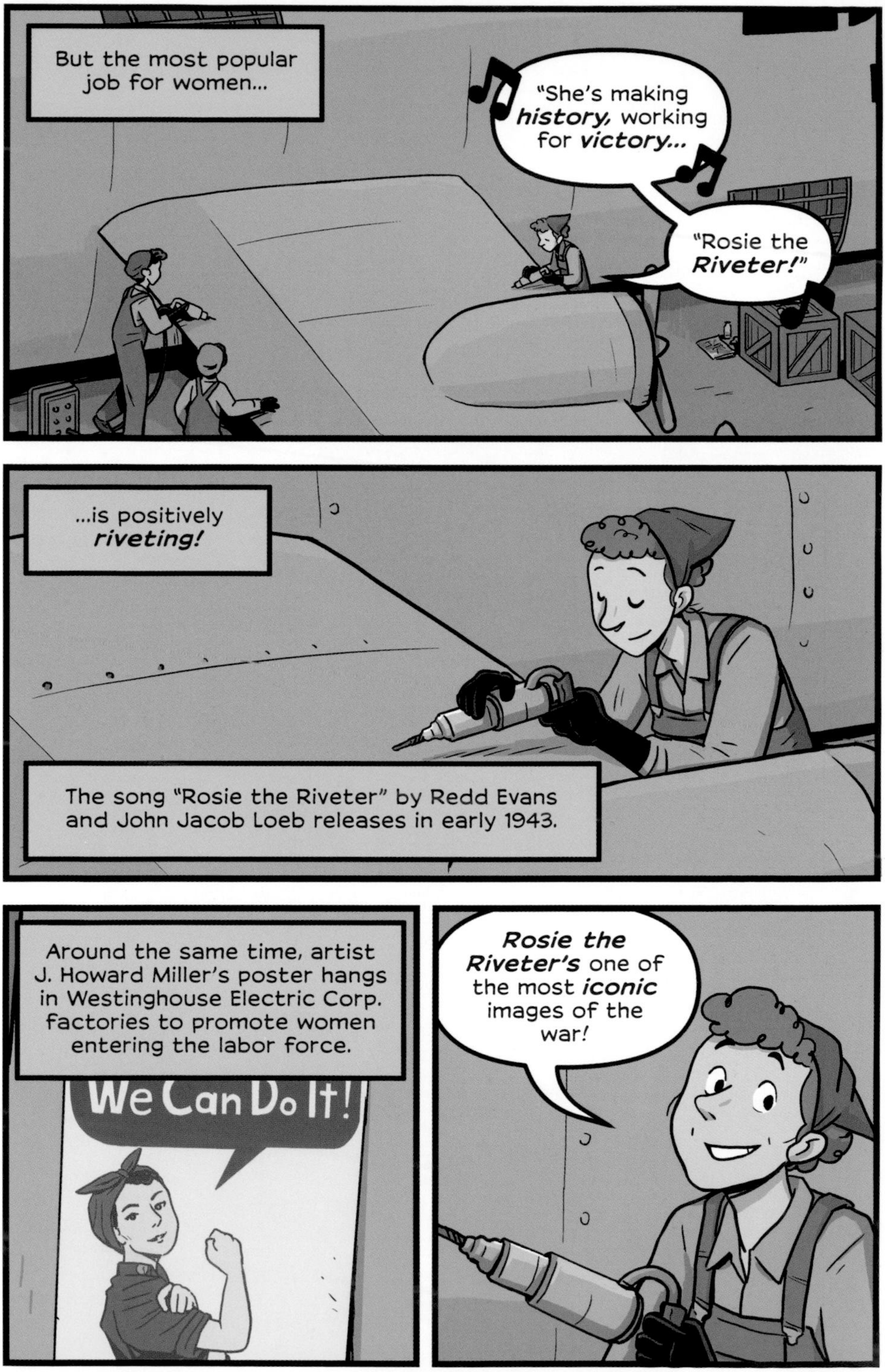
But the most popular job for women...
"She's making *history,* working for *victory...*
"Rosie the *Riveter!"*
...is positively *riveting!*
The song "Rosie the Riveter" by Redd Evans and John Jacob Loeb releases in early 1943.
Around the same time, artist J. Howard Miller's poster hangs in Westinghouse Electric Corp. factories to promote women entering the labor force.
We Can Do It!
Rosie the Riveter's one of the most *iconic* images of the war!

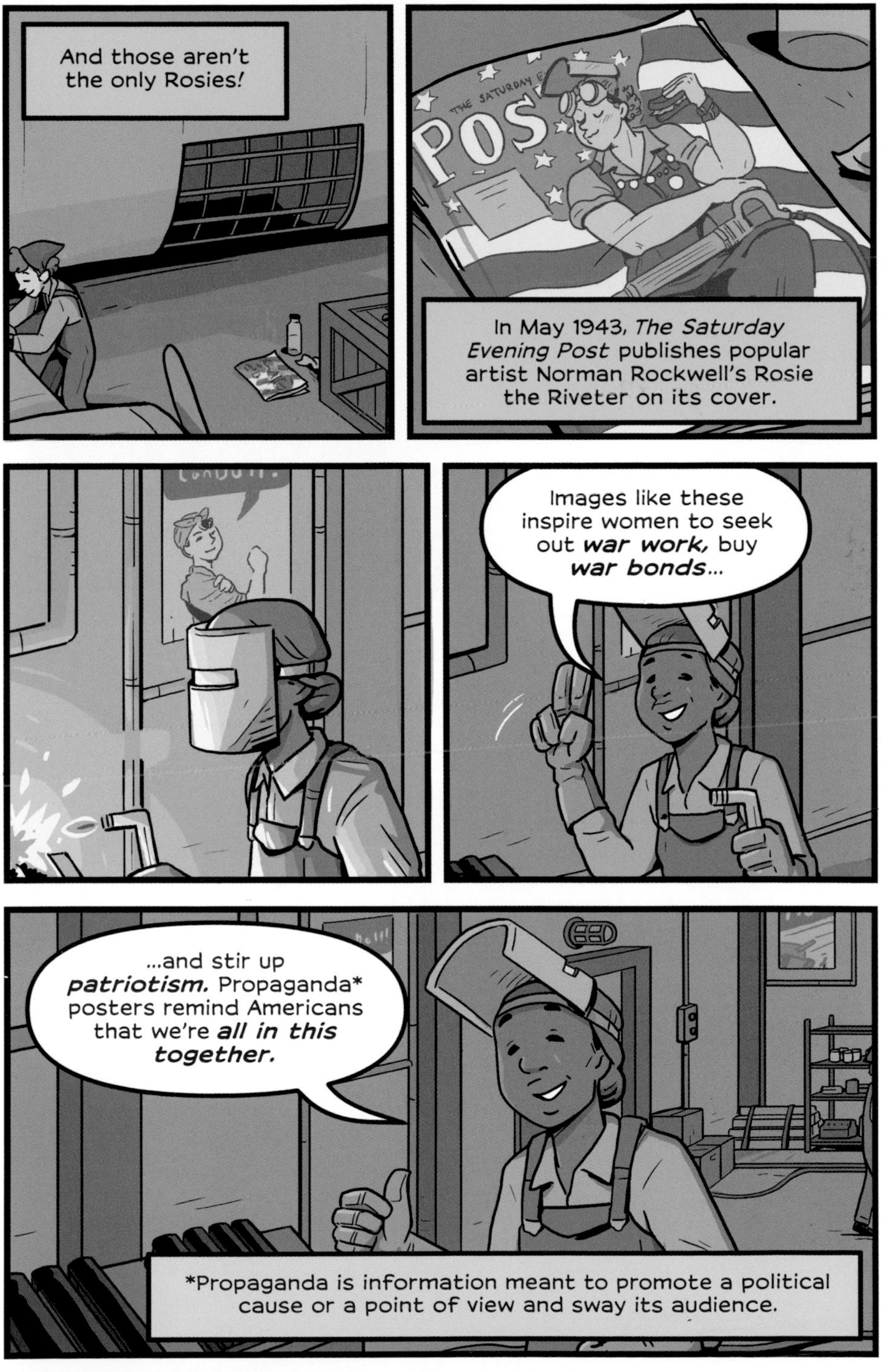
And those aren't the only Rosies!
In May 1943, The Saturday Evening Post publishes popular artist Norman Rockwell's Rosie the Riveter on its cover.
Images like these inspire women to seek out war work, buy war bonds...
...and stir up patriotism. Propaganda* posters remind Americans that we're all in this together.
*Propaganda is information meant to promote a political cause or a point of view and sway its audience.

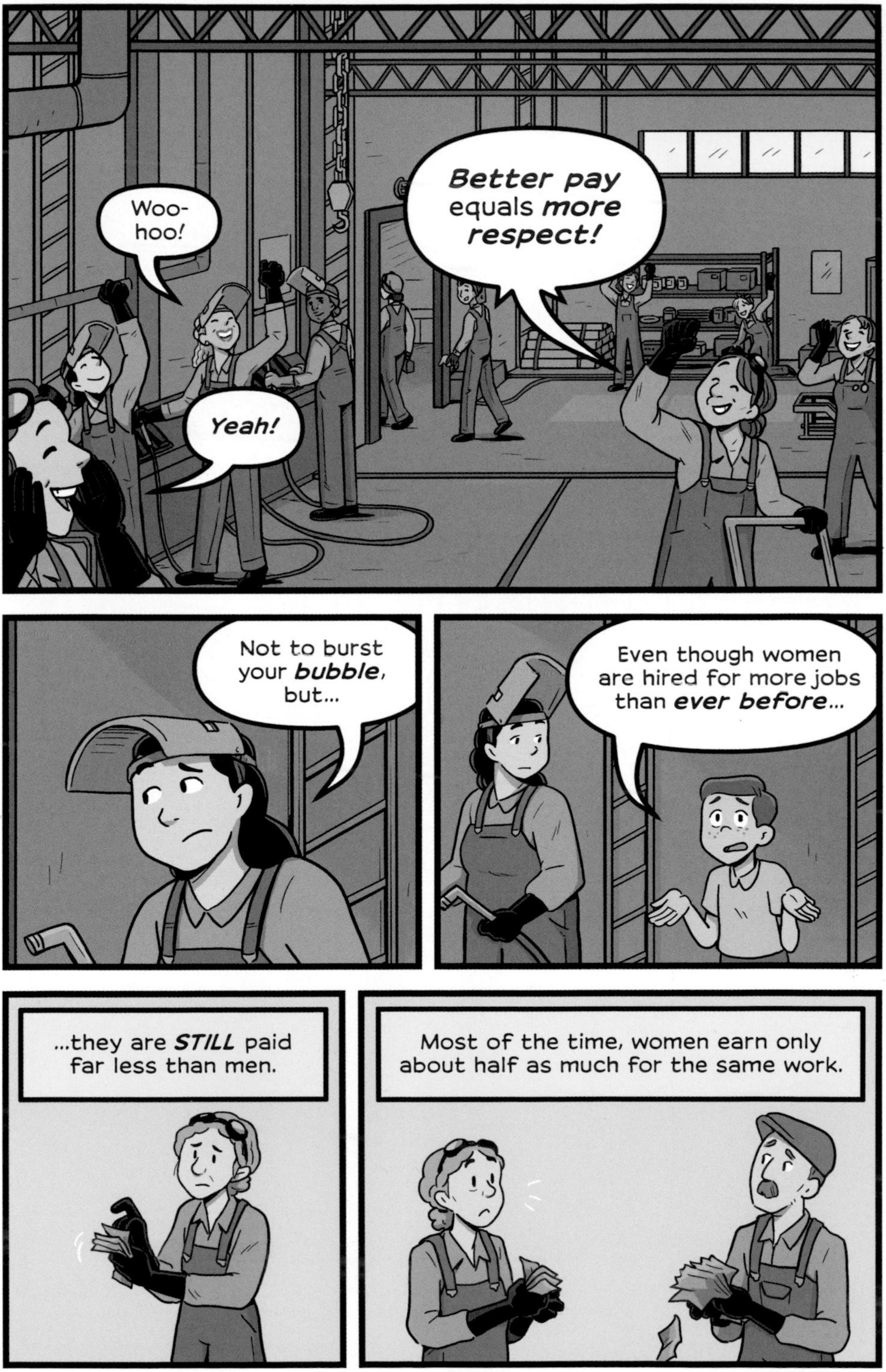

Woo-hoo!
Yeah!
Better pay equals more respect!
Not to burst your bubble, but...
Even though women are hired for more jobs than ever before...
...they are STILL paid far less than men.
Most of the time, women earn only about half as much for the same work.

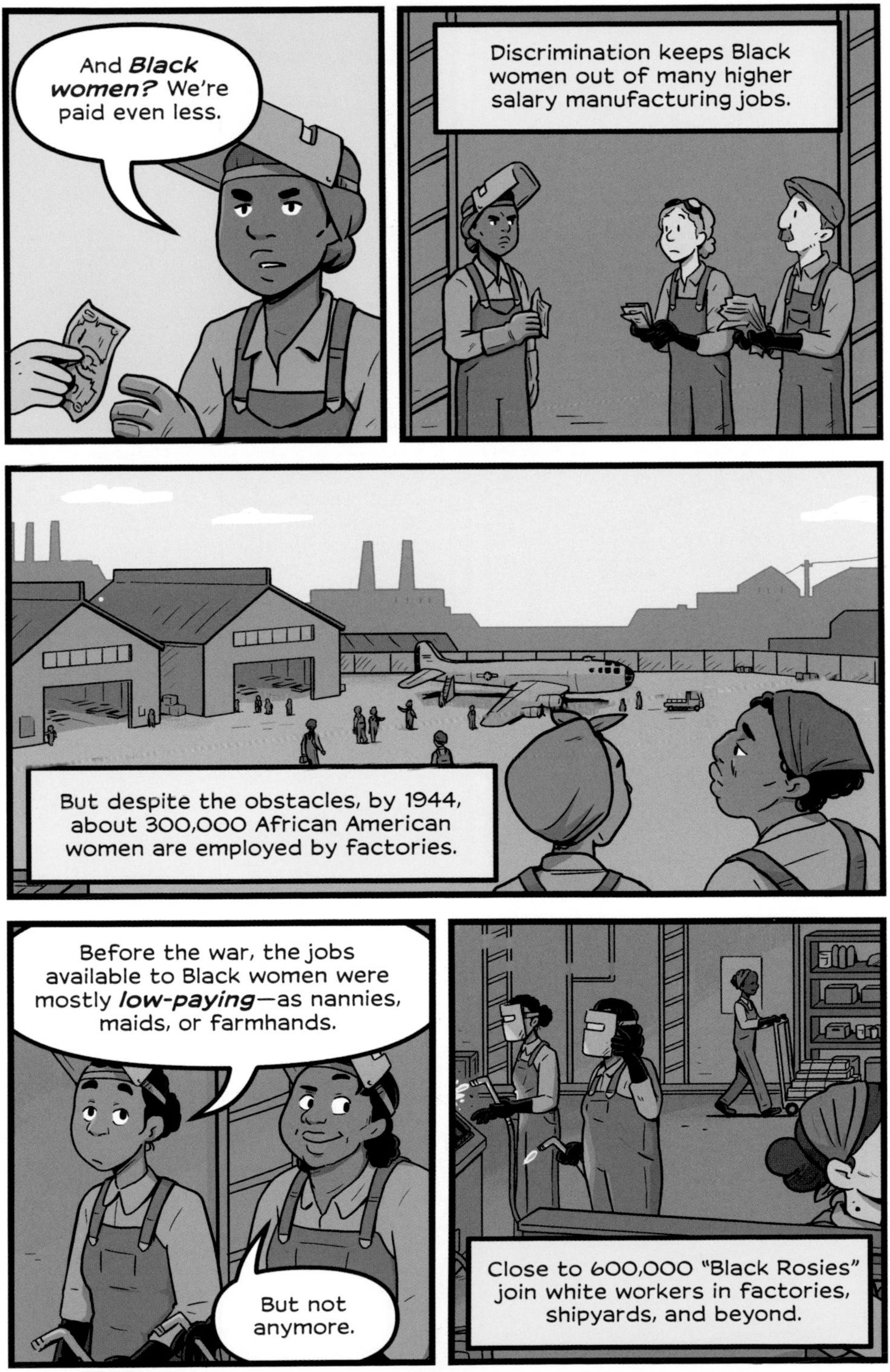
And *Black women?* We're paid even less.
Discrimination keeps Black women out of many higher salary manufacturing jobs.
But despite the obstacles, by 1944, about 300,000 African American women are employed by factories.
Before the war, the jobs available to Black women were mostly *low-paying*—as nannies, maids, or farmhands.
But not anymore.
Close to 600,000 "Black Rosies" join white workers in factories, shipyards, and beyond.

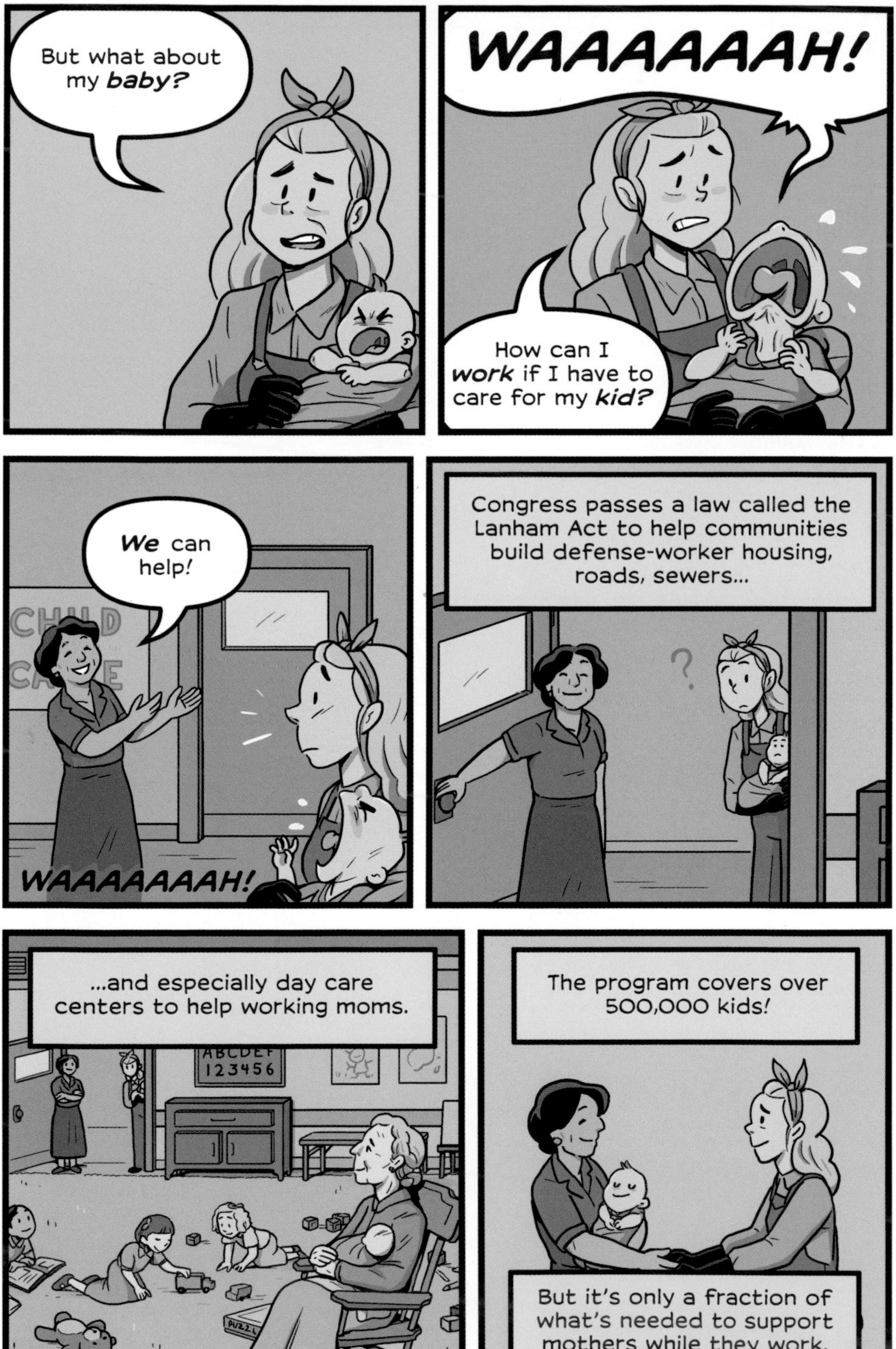
But what about my ***baby?***
WAAAAAAH!
How can I ***work*** if I have to care for my ***kid?***
We can help!
WAAAAAAAH!
Congress passes a law called the Lanham Act to help communities build defense-worker housing, roads, sewers...
...and especially day care centers to help working moms.
ABCDEF
123456
The program covers over 500,000 kids!
But it's only a fraction of what's needed to support mothers while they work.

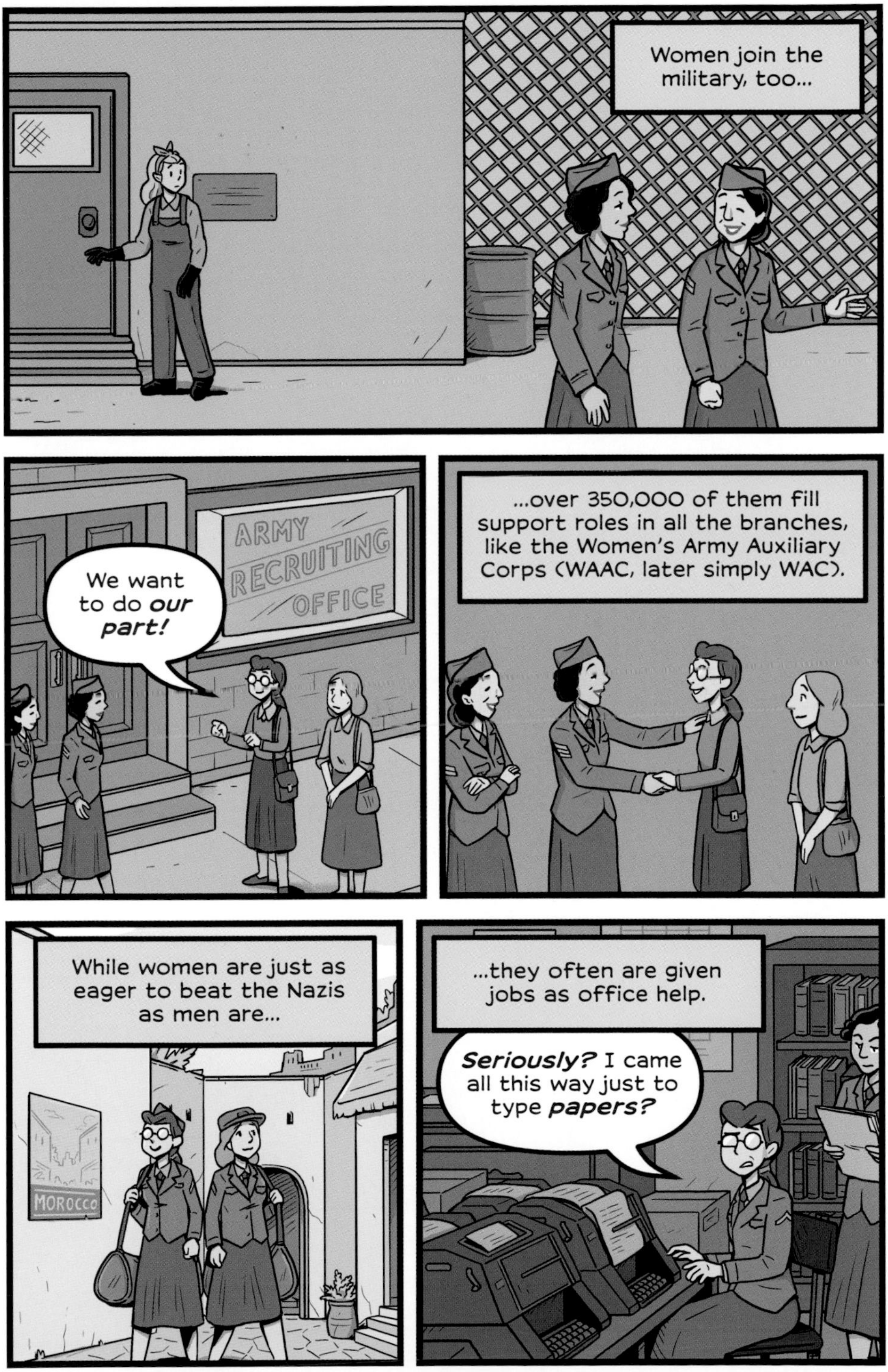
Women join the military, too...
We want to do *our part!*
ARMY RECRUITING OFFICE
...over 350,000 of them fill support roles in all the branches, like the Women's Army Auxiliary Corps (WAAC, later simply WAC).
While women are just as eager to beat the Nazis as men are...
MOROCCO
...they often are given jobs as office help.
Seriously? I came all this way just to type *papers?*

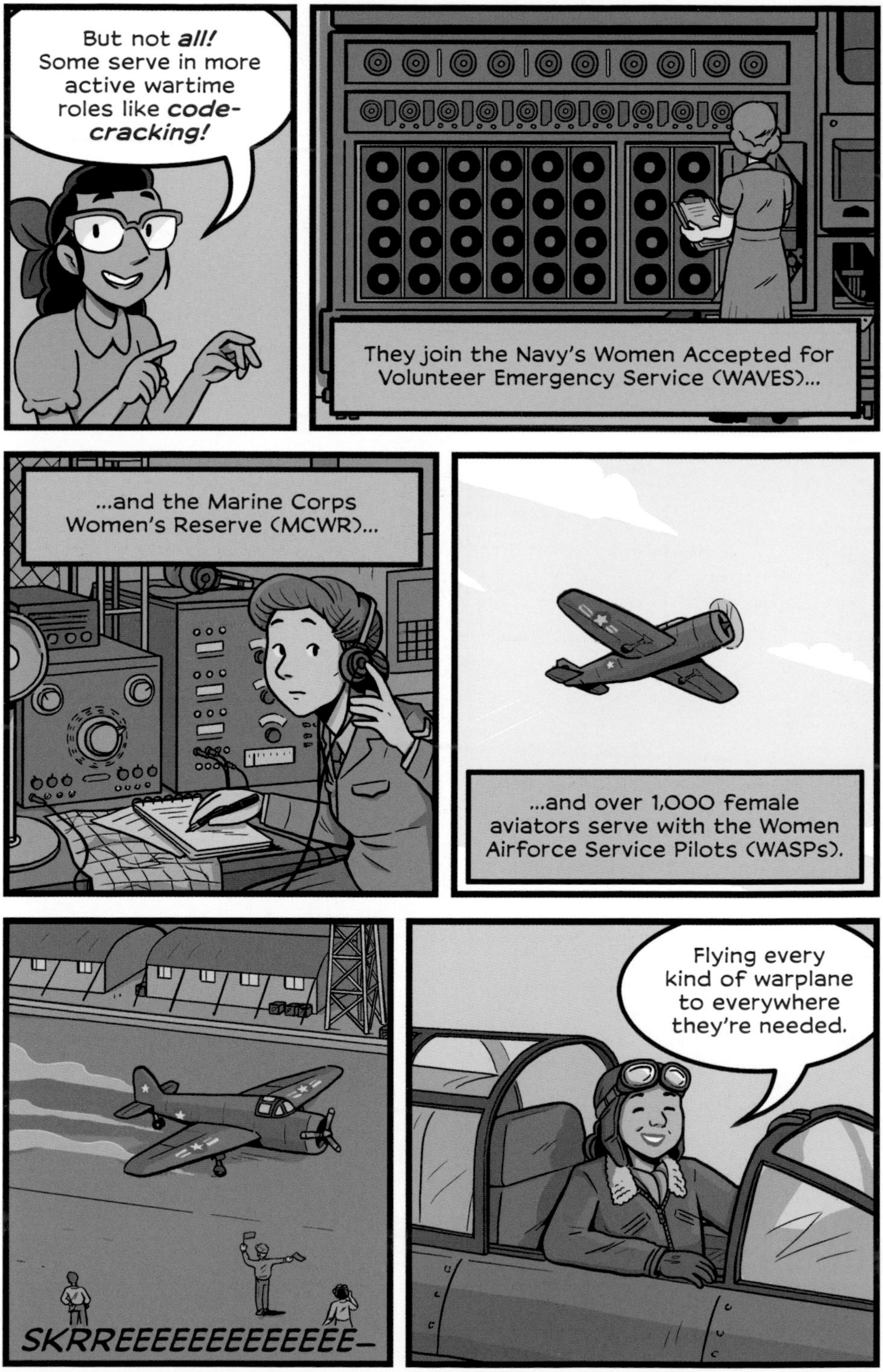
But not *all!* Some serve in more active wartime roles like *code-cracking!*
They join the Navy's Women Accepted for Volunteer Emergency Service (WAVES)...
...and the Marine Corps Women's Reserve (MCWR)...
...and over 1,000 female aviators serve with the Women Airforce Service Pilots (WASPs).
SKRREEEEEEEEEEEEEE–
Flying every kind of warplane to everywhere they're needed.

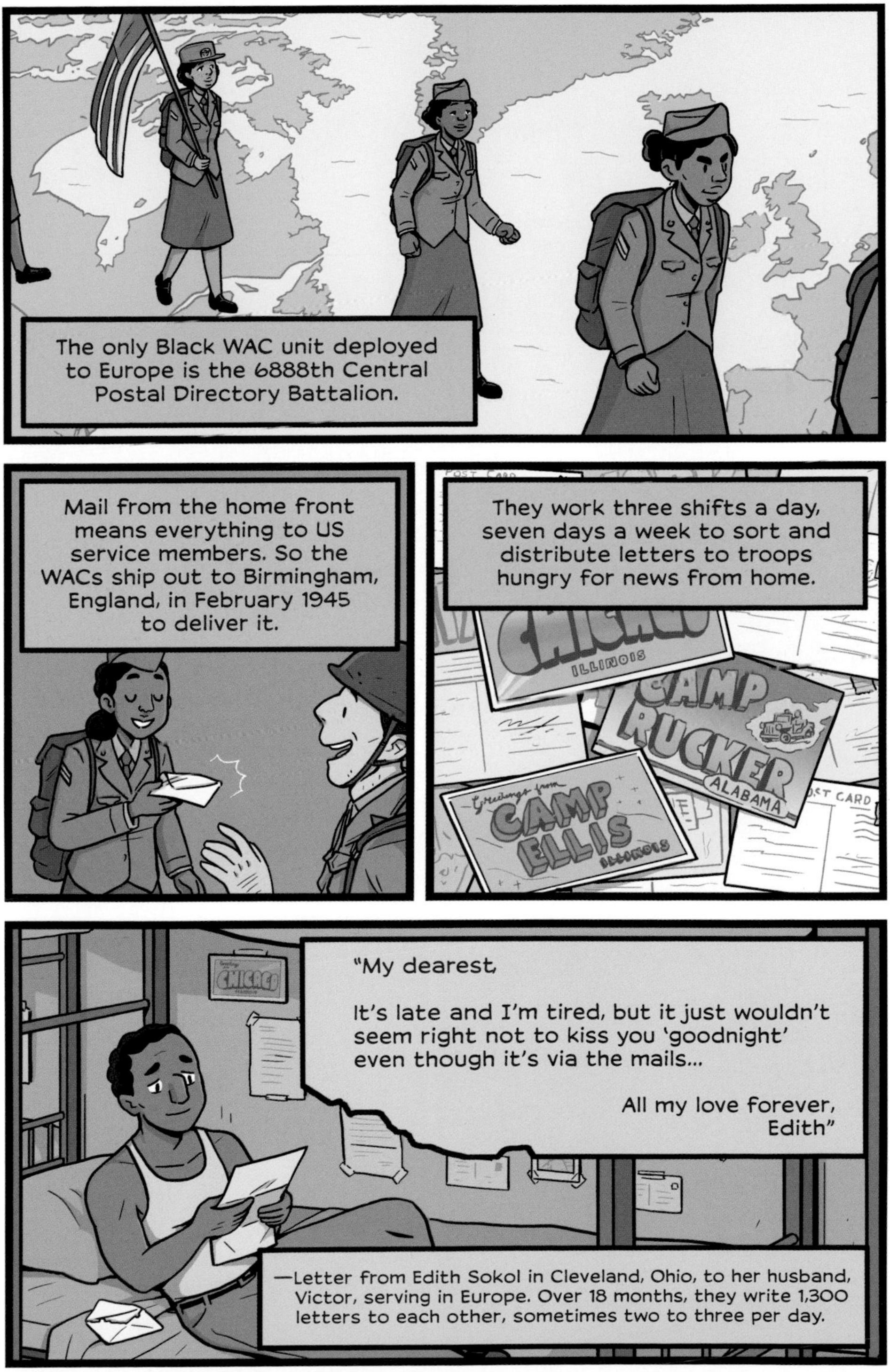
The only Black WAC unit deployed to Europe is the 6888th Central Postal Directory Battalion.
Mail from the home front means everything to US service members. So the WACs ship out to Birmingham, England, in February 1945 to deliver it.
They work three shifts a day, seven days a week to sort and distribute letters to troops hungry for news from home.
ILLINOIS
CAMP RUCKER
ALABAMA
CAMP ELLIS
ILLINOIS
"My dearest,
It's late and I'm tired, but it just wouldn't seem right not to kiss you 'goodnight' even though it's via the mails...
All my love forever,
Edith"
—Letter from Edith Sokol in Cleveland, Ohio, to her husband, Victor, serving in Europe. Over 18 months, they write 1,300 letters to each other, sometimes two to three per day.

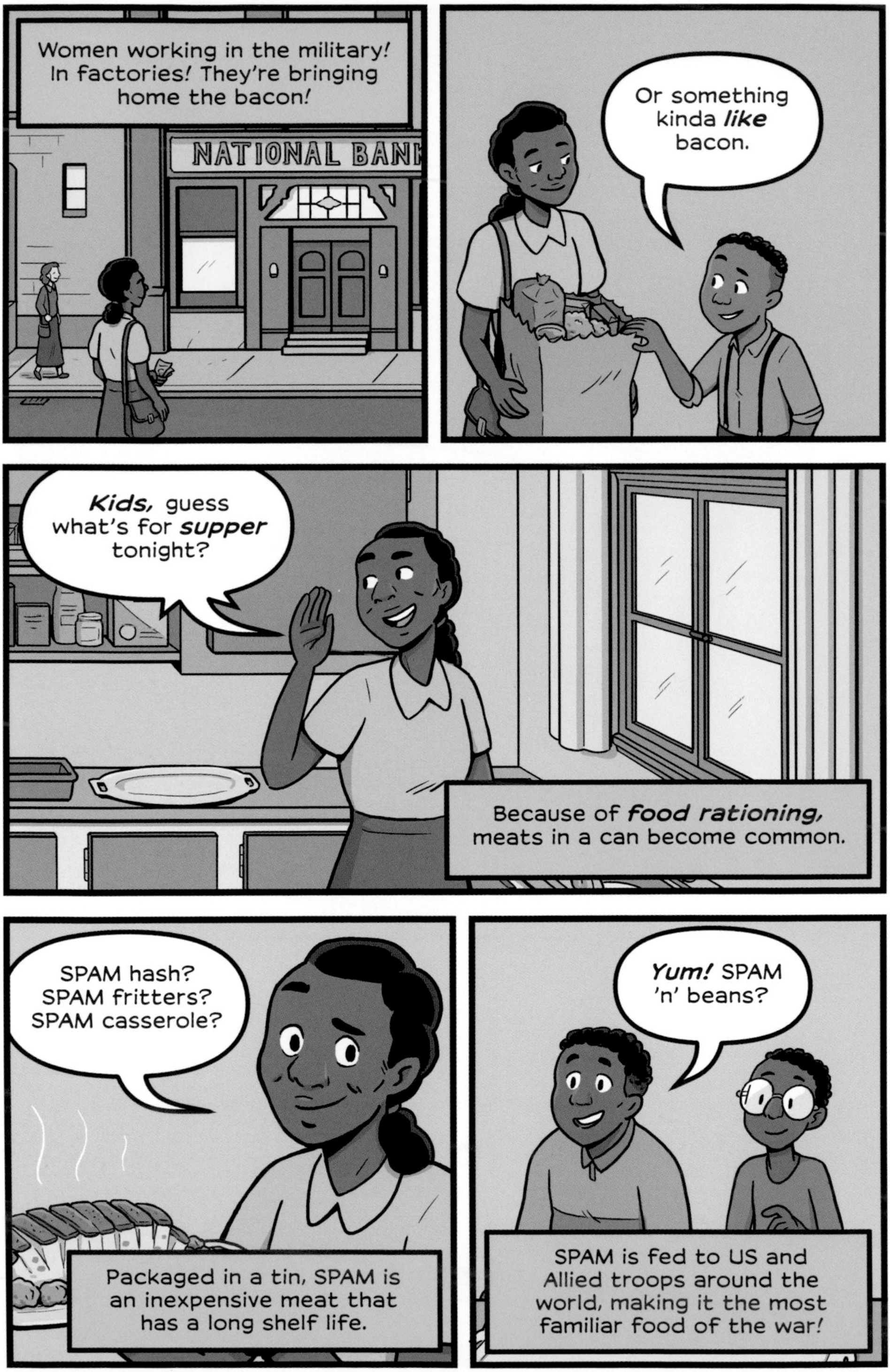
Women working in the military! In factories! They're bringing home the bacon!
NATIONAL BANK
Or something kinda *like* bacon.
Kids, guess what's for *supper* tonight?
Because of *food rationing,* meats in a can become common.
SPAM hash? SPAM fritters? SPAM casserole?
Packaged in a tin, SPAM is an inexpensive meat that has a long shelf life.
Yum! SPAM 'n' beans?
SPAM is fed to US and Allied troops around the world, making it the most familiar food of the war!

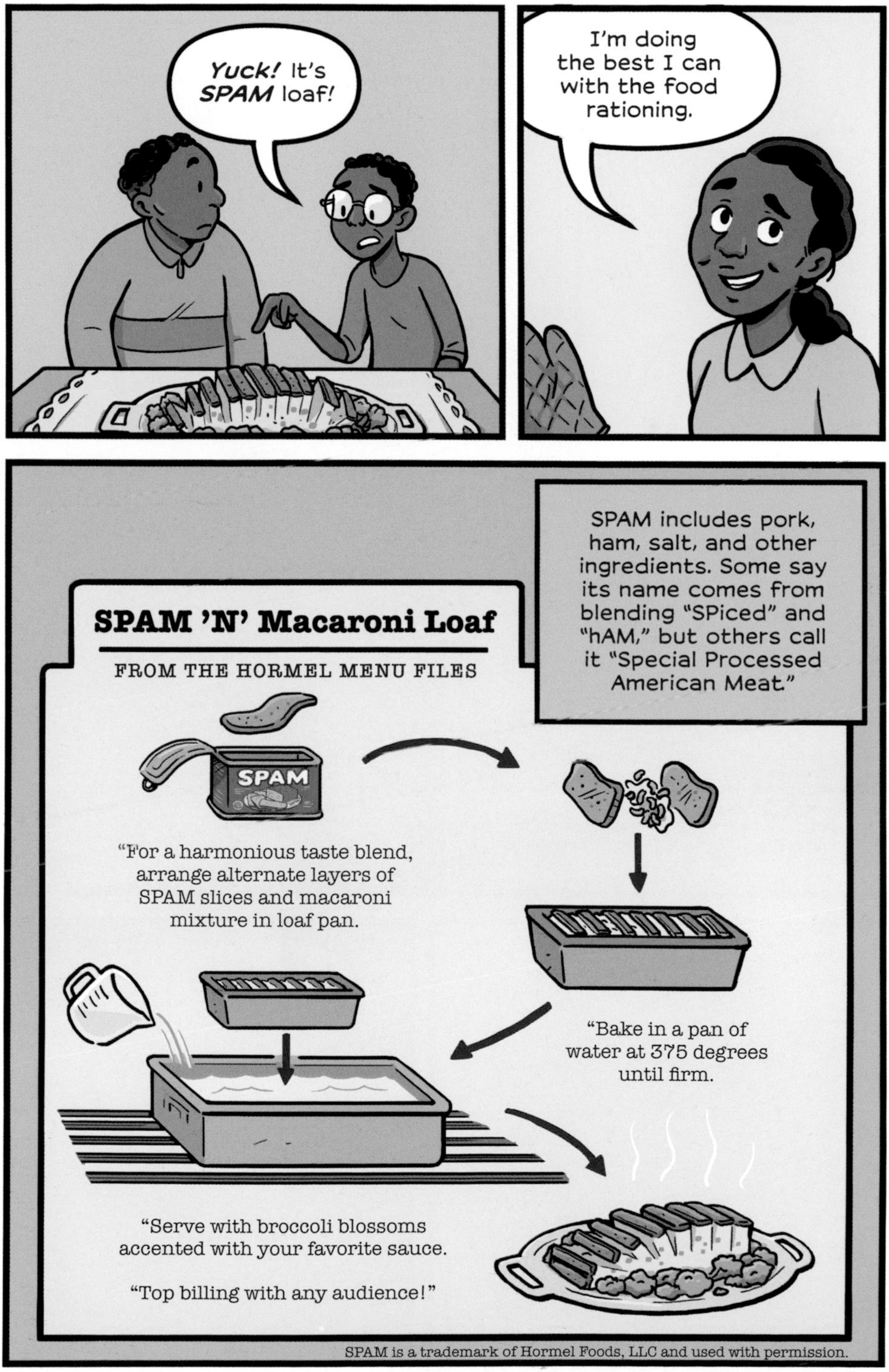

Yuck! It's *SPAM* loaf!
I'm doing the best I can with the food rationing.
SPAM includes pork, ham, salt, and other ingredients. Some say its name comes from blending "SPiced" and "hAM," but others call it "Special Processed American Meat."
SPAM 'N' Macaroni Loaf
FROM THE HORMEL MENU FILES
SPAM
"For a harmonious taste blend, arrange alternate layers of SPAM slices and macaroni mixture in loaf pan.
"Bake in a pan of water at 375 degrees until firm.
"Serve with broccoli blossoms accented with your favorite sauce.
"Top billing with any audience!"
SPAM is a trademark of Hormel Foods, LLC and used with permission.

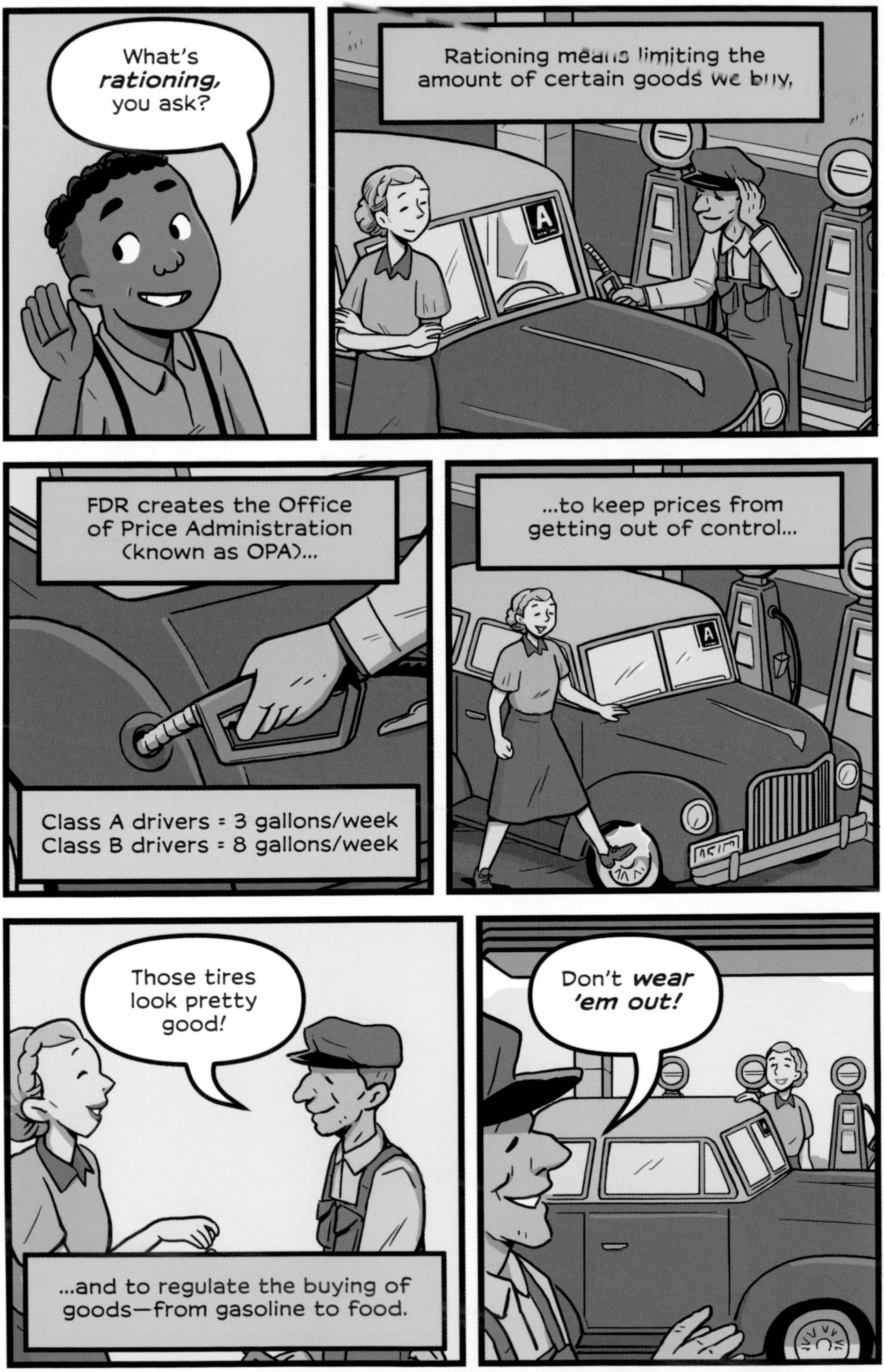
What's *rationing,* you ask?
Rationing means limiting the amount of certain goods we buy,
A
FDR creates the Office of Price Administration (known as OPA)...
Class A drivers = 3 gallons/week
Class B drivers = 8 gallons/week
...to keep prices from getting out of control...
A
Those tires look pretty good!
...and to regulate the buying of goods—from gasoline to food.
Don't ***wear 'em out!***

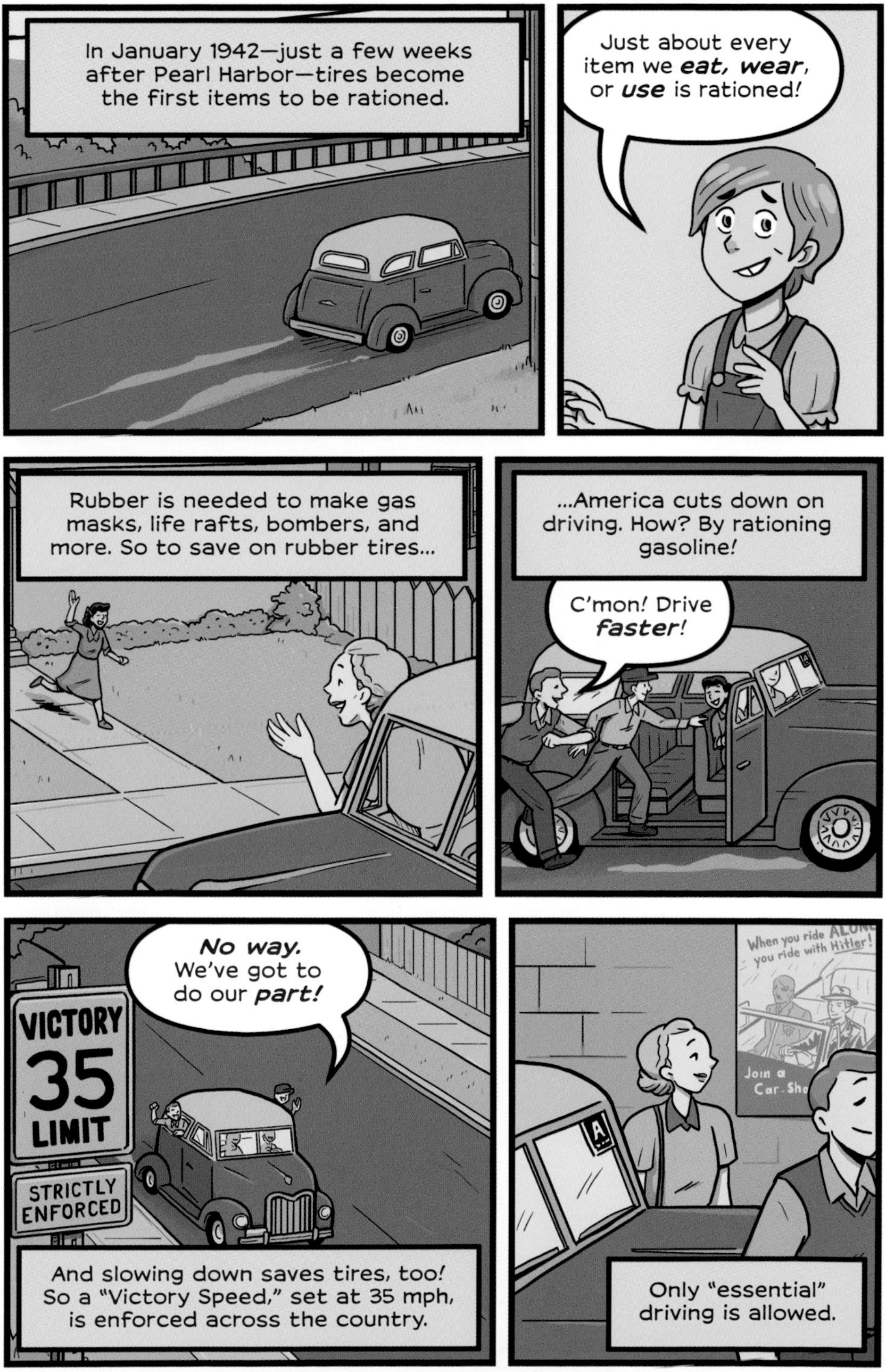

In January 1942—just a few weeks after Pearl Harbor—tires become the first items to be rationed.
Just about every item we ***eat, wear***, or ***use*** is rationed!
Rubber is needed to make gas masks, life rafts, bombers, and more. So to save on rubber tires...
...America cuts down on driving. How? By rationing gasoline!
C'mon! Drive ***faster***!
No way. We've got to do our ***part!***
VICTORY 35 LIMIT
STRICTLY ENFORCED
And slowing down saves tires, too! So a "Victory Speed," set at 35 mph, is enforced across the country.
When you ride ALON
you ride with Hitler!
Join a Car-Sha
A
Only "essential" driving is allowed.

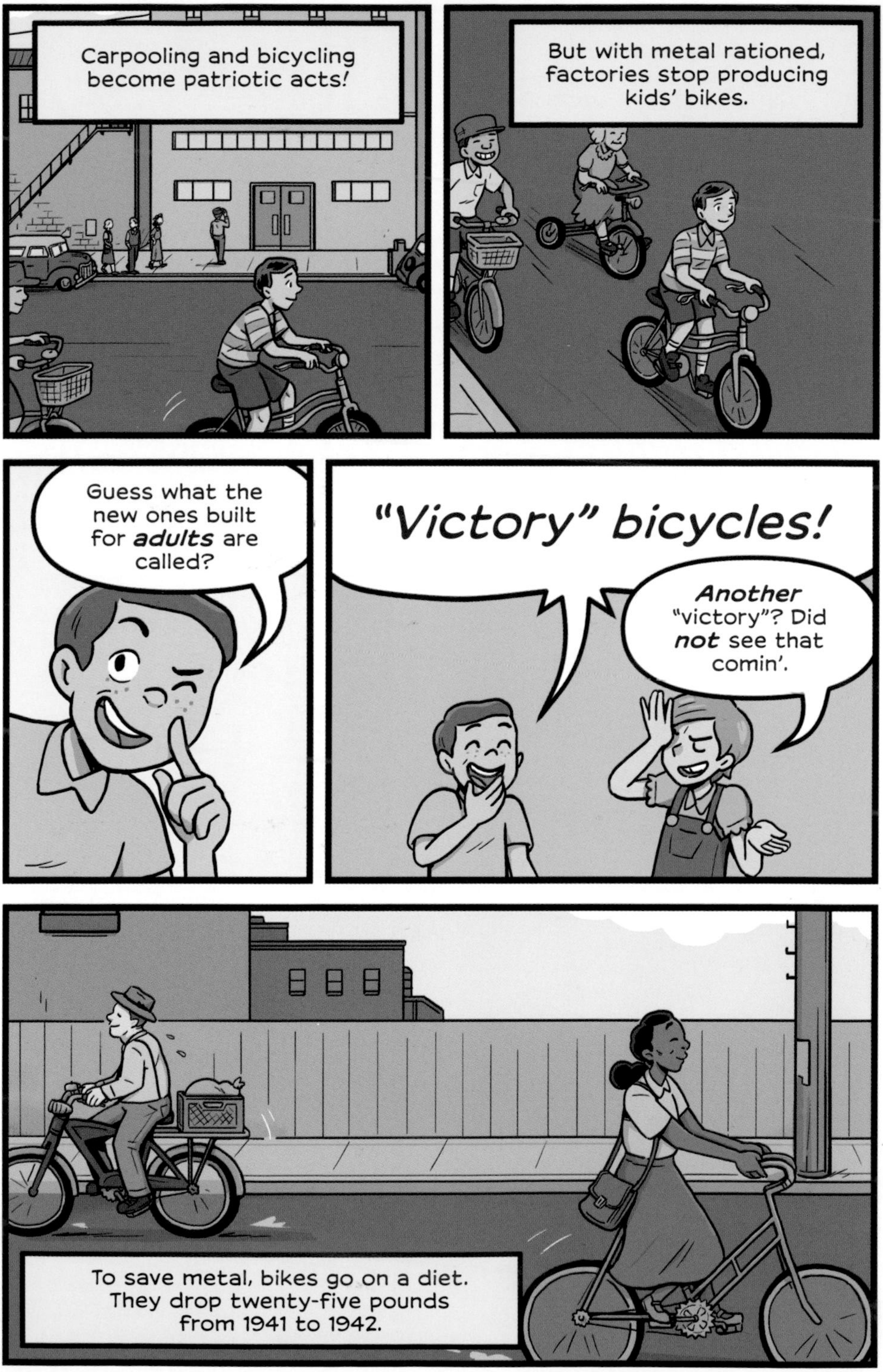
Carpooling and bicycling become patriotic acts!
But with metal rationed, factories stop producing kids' bikes.
Guess what the new ones built for *adults* are called?
"Victory" bicycles!
Another "victory"? Did *not* see that comin'.
To save metal, bikes go on a diet. They drop twenty-five pounds from 1941 to 1942.

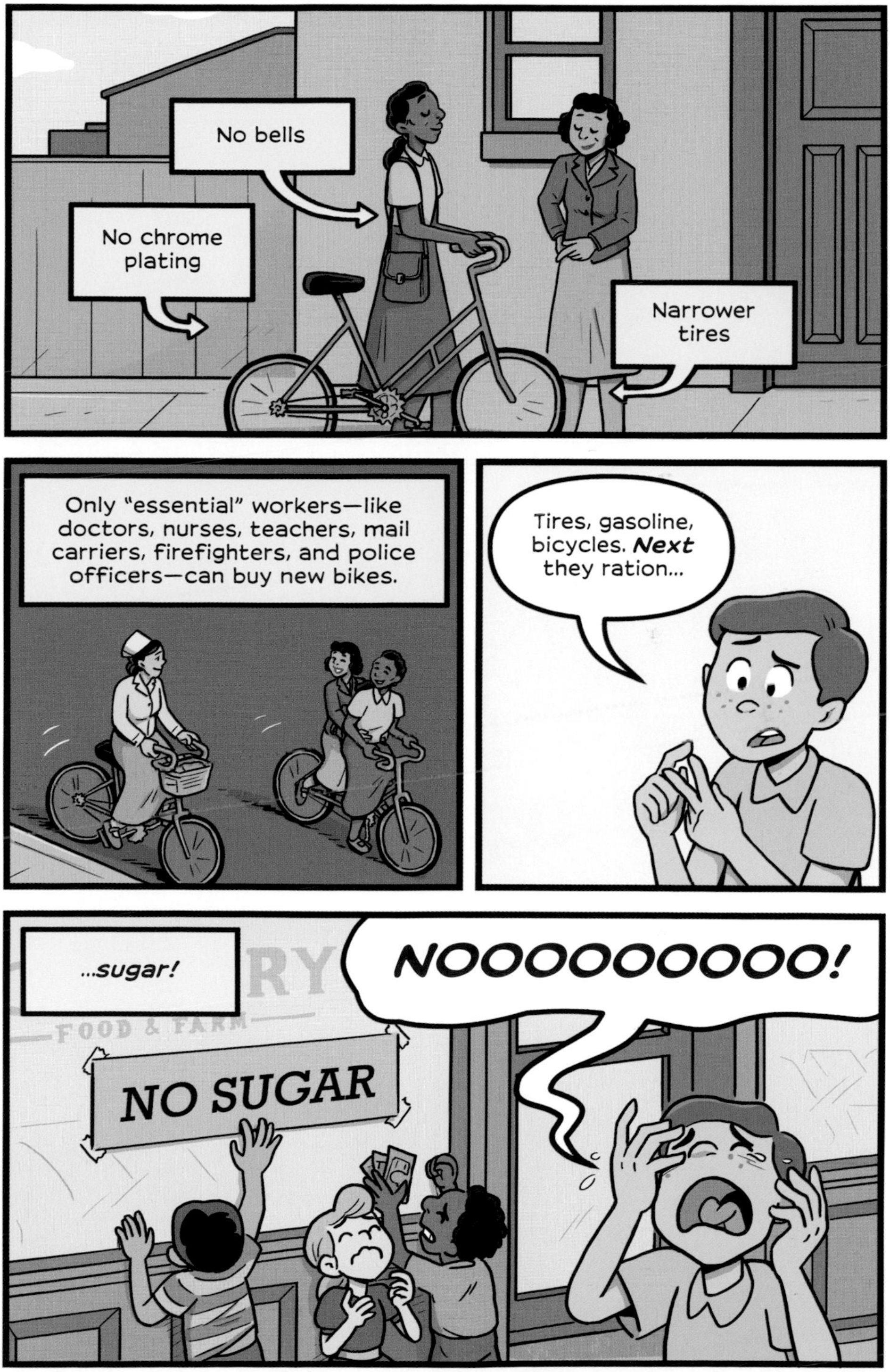
No bells
No chrome plating
Narrower tires
Only "essential" workers—like doctors, nurses, teachers, mail carriers, firefighters, and police officers—can buy new bikes.
Tires, gasoline, bicycles. ***Next*** they ration...
...sugar!
NOOOOOOOOOO!
FOOD & FARM
NO SUGAR

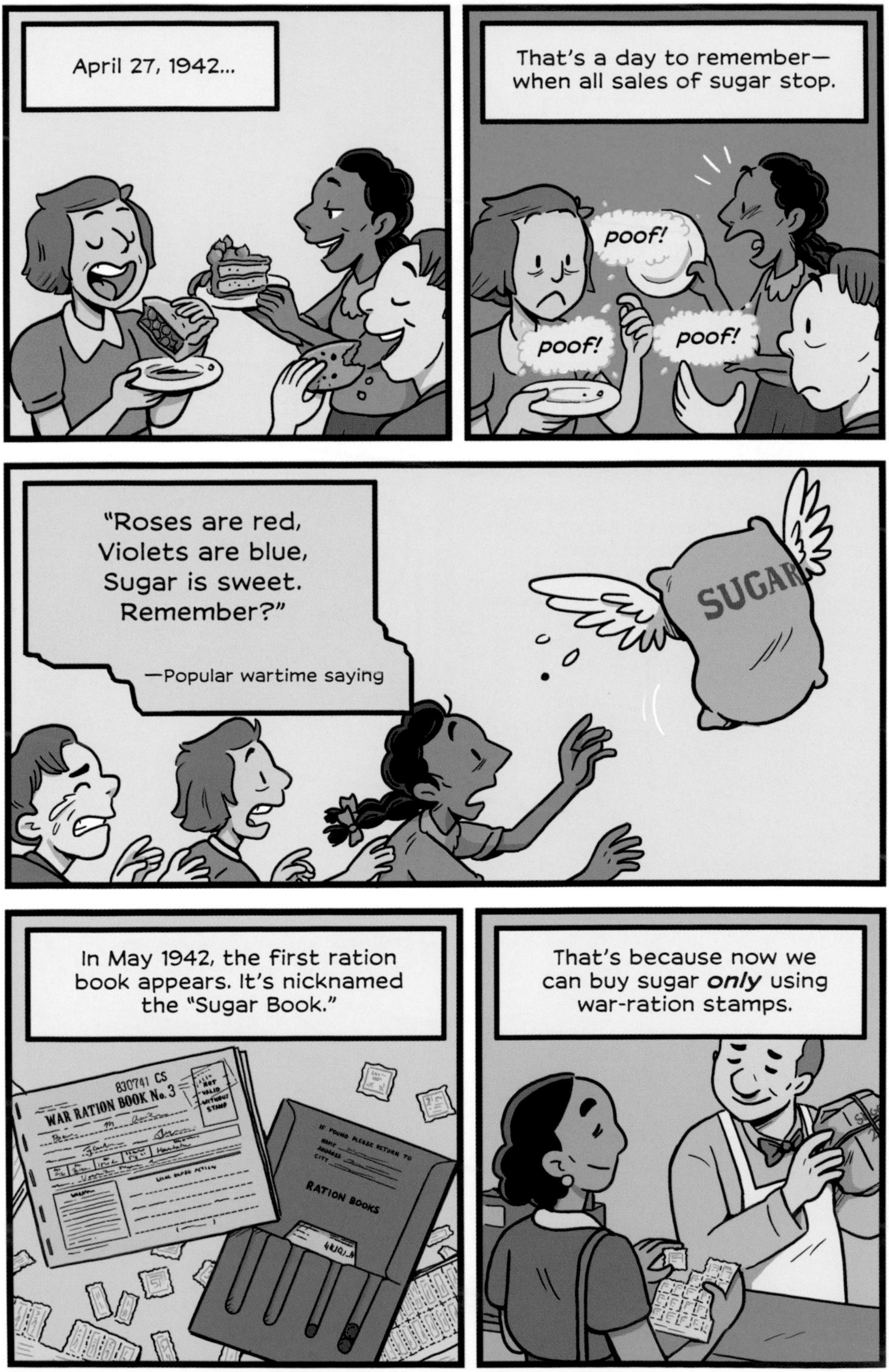
April 27, 1942...
That's a day to remember—when all sales of sugar stop.
poof!
poof!
poof!
"Roses are red, Violets are blue, Sugar is sweet. Remember?"
—Popular wartime saying
SUGAR
In May 1942, the first ration book appears. It's nicknamed the "Sugar Book."
830741 CS
WAR RATION BOOK No. 3
RATION BOOKS
That's because now we can buy sugar *only* using war-ration stamps.

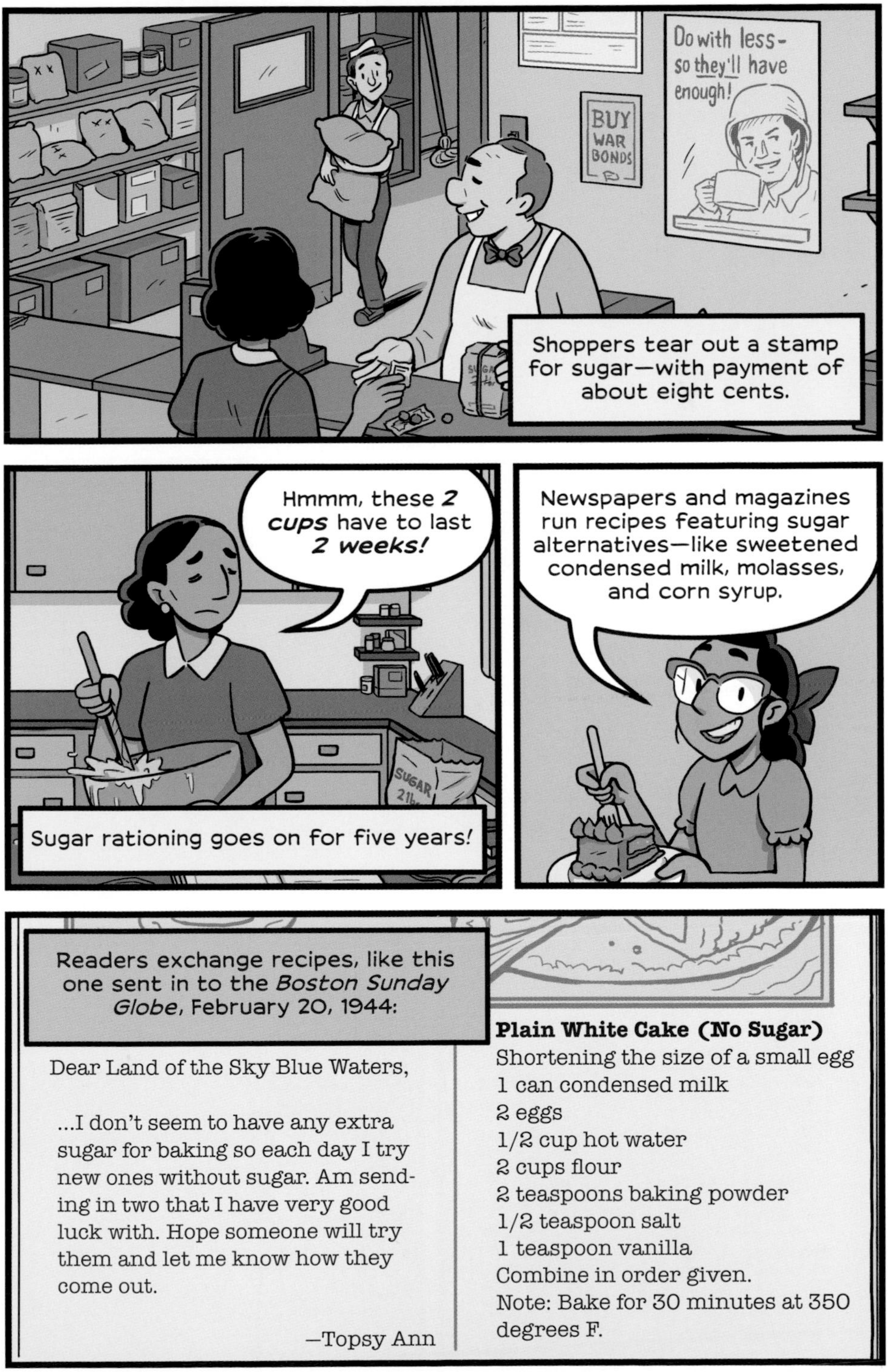
Do with less-so they'll have enough!
BUY WAR BONDS
Shoppers tear out a stamp for sugar—with payment of about eight cents.
Hmmm, these *2 cups* have to last *2 weeks!*
SUGAR
Sugar rationing goes on for five years!
Newspapers and magazines run recipes featuring sugar alternatives—like sweetened condensed milk, molasses, and corn syrup.
Readers exchange recipes, like this one sent in to the *Boston Sunday Globe*, February 20, 1944:
Dear Land of the Sky Blue Waters,
...I don't seem to have any extra sugar for baking so each day I try new ones without sugar. Am sending in two that I have very good luck with. Hope someone will try them and let me know how they come out.
—Topsy Ann
Plain White Cake (No Sugar)
Shortening the size of a small egg
1 can condensed milk
2 eggs
1/2 cup hot water
2 cups flour
2 teaspoons baking powder
1/2 teaspoon salt
1 teaspoon vanilla
Combine in order given.
Note: Bake for 30 minutes at 350 degrees F.

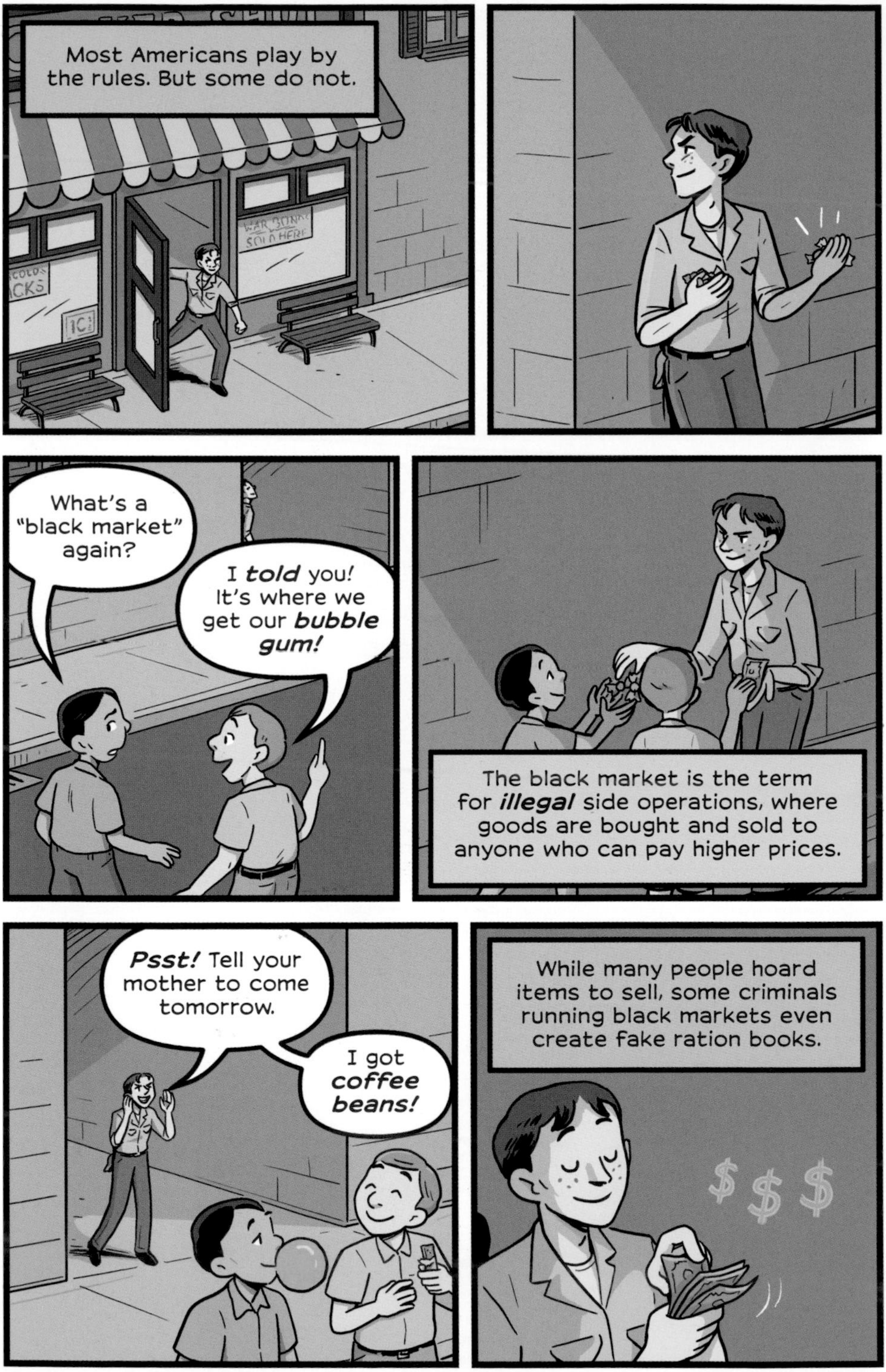
Most Americans play by the rules. But some do not.
WAR BONDS SOLD HERE
What's a "black market" again?
I ***told*** you! It's where we get our ***bubble gum!***
The black market is the term for ***illegal*** side operations, where goods are bought and sold to anyone who can pay higher prices.
Psst! Tell your mother to come tomorrow.
I got ***coffee beans!***
While many people hoard items to sell, some criminals running black markets even create fake ration books.
$ $ $

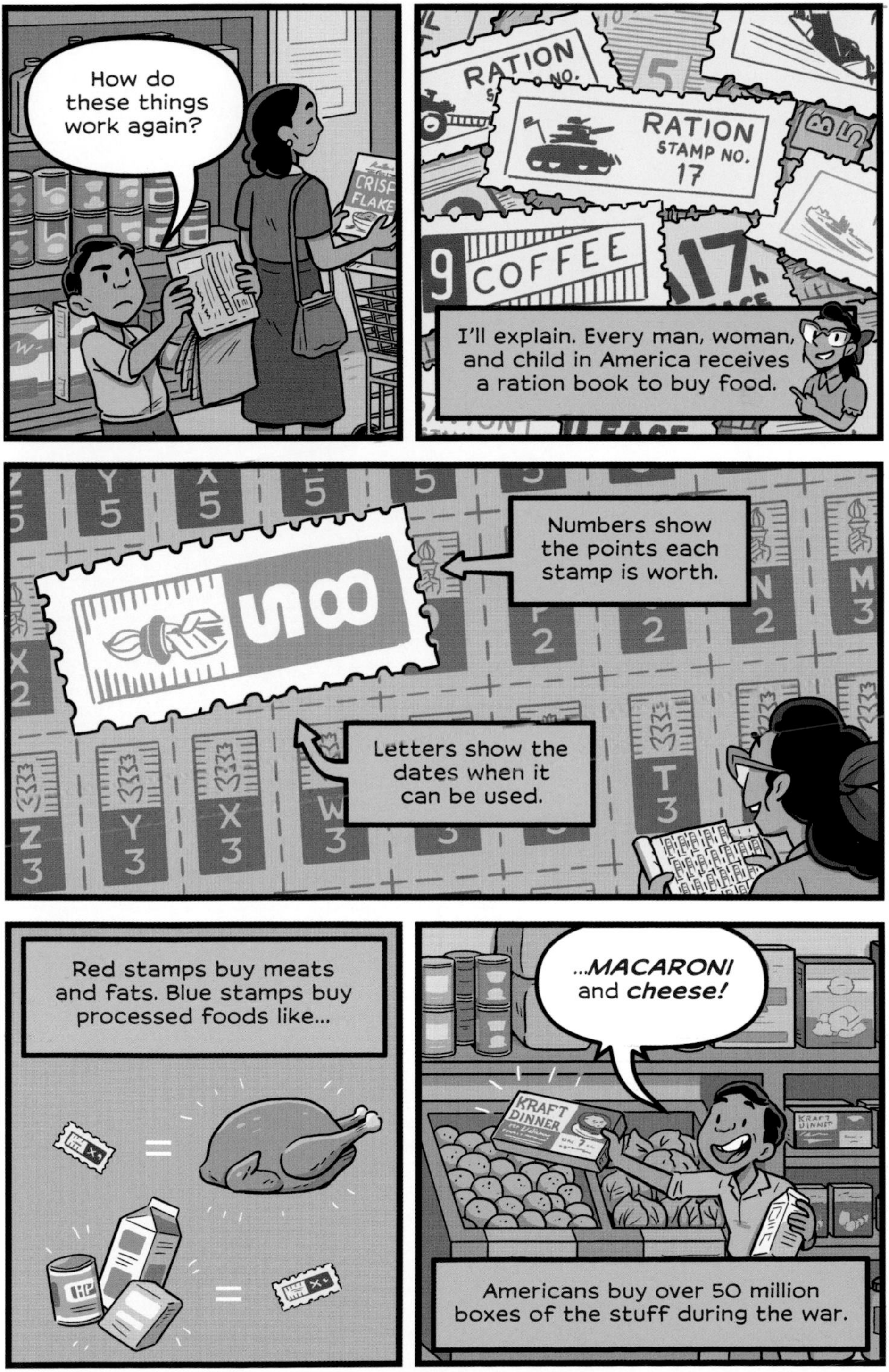
How do these things work again?
RATION STAMP NO. 17
COFFEE
I'll explain. Every man, woman, and child in America receives a ration book to buy food.
Numbers show the points each stamp is worth.
Letters show the dates when it can be used.
Red stamps buy meats and fats. Blue stamps buy processed foods like...
...*MACARONI* and *cheese!*
KRAFT DINNER
Americans buy over 50 million boxes of the stuff during the war.

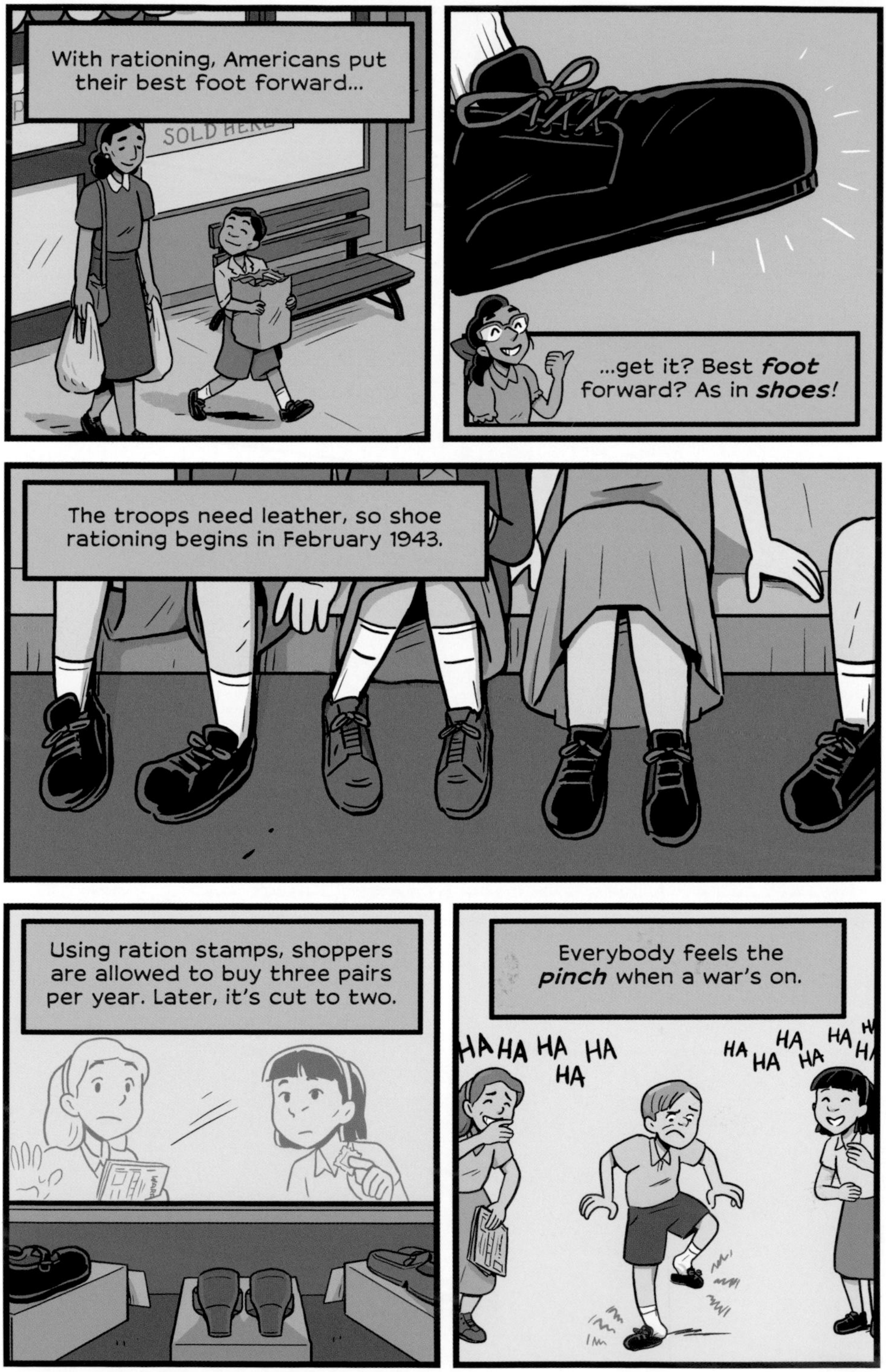
With rationing, Americans put their best foot forward...
SOLD HERE
...get it? Best *foot* forward? As in *shoes!*
The troops need leather, so shoe rationing begins in February 1943.
Using ration stamps, shoppers are allowed to buy three pairs per year. Later, it's cut to two.
Everybody feels the *pinch* when a war's on.
HA HA HA HA HA
HA
HA HA HA HA HA HA

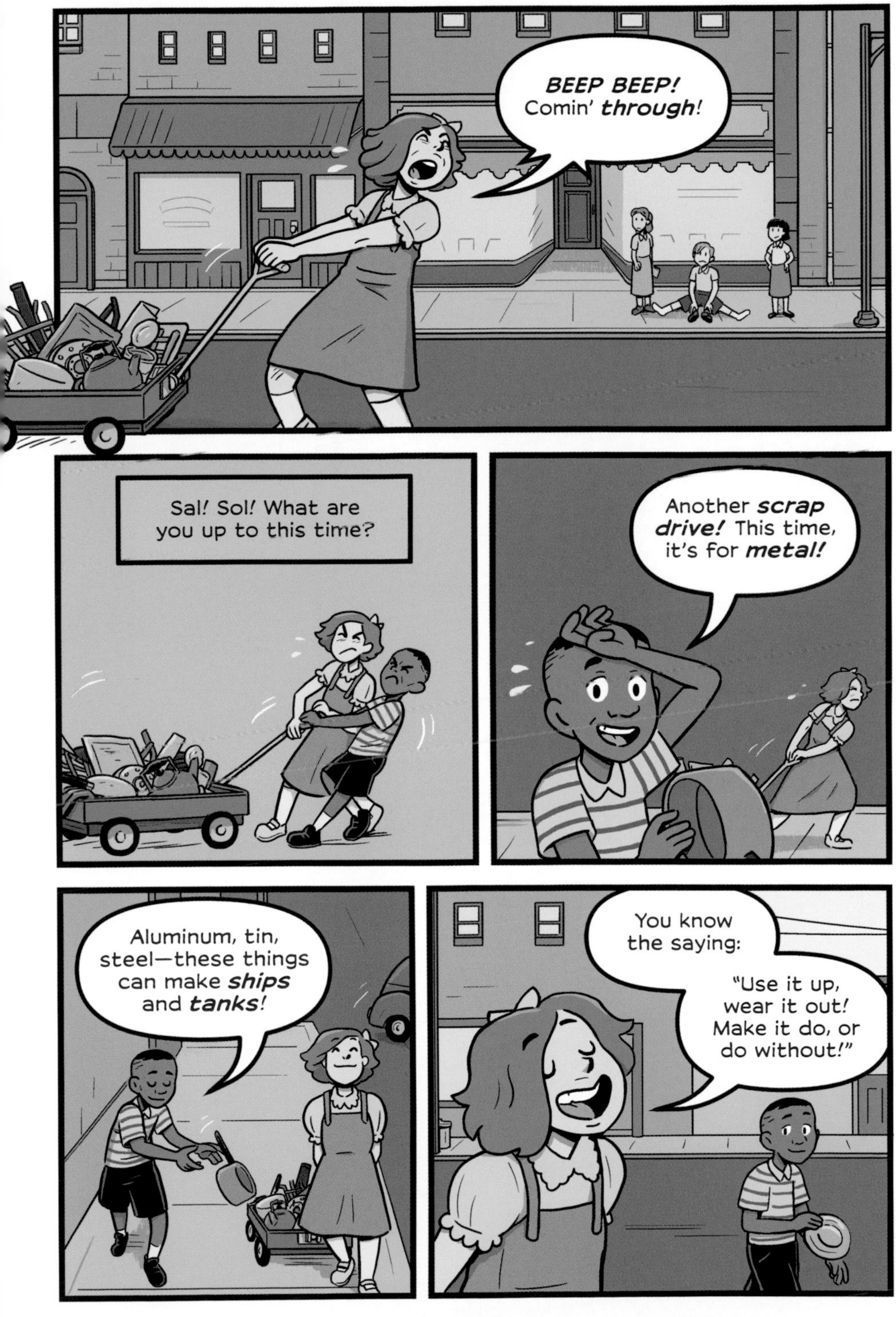
BEEP BEEP! Comin' through!
Sal! Sol! What are you up to this time?
Another scrap drive! This time, it's for metal!
Aluminum, tin, steel—these things can make ships and tanks!
You know the saying:
"Use it up, wear it out! Make it do, or do without!"

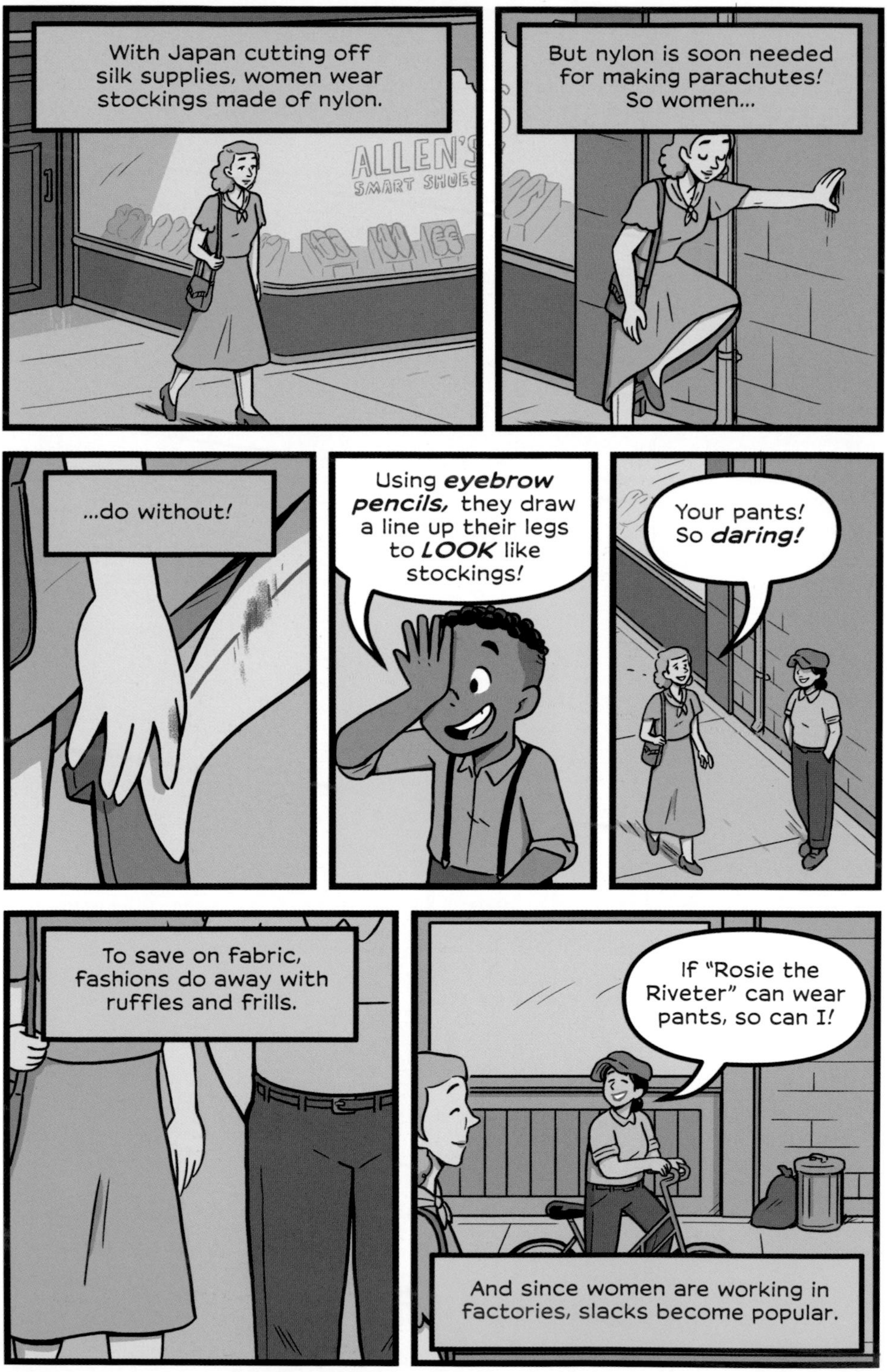
With Japan cutting off silk supplies, women wear stockings made of nylon.
ALLEN'S
SMART SHOES
But nylon is soon needed for making parachutes! So women...
...do without!
Using *eyebrow pencils,* they draw a line up their legs to ***LOOK*** like stockings!
Your pants! So ***daring!***
To save on fabric, fashions do away with ruffles and frills.
If "Rosie the Riveter" can wear pants, so can I!
And since women are working in factories, slacks become popular.

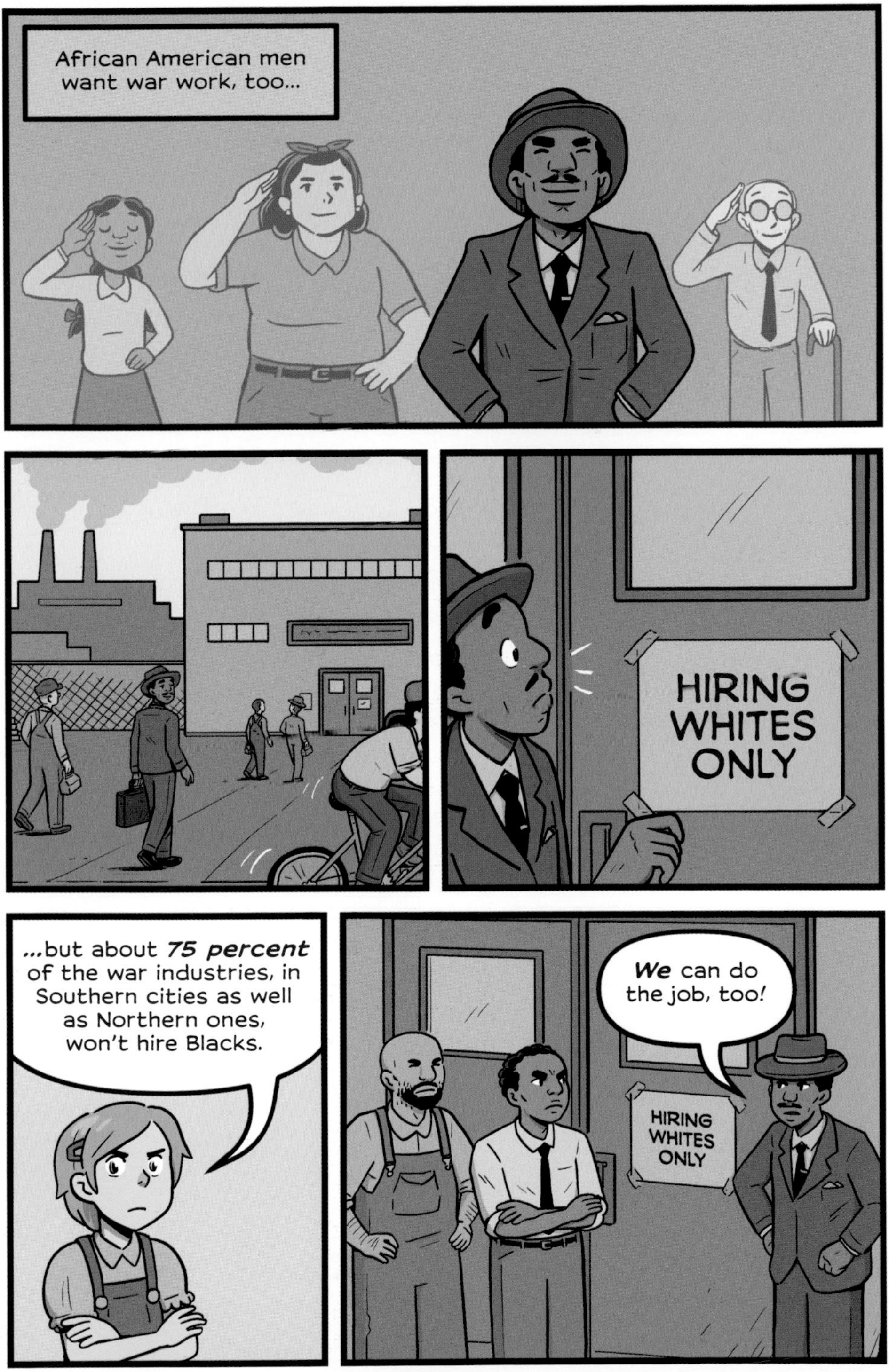
African American men want war work, too...
HIRING WHITES ONLY
...but about *75 percent* of the war industries, in Southern cities as well as Northern ones, won't hire Blacks.
HIRING WHITES ONLY
We can do the job, too!

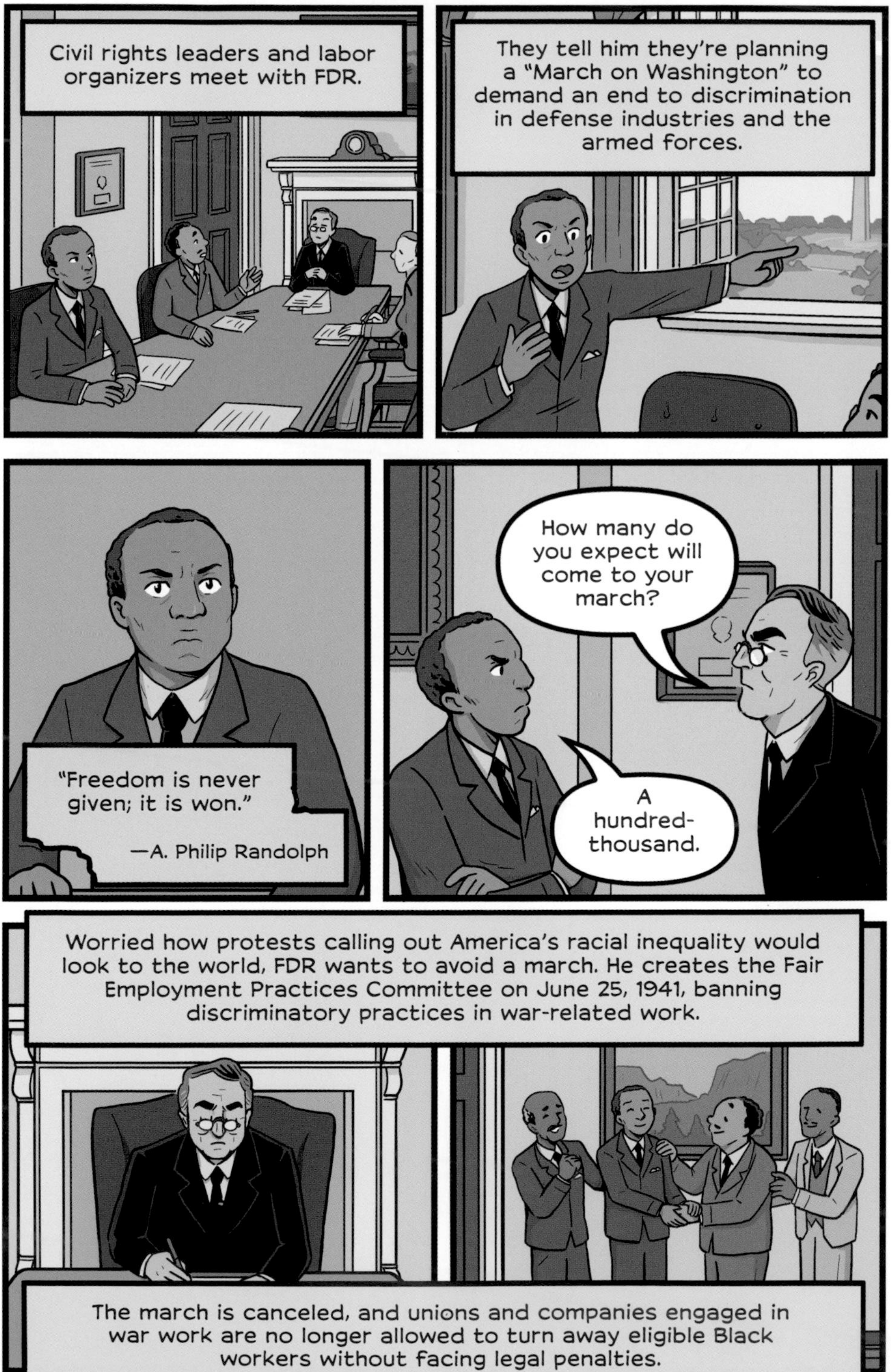
Civil rights leaders and labor organizers meet with FDR.
They tell him they're planning a "March on Washington" to demand an end to discrimination in defense industries and the armed forces.
"Freedom is never given; it is won."
—A. Philip Randolph
How many do you expect will come to your march?
A hundred-thousand.
Worried how protests calling out America's racial inequality would look to the world, FDR wants to avoid a march. He creates the Fair Employment Practices Committee on June 25, 1941, banning discriminatory practices in war-related work.
The march is canceled, and unions and companies engaged in war work are no longer allowed to turn away eligible Black workers without facing legal penalties.

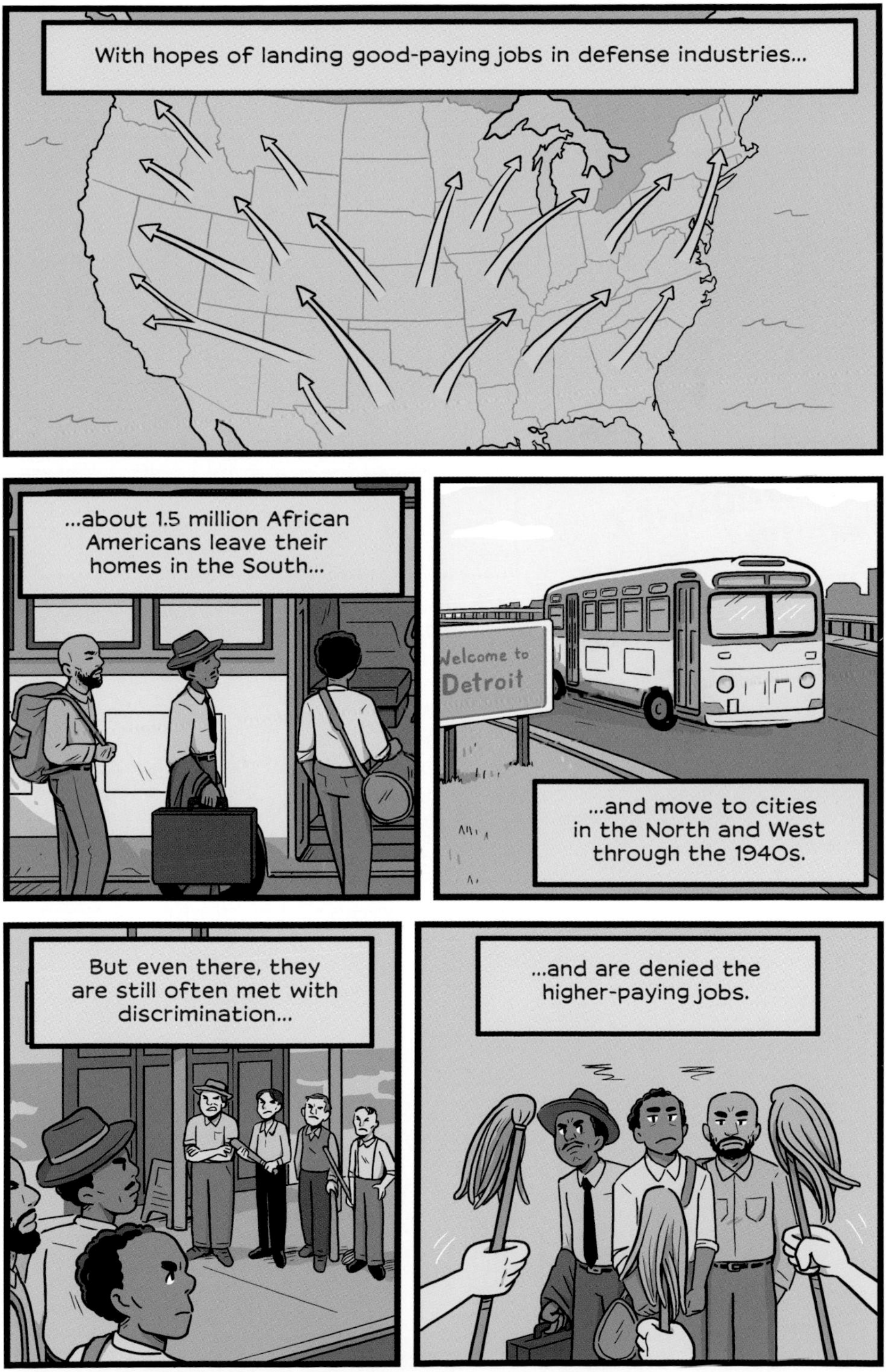

With hopes of landing good-paying jobs in defense industries...
...about 1.5 million African Americans leave their homes in the South...
Welcome to Detroit
...and move to cities in the North and West through the 1940s.
But even there, they are still often met with discrimination...
...and are denied the higher-paying jobs.

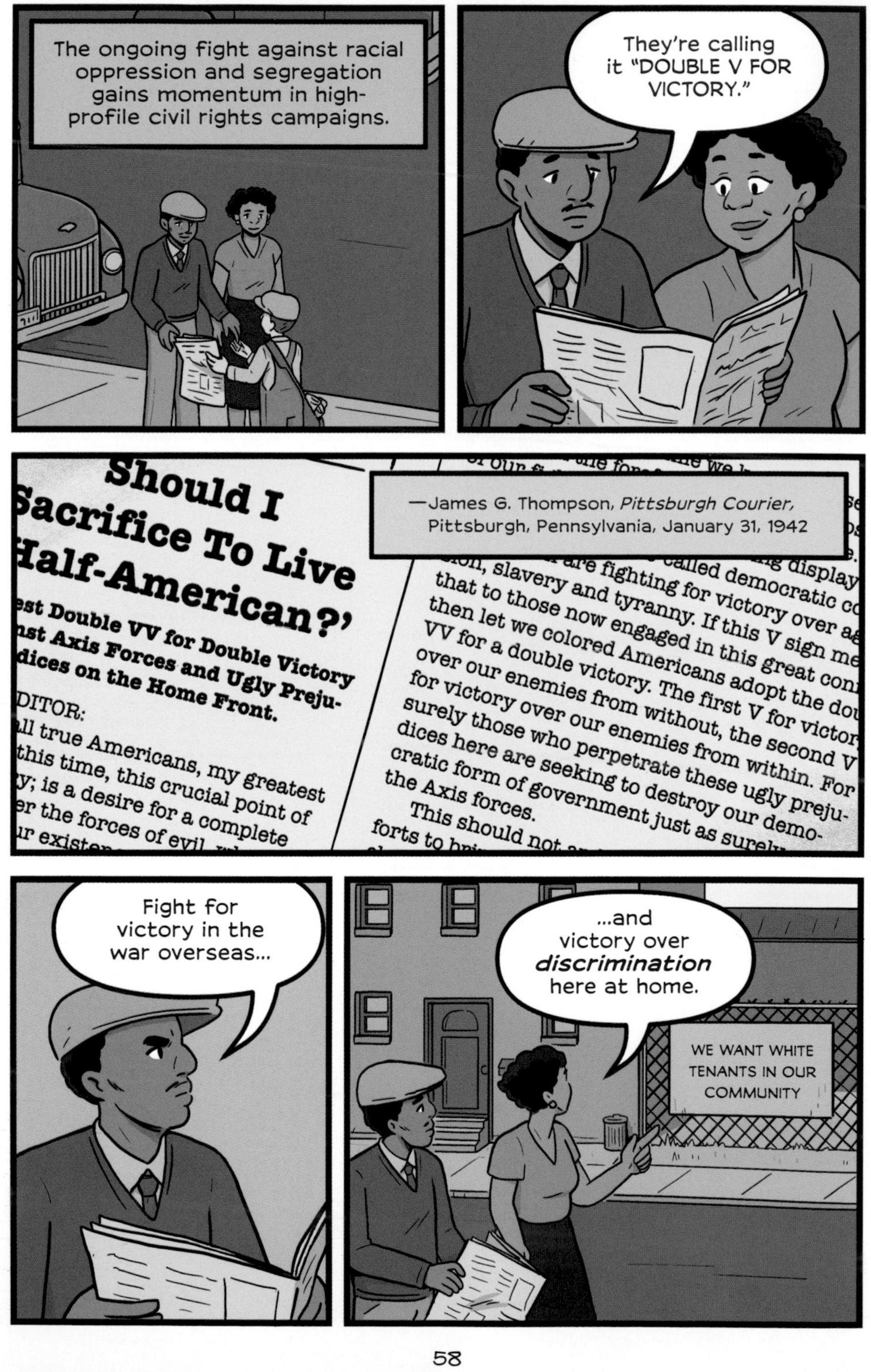
The ongoing fight against racial oppression and segregation gains momentum in high-profile civil rights campaigns.
They're calling it "DOUBLE V FOR VICTORY."
Should I Sacrifice To Live Half-American?'
Double VV for Double Victory
Axis Forces and Ugly Prejudices on the Home Front.
DITOR:
ll true Americans, my greatest
this time, this crucial point of
y; is a desire for a complete
er the forces of evil,
on, slavery and tyranny. If this V sign me
that to those now engaged in this great con
then let we colored Americans adopt the dou
VV for a double victory. The first V for victor
over our enemies from without, the second V
for victory over our enemies from within. For
surely those who perpetrate these ugly prejudices here are seeking to destroy our demo-
cratic form of government just as surely
the Axis forces.
This should not
—James G. Thompson, *Pittsburgh Courier,* Pittsburgh, Pennsylvania, January 31, 1942
Fight for victory in the war overseas...
...and victory over ***discrimination*** here at home.
WE WANT WHITE TENANTS IN OUR COMMUNITY

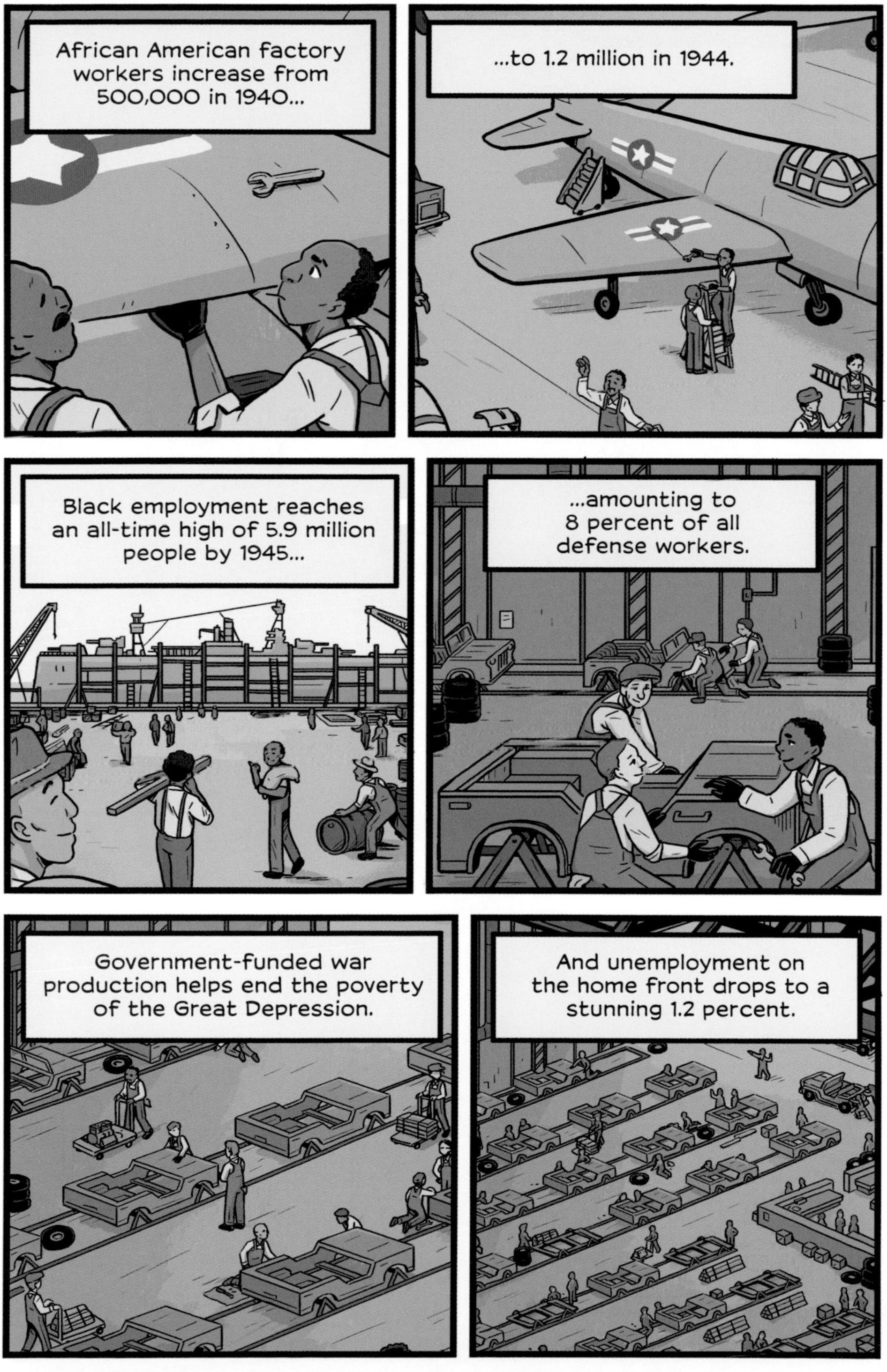
African American factory workers increase from 500,000 in 1940...
...to 1.2 million in 1944.
Black employment reaches an all-time high of 5.9 million people by 1945...
...amounting to 8 percent of all defense workers.
Government-funded war production helps end the poverty of the Great Depression.
And unemployment on the home front drops to a stunning 1.2 percent.

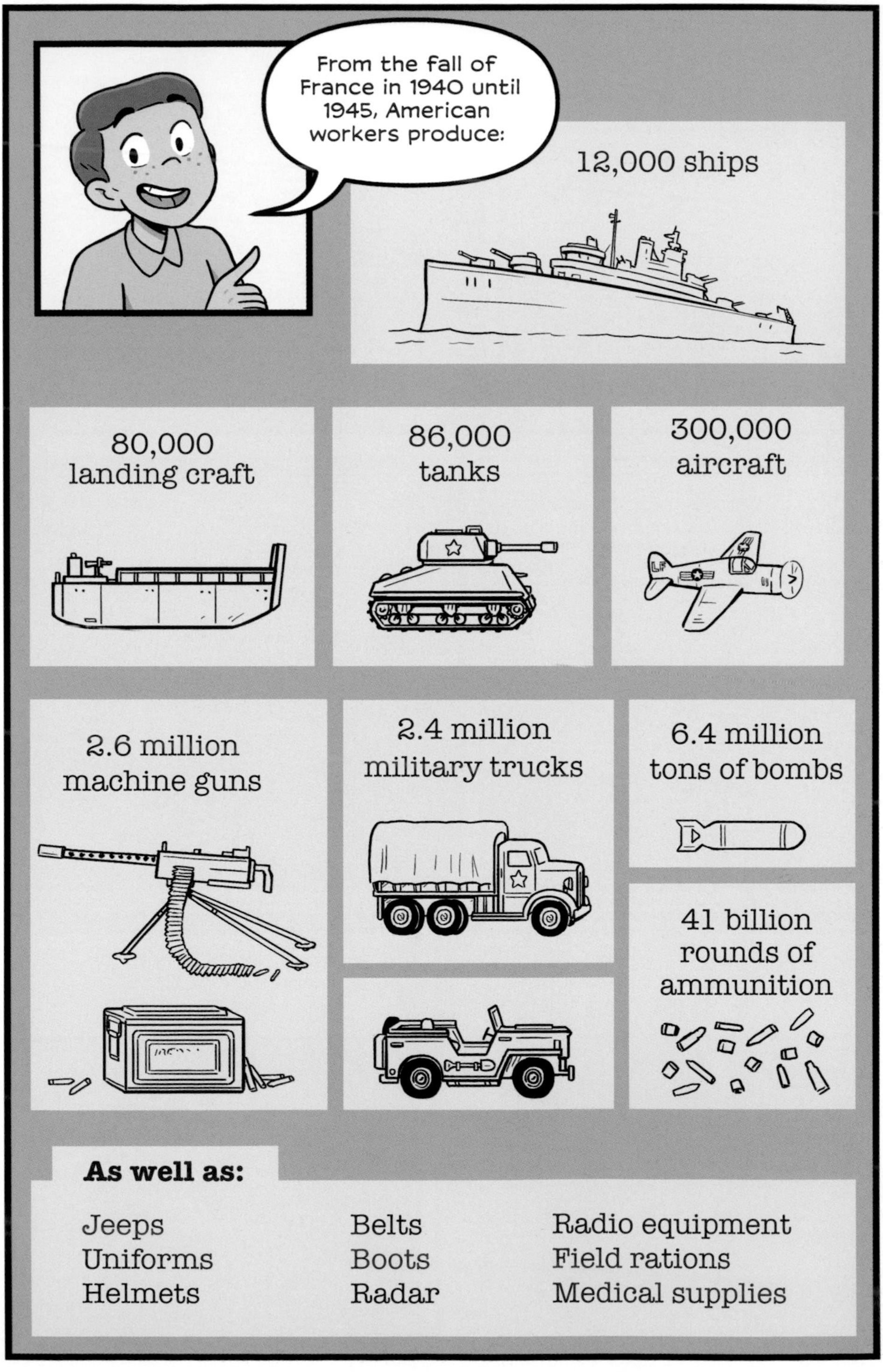
From the fall of France in 1940 until 1945, American workers produce:
12,000 ships
80,000 landing craft
86,000 tanks
300,000 aircraft
2.6 million machine guns
2.4 million military trucks
6.4 million tons of bombs
41 billion rounds of ammunition
As well as:
Jeeps
Uniforms
Helmets
Belts
Boots
Radar
Radio equipment
Field rations
Medical supplies

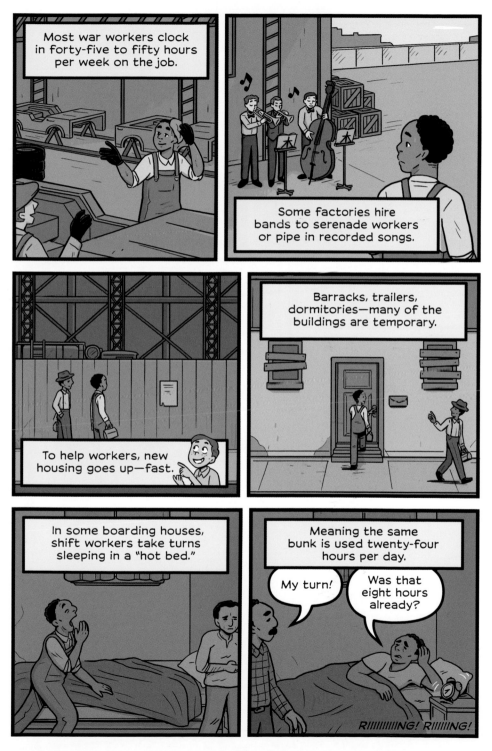

Most war workers clock in forty-five to fifty hours per week on the job.

Some factories hire bands to serenade workers or pipe in recorded songs.

To help workers, new housing goes up—fast.

Barracks, trailers, dormitories—many of the buildings are temporary.

In some boarding houses, shift workers take turns sleeping in a "hot bed."

Meaning the same bunk is used twenty-four hours per day.

My turn!

Was that eight hours already?

RIIIIIIIIING! RIIIIING!

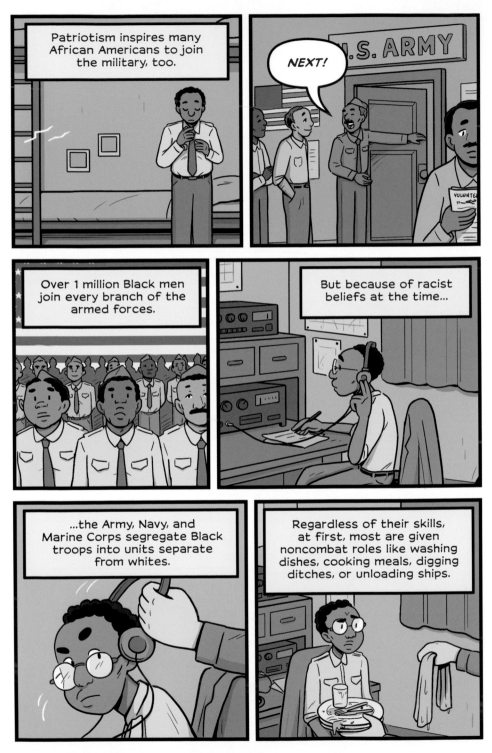

Patriotism inspires many African Americans to join the military, too.

NEXT!

U.S. ARMY

VOLUNTE

Over 1 million Black men join every branch of the armed forces.

But because of racist beliefs at the time...

...the Army, Navy, and Marine Corps segregate Black troops into units separate from whites.

Regardless of their skills, at first, most are given noncombat roles like washing dishes, cooking meals, digging ditches, or unloading ships.

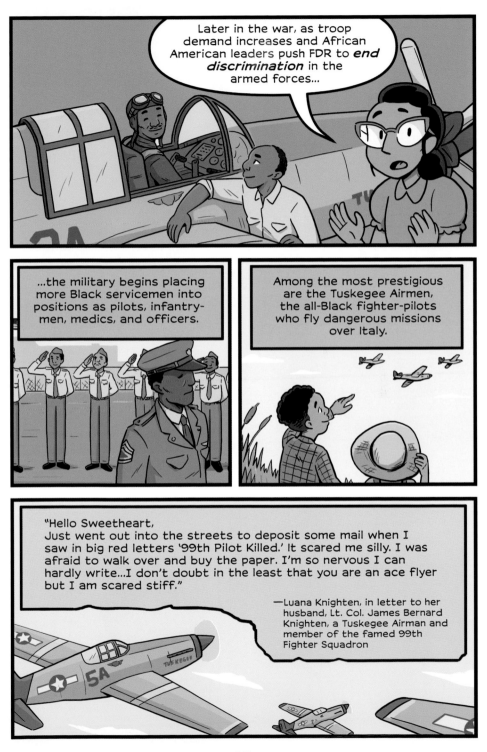

Later in the war, as troop demand increases and African American leaders push FDR to **end *discrimination*** in the armed forces...

...the military begins placing more Black servicemen into positions as pilots, infantrymen, medics, and officers.

Among the most prestigious are the Tuskegee Airmen, the all-Black fighter-pilots who fly dangerous missions over Italy.

"Hello Sweetheart,
Just went out into the streets to deposit some mail when I saw in big red letters '99th Pilot Killed.' It scared me silly. I was afraid to walk over and buy the paper. I'm so nervous I can hardly write...I don't doubt in the least that you are an ace flyer but I am scared stiff."

—Luana Knighten, in letter to her husband, Lt. Col. James Bernard Knighten, a Tuskegee Airman and member of the famed 99th Fighter Squadron

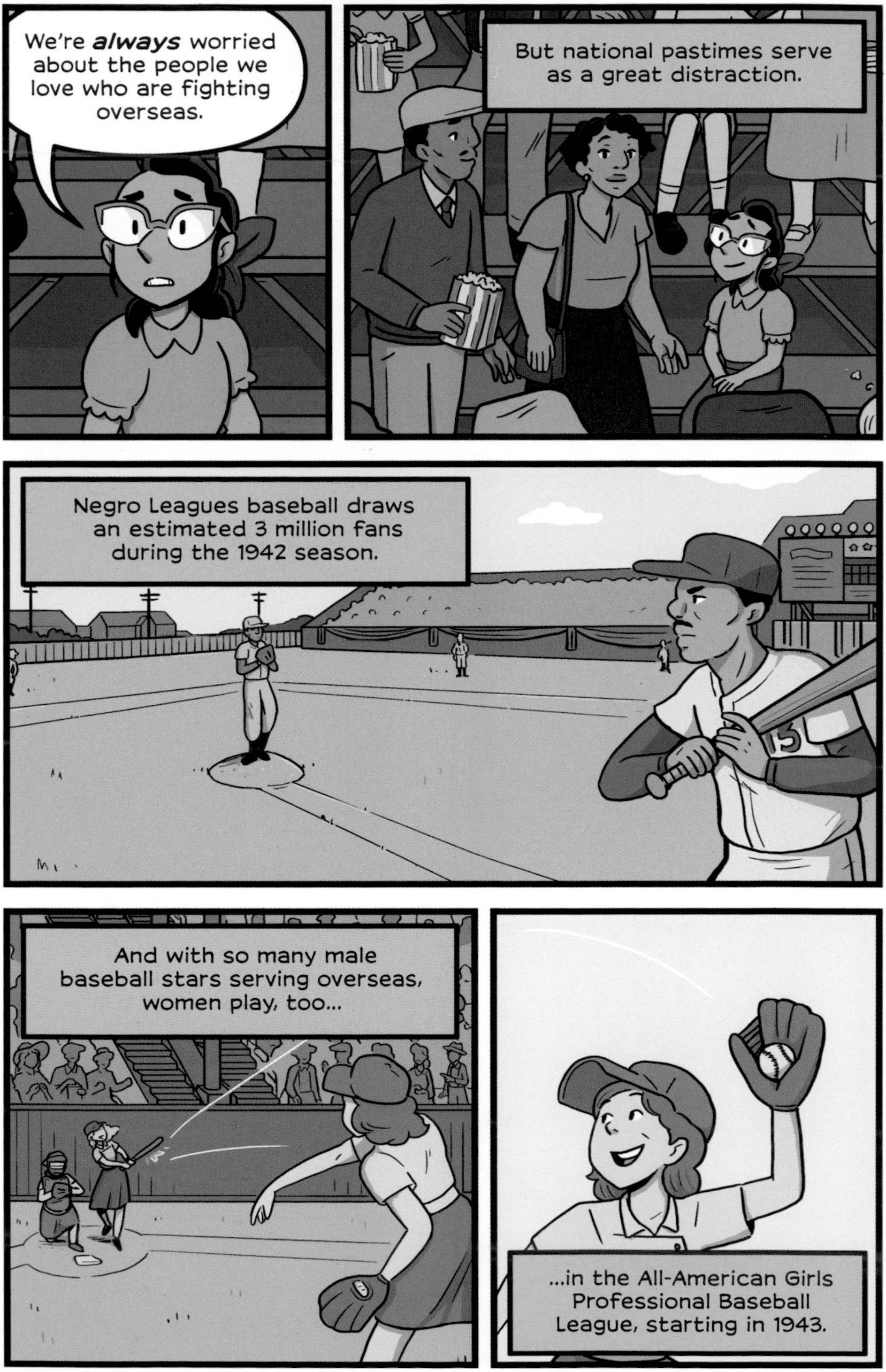
We're ***always*** worried about the people we love who are fighting overseas.
But national pastimes serve as a great distraction.
Negro Leagues baseball draws an estimated 3 million fans during the 1942 season.
And with so many male baseball stars serving overseas, women play, too...
...in the All-American Girls Professional Baseball League, starting in 1943.

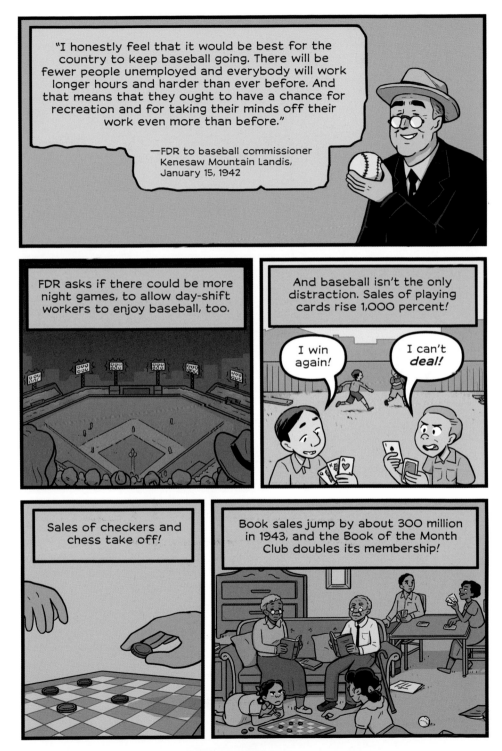

"I honestly feel that it would be best for the country to keep baseball going. There will be fewer people unemployed and everybody will work longer hours and harder than ever before. And that means that they ought to have a chance for recreation and for taking their minds off their work even more than before."

—FDR to baseball commissioner Kenesaw Mountain Landis, January 15, 1942

FDR asks if there could be more night games, to allow day-shift workers to enjoy baseball, too.

And baseball isn't the only distraction. Sales of playing cards rise 1,000 percent!

I win again!

I can't *deal!*

Sales of checkers and chess take off!

Book sales jump by about 300 million in 1943, and the Book of the Month Club doubles its membership!

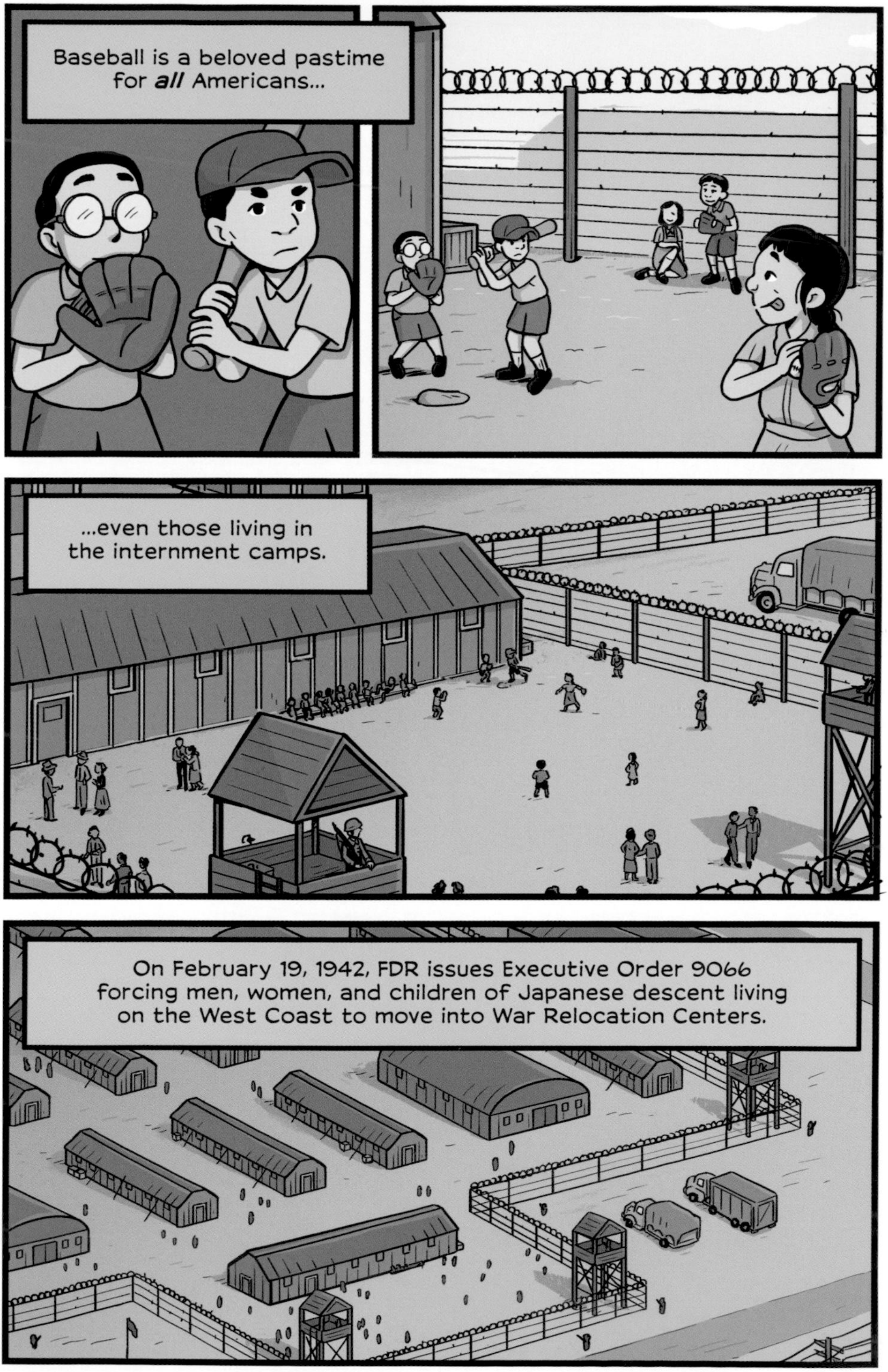
Baseball is a beloved pastime for *all* Americans...
...even those living in the internment camps.
On February 19, 1942, FDR issues Executive Order 9066 forcing men, women, and children of Japanese descent living on the West Coast to move into War Relocation Centers.

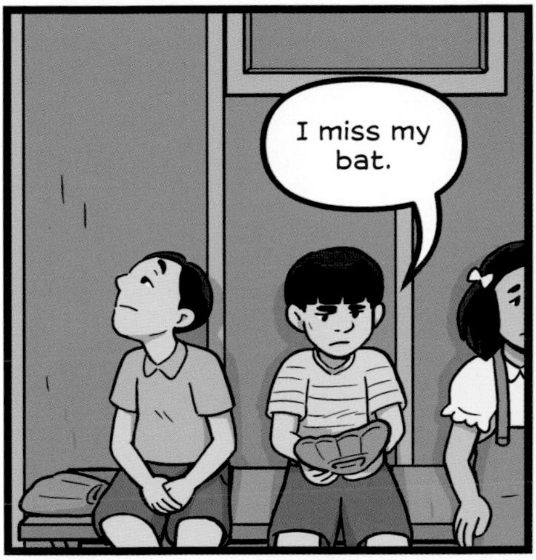
I miss my bat.

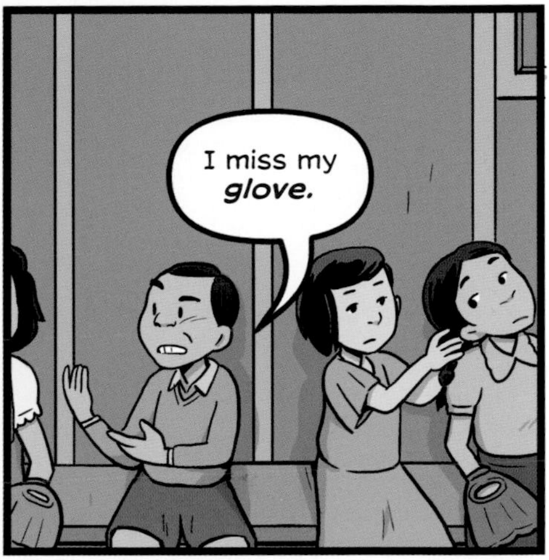
I miss my *glove.*

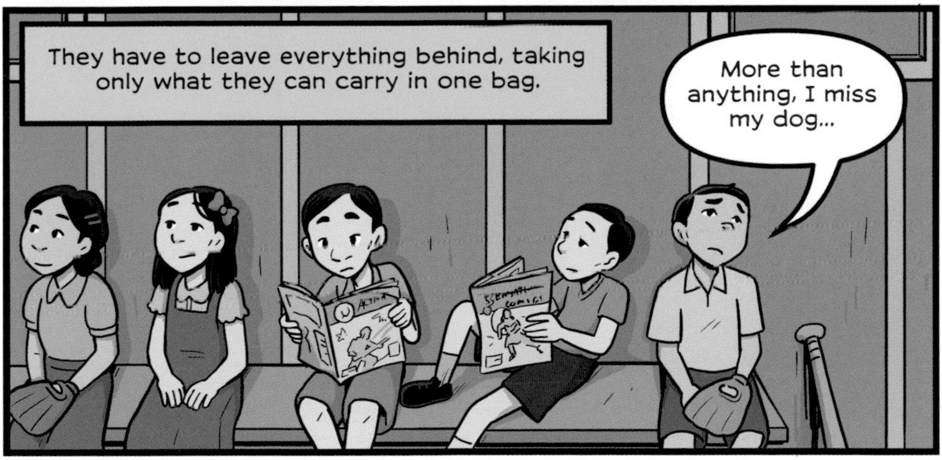
They have to leave everything behind, taking only what they can carry in one bag.
More than anything, I miss my dog...

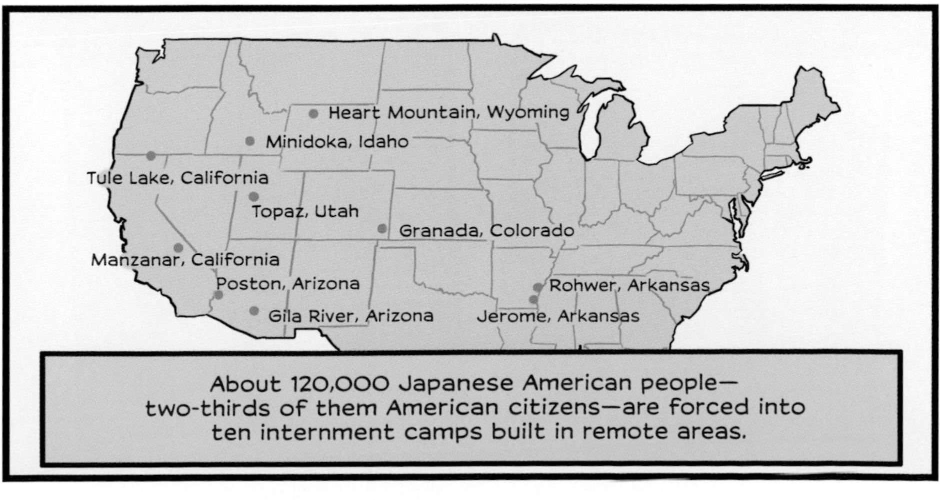
Heart Mountain, Wyoming
Minidoka, Idaho
Tule Lake, California
Topaz, Utah
Granada, Colorado
Manzanar, California
Poston, Arizona
Gila River, Arizona
Rohwer, Arkansas
Jerome, Arkansas
About 120,000 Japanese American people—two-thirds of them American citizens—are forced into ten internment camps built in remote areas.

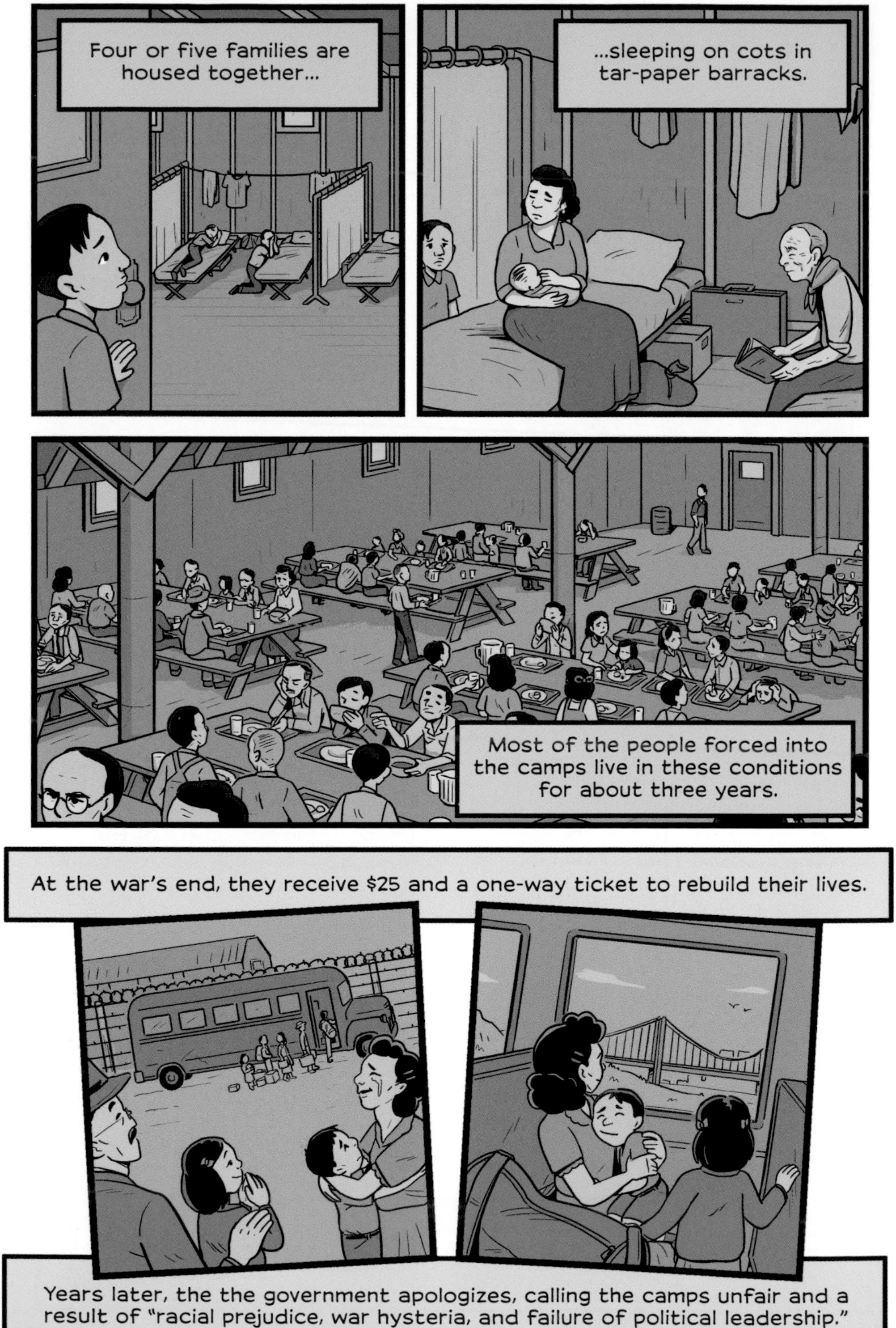
Four or five families are housed together...
...sleeping on cots in tar-paper barracks.
Most of the people forced into the camps live in these conditions for about three years.
At the war's end, they receive $25 and a one-way ticket to rebuild their lives.
Years later, the the government apologizes, calling the camps unfair and a result of "racial prejudice, war hysteria, and failure of political leadership."

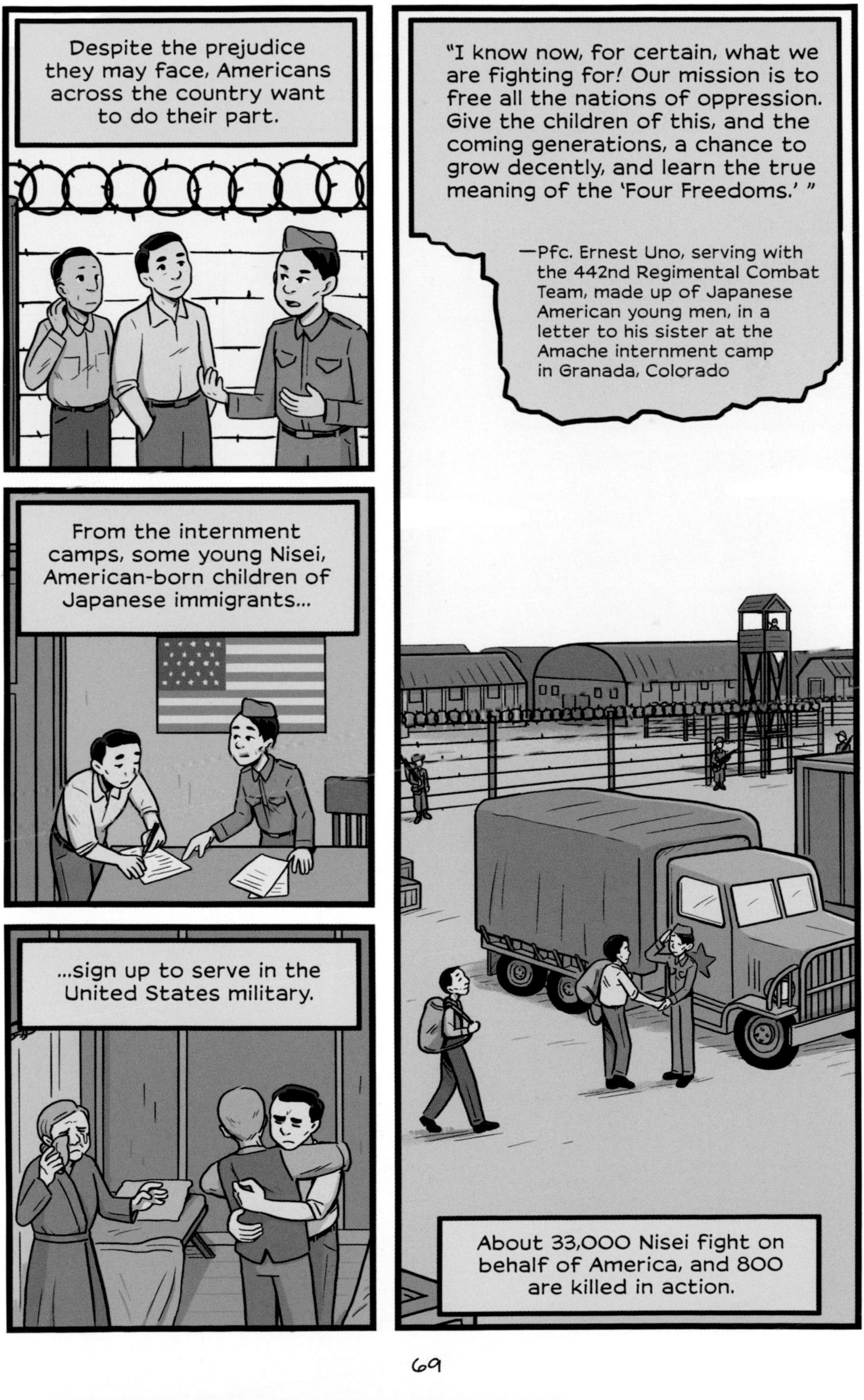
Despite the prejudice they may face, Americans across the country want to do their part.
From the internment camps, some young Nisei, American-born children of Japanese immigrants...
...sign up to serve in the United States military.
"I know now, for certain, what we are fighting for! Our mission is to free all the nations of oppression. Give the children of this, and the coming generations, a chance to grow decently, and learn the true meaning of the 'Four Freedoms.' "
—Pfc. Ernest Uno, serving with the 442nd Regimental Combat Team, made up of Japanese American young men, in a letter to his sister at the Amache internment camp in Granada, Colorado
About 33,000 Nisei fight on behalf of America, and 800 are killed in action.

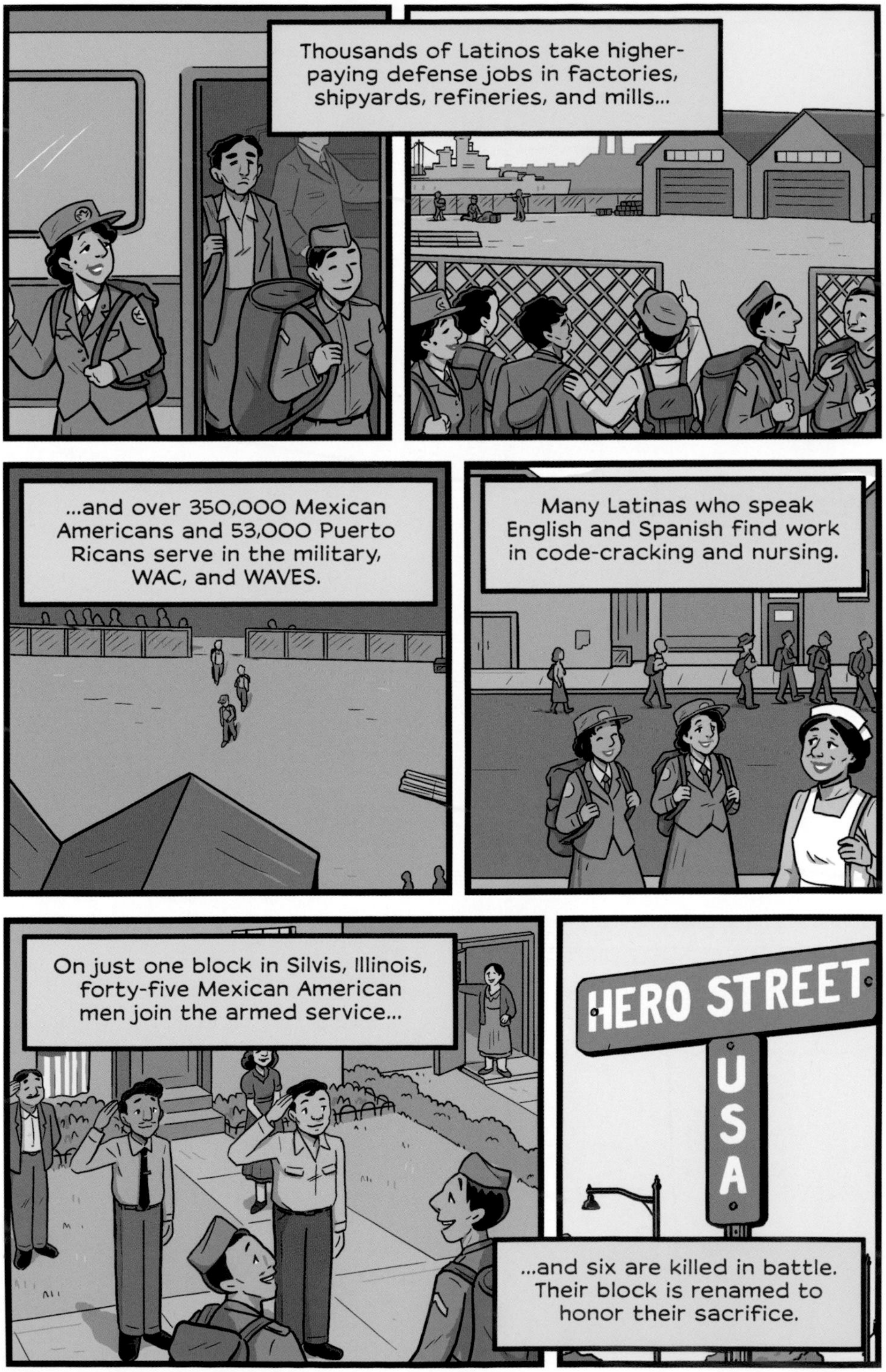
Thousands of Latinos take higher-paying defense jobs in factories, shipyards, refineries, and mills...
...and over 350,000 Mexican Americans and 53,000 Puerto Ricans serve in the military, WAC, and WAVES.
Many Latinas who speak English and Spanish find work in code-cracking and nursing.
On just one block in Silvis, Illinois, forty-five Mexican American men join the armed service...
HERO STREET
USA
...and six are killed in battle. Their block is renamed to honor their sacrifice.

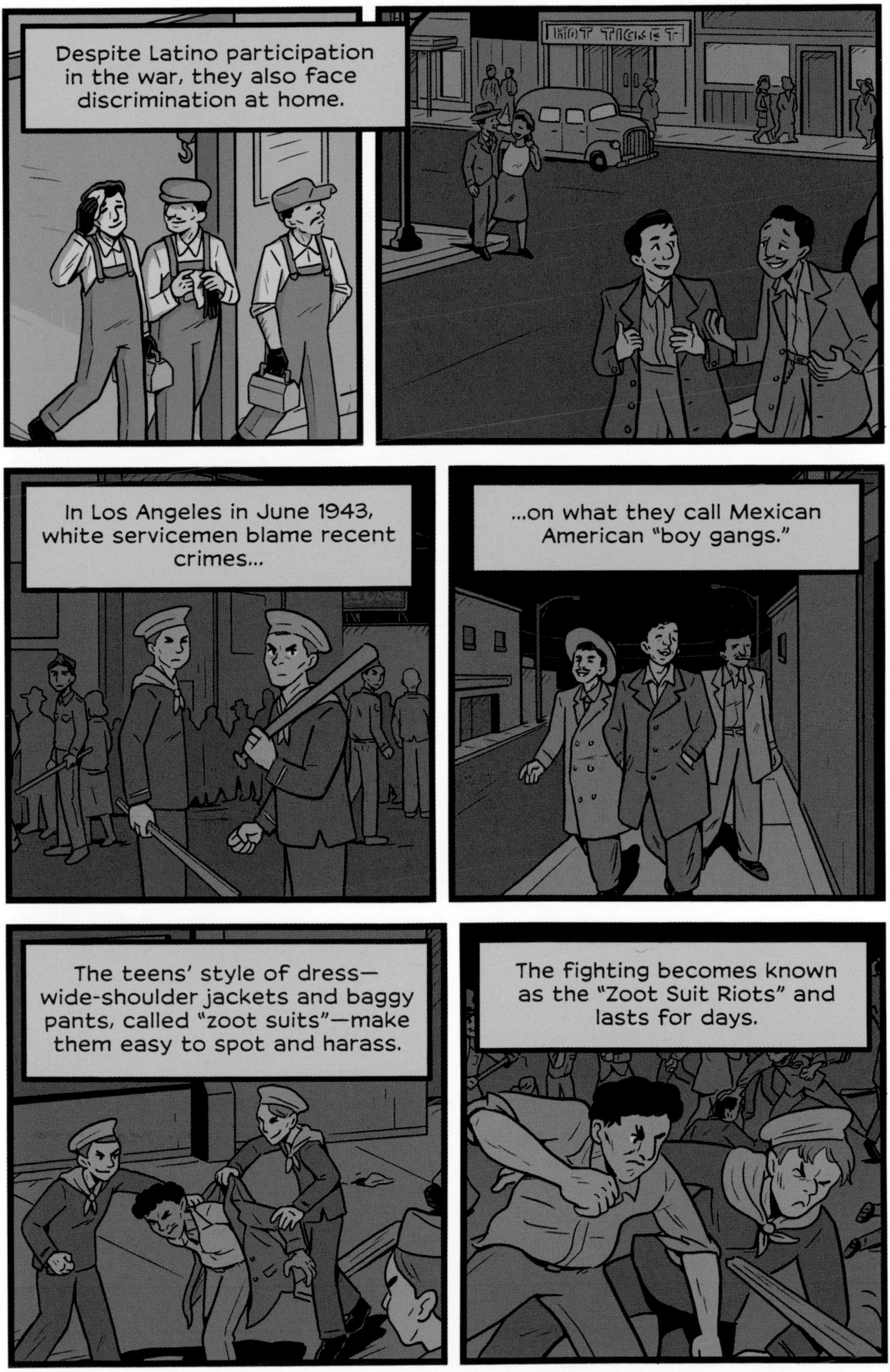
Despite Latino participation in the war, they also face discrimination at home.
HOT TICKET
In Los Angeles in June 1943, white servicemen blame recent crimes...
...on what they call Mexican American "boy gangs."
The teens' style of dress—wide-shoulder jackets and baggy pants, called "zoot suits"—make them easy to spot and harass.
The fighting becomes known as the "Zoot Suit Riots" and lasts for days.

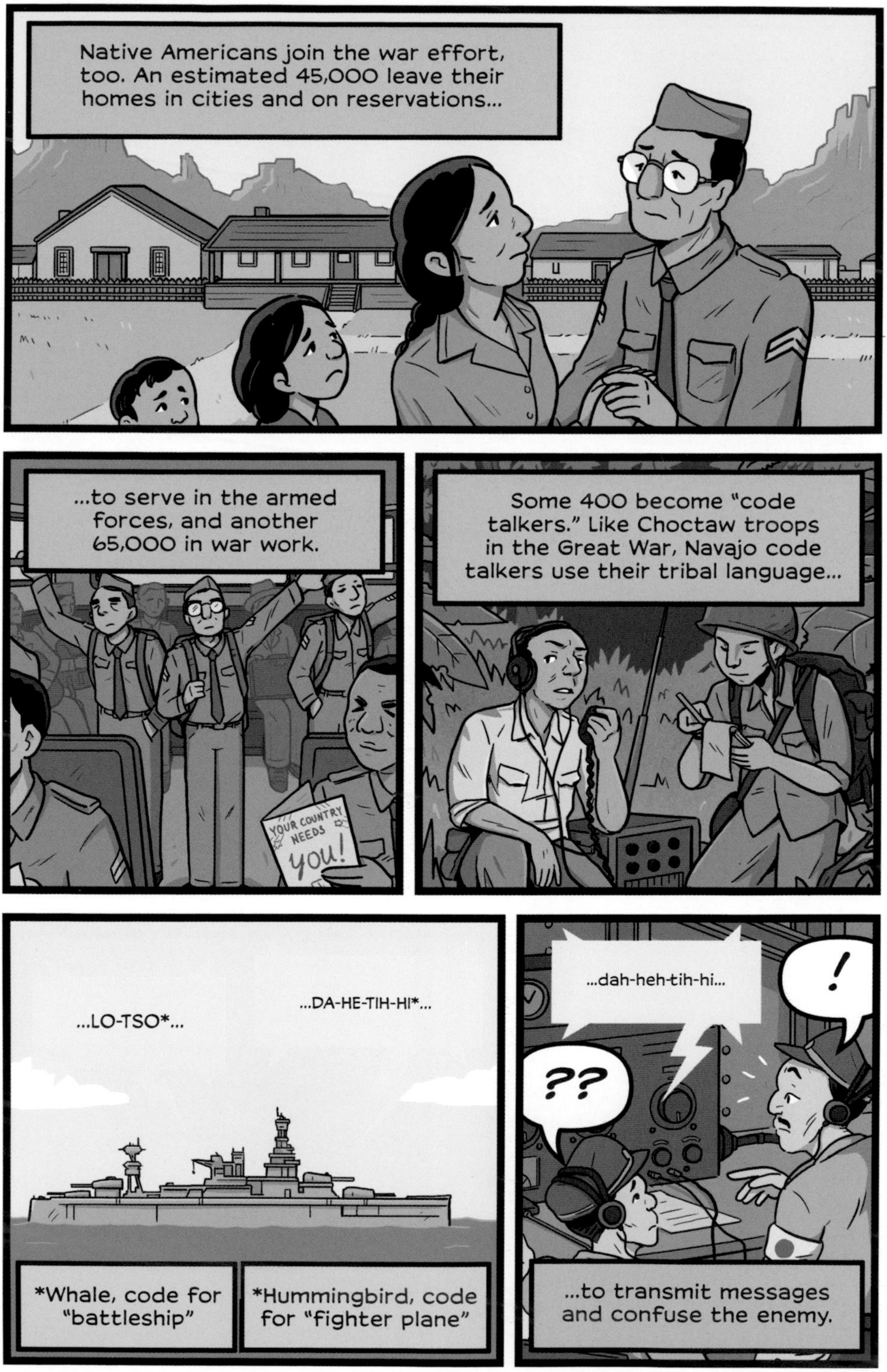

Native Americans join the war effort, too. An estimated 45,000 leave their homes in cities and on reservations...
...to serve in the armed forces, and another 65,000 in war work.
YOUR COUNTRY NEEDS YOU!
Some 400 become "code talkers." Like Choctaw troops in the Great War, Navajo code talkers use their tribal language...
...LO-TSO*...
...DA-HE-TIH-HI*...
*Whale, code for "battleship"
*Hummingbird, code for "fighter plane"
...dah-heh-tih-hi...
!
??
...to transmit messages and confuse the enemy.

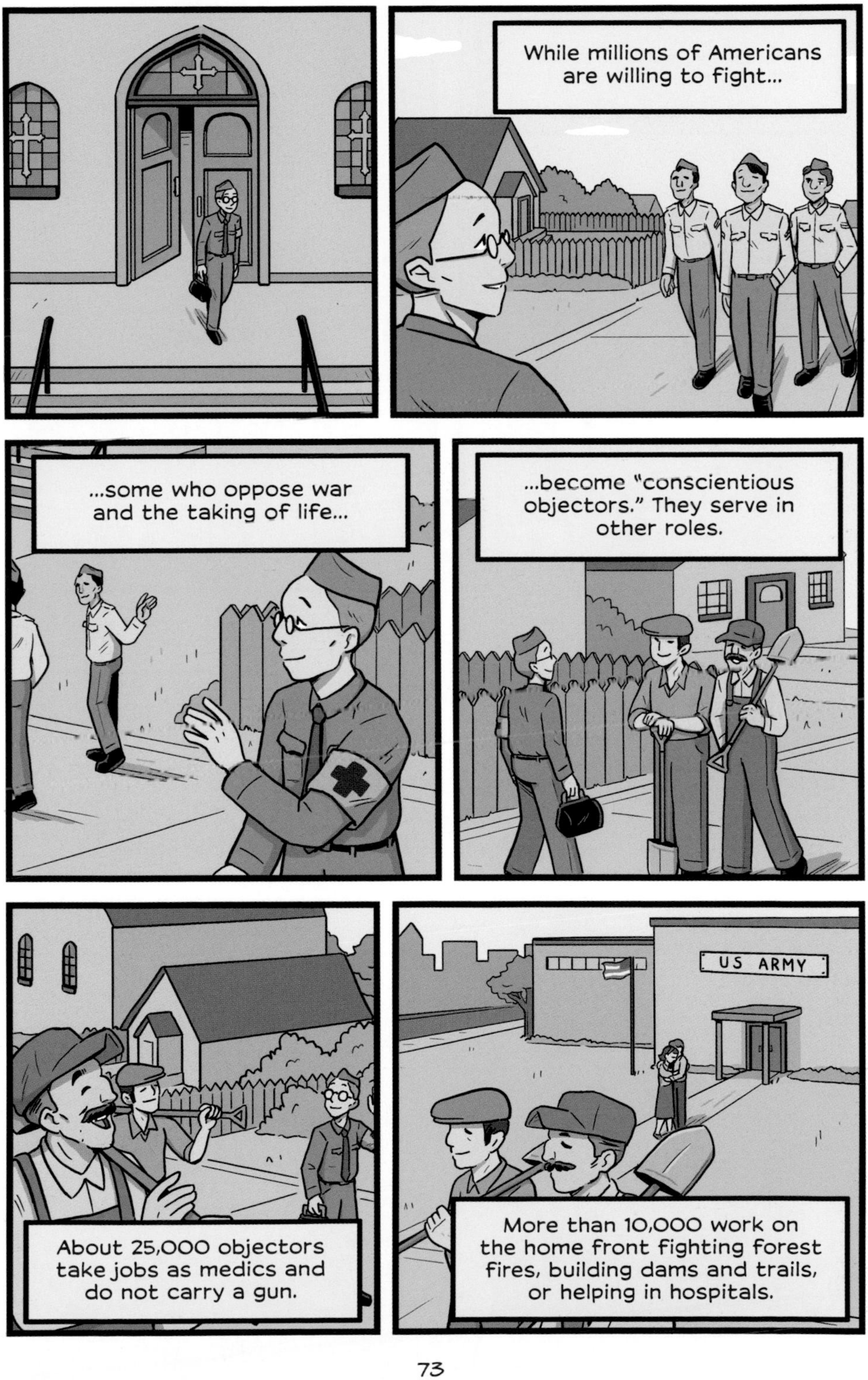
While millions of Americans are willing to fight...
...some who oppose war and the taking of life...
...become "conscientious objectors." They serve in other roles.
About 25,000 objectors take jobs as medics and do not carry a gun.
US ARMY
More than 10,000 work on the home front fighting forest fires, building dams and trails, or helping in hospitals.

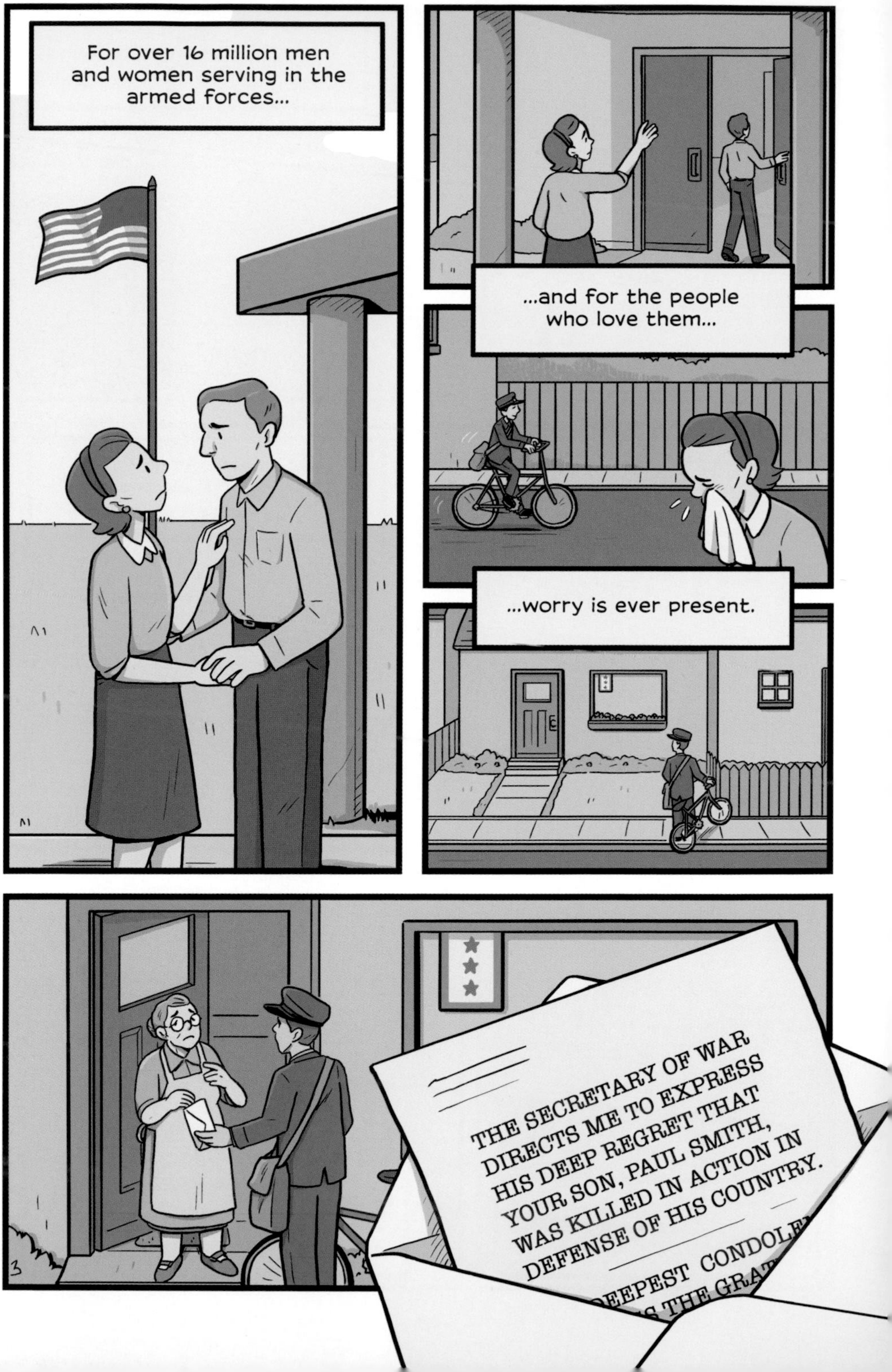
For over 16 million men and women serving in the armed forces...
...and for the people who love them...
...worry is ever present.
THE SECRETARY OF WAR
DIRECTS ME TO EXPRESS
HIS DEEP REGRET THAT
YOUR SON, PAUL SMITH,
WAS KILLED IN ACTION IN
DEFENSE OF HIS COUNTRY.

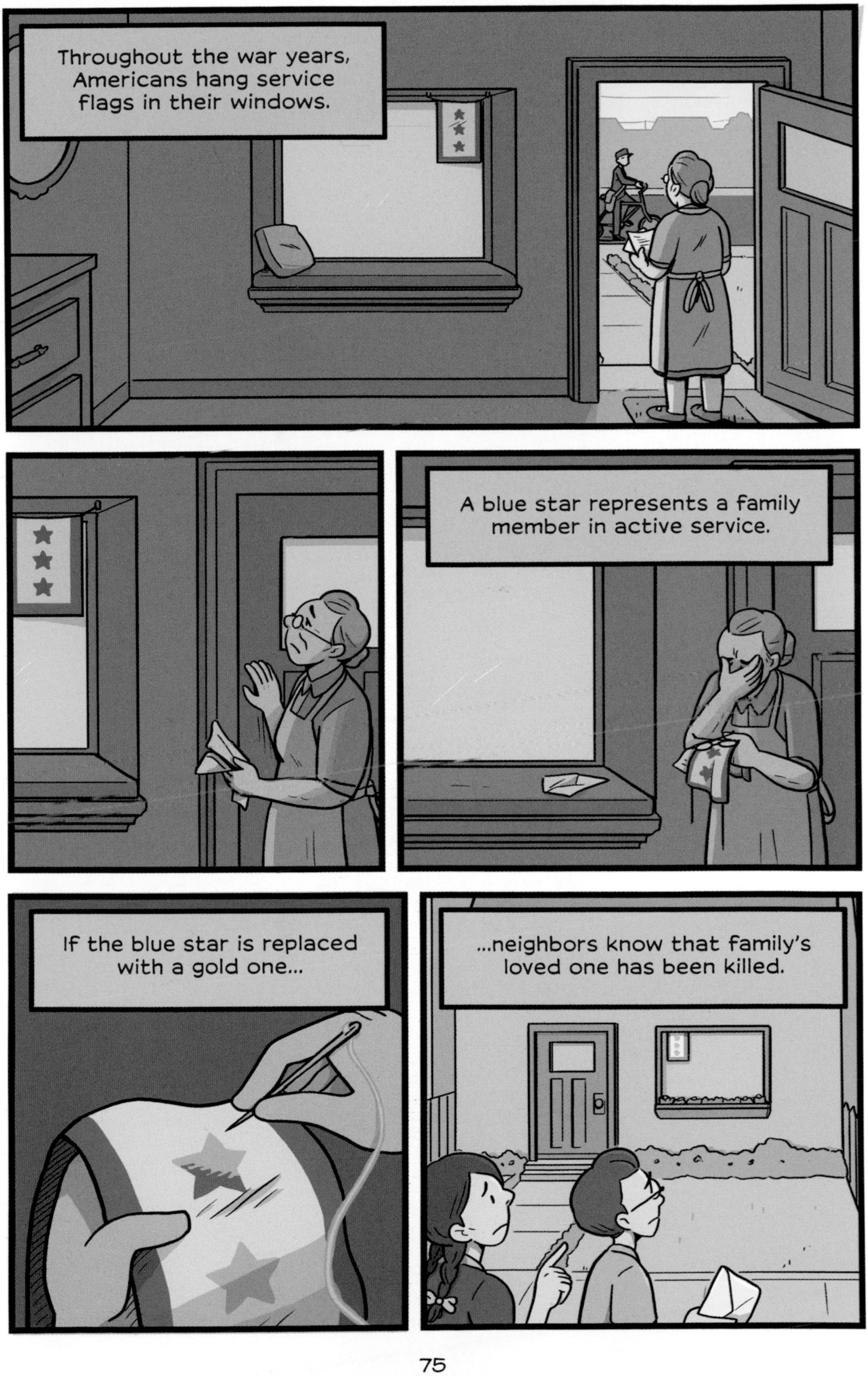

Throughout the war years, Americans hang service flags in their windows.
A blue star represents a family member in active service.
If the blue star is replaced with a gold one...
...neighbors know that family's loved one has been killed.

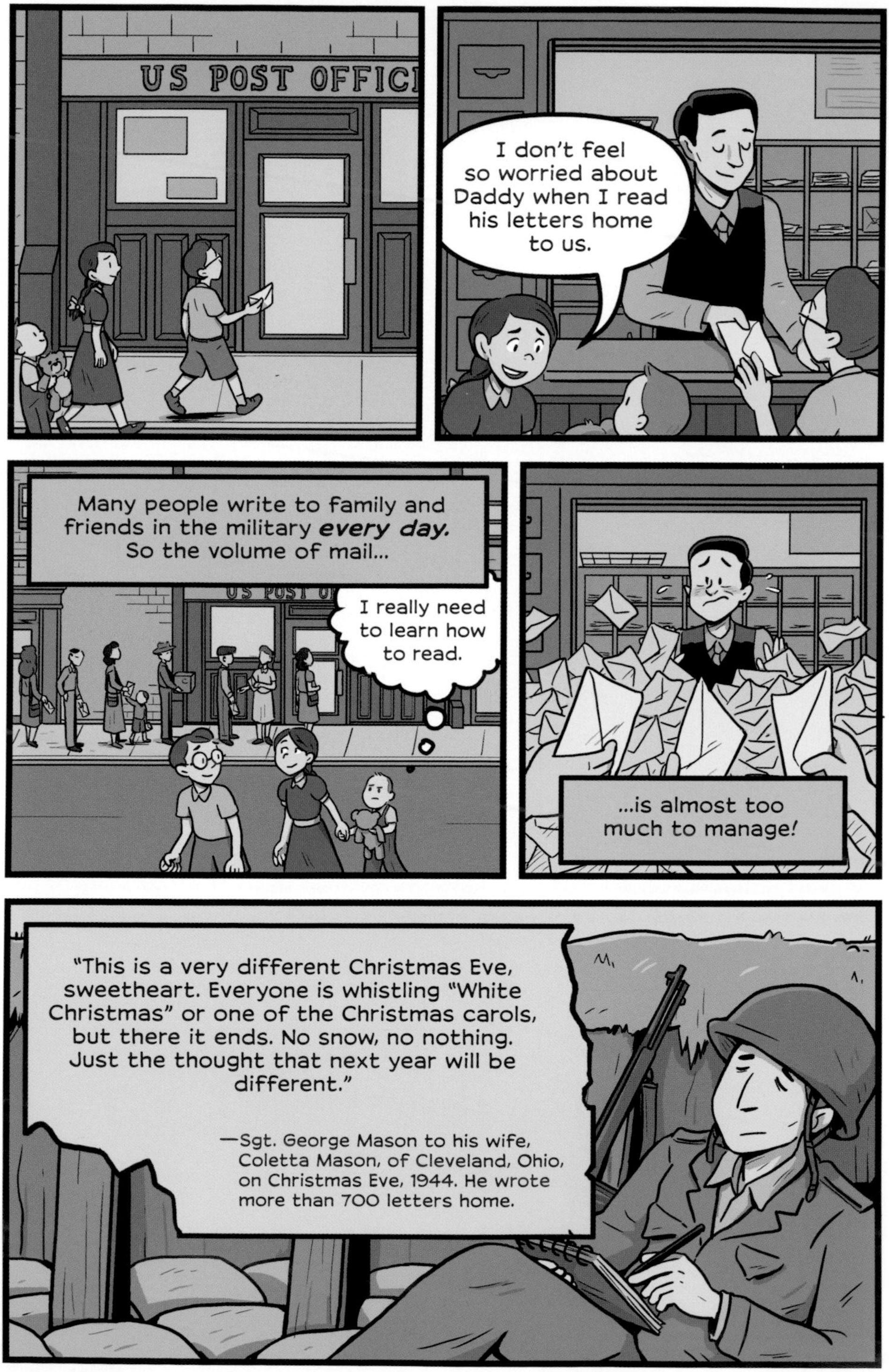
US POST OFFICE
I don't feel so worried about Daddy when I read his letters home to us.
Many people write to family and friends in the military ***every day.*** So the volume of mail...
US POST OF
I really need to learn how to read.
...is almost too much to manage!
"This is a very different Christmas Eve, sweetheart. Everyone is whistling "White Christmas" or one of the Christmas carols, but there it ends. No snow, no nothing. Just the thought that next year will be different."
—Sgt. George Mason to his wife, Coletta Mason, of Cleveland, Ohio, on Christmas Eve, 1944. He wrote more than 700 letters home.

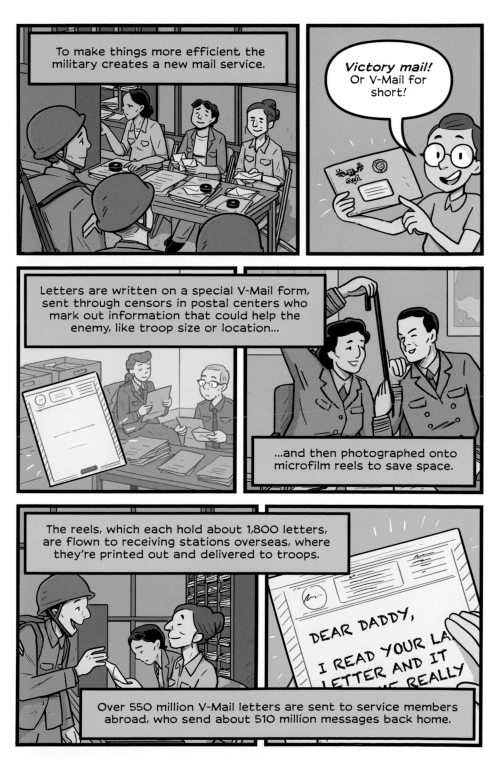

To make things more efficient, the military creates a new mail service.

Victory mail! Or V-Mail for short*!*

Letters are written on a special V-Mail form, sent through censors in postal centers who mark out information that could help the enemy, like troop size or location...

...and then photographed onto microfilm reels to save space.

The reels, which each hold about 1,800 letters, are flown to receiving stations overseas, where they're printed out and delivered to troops.

DEAR DADDY,
I READ YOUR LA[
ETTER AND IT
REALLY

Over 550 million V-Mail letters are sent to service members abroad, who send about 510 million messages back home.

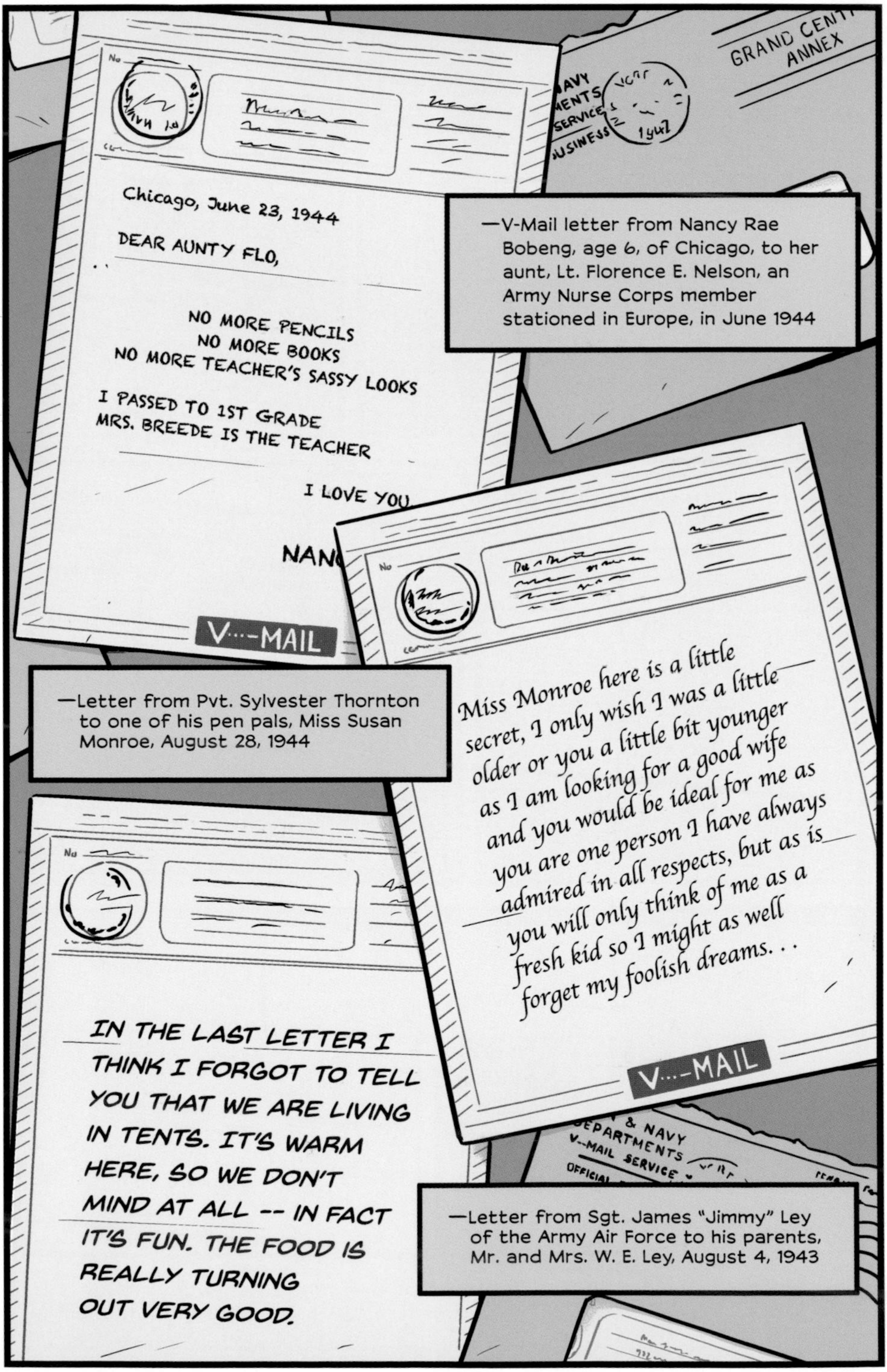
Chicago, June 23, 1944
DEAR AUNTY FLO,
NO MORE PENCILS
NO MORE BOOKS
NO MORE TEACHER'S SASSY LOOKS
I PASSED TO 1ST GRADE
MRS. BREEDE IS THE TEACHER
I LOVE YOU
V...-MAIL
—V-Mail letter from Nancy Rae Bobeng, age 6, of Chicago, to her aunt, Lt. Florence E. Nelson, an Army Nurse Corps member stationed in Europe, in June 1944
Miss Monroe here is a little secret, I only wish I was a little older or you a little bit younger as I am looking for a good wife and you would be ideal for me as you are one person I have always admired in all respects, but as is you will only think of me as a fresh kid so I might as well forget my foolish dreams. . .
V...-MAIL
—Letter from Pvt. Sylvester Thornton to one of his pen pals, Miss Susan Monroe, August 28, 1944
IN THE LAST LETTER I THINK I FORGOT TO TELL YOU THAT WE ARE LIVING IN TENTS. IT'S WARM HERE, SO WE DON'T MIND AT ALL -- IN FACT IT'S FUN. THE FOOD IS REALLY TURNING OUT VERY GOOD.
—Letter from Sgt. James "Jimmy" Ley of the Army Air Force to his parents, Mr. and Mrs. W. E. Ley, August 4, 1943

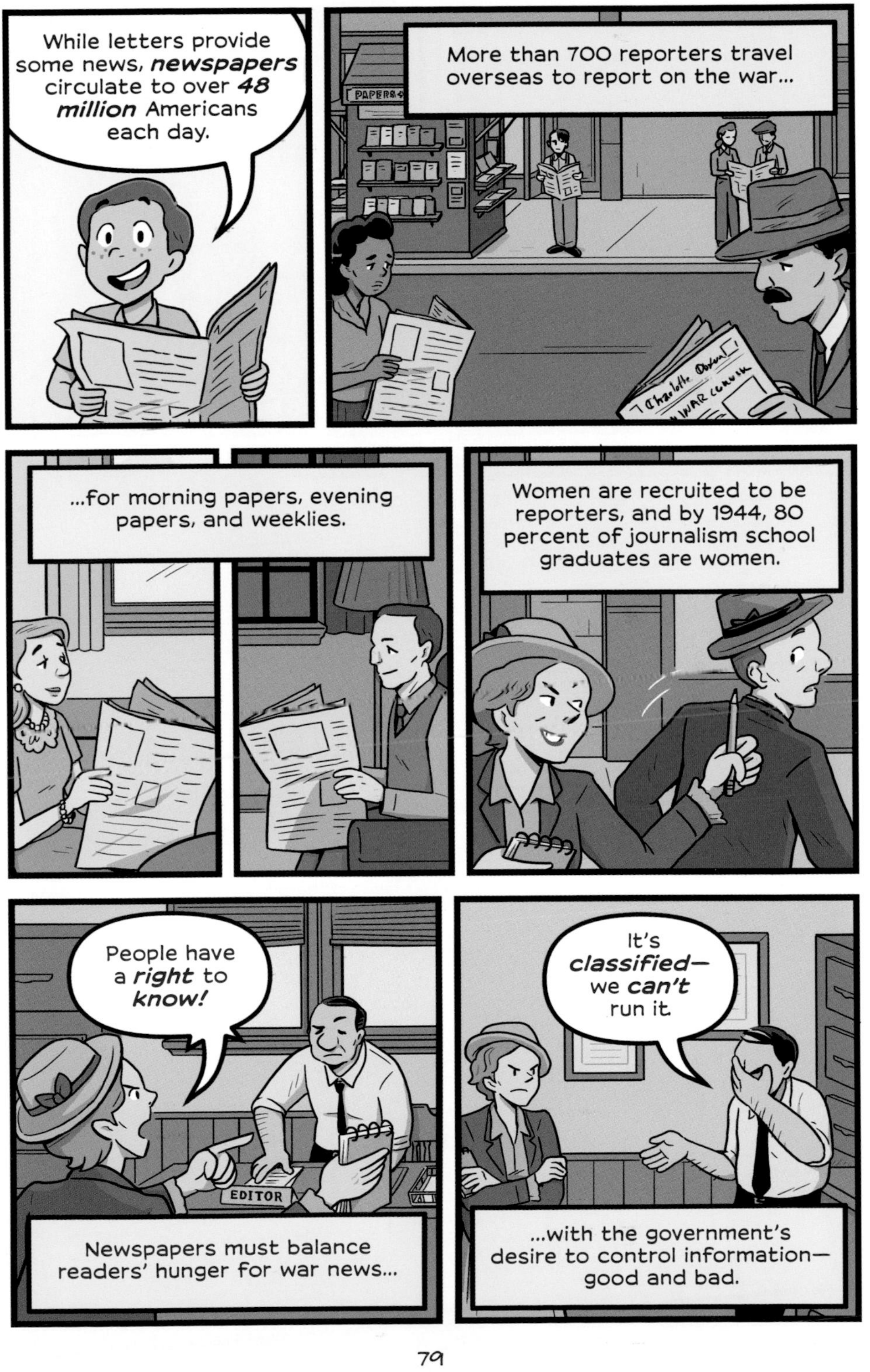
While letters provide some news, *newspapers* circulate to over *48 million* Americans each day.
More than 700 reporters travel overseas to report on the war...
PAPERS
...for morning papers, evening papers, and weeklies.
Women are recruited to be reporters, and by 1944, 80 percent of journalism school graduates are women.
People have a *right* to *know!*
EDITOR
Newspapers must balance readers' hunger for war news...
It's *classified*— we *can't* run it.
...with the government's desire to control information— good and bad.

Pew!

War correspondents report news back to the home front—and risk their lives.

Their stories are first sent to military censors, then on to news outlets via radio or telephone.

CBC

One of the home front's favorites is Ernie Pyle. He writes about ordinary servicemen, and 12 million readers devour his stories in hundreds of papers.

...DIVISION DESERVES
PRAISE FOR BRUTAL BATTLE
by Ernie Pyle

...THERN TUNISIA, April 22,
—I was away from the
lines for a while this
living with other troop
siderable right...
ile I w...
to K...
the...
...ense...

Even after a wint...
wholesa...

...ite...

...hange is...

While covering fighting in the Pacific, Ernie is hit by Japanese fire. He dies on April 18, 1945. America mourns him as if he's family.

"...that faint-red, angry snap of anti-aircraft bursts against the steel-blue sky...the sound of guns off in the distance very faintly, like someone kicking a tub...four searchlights reach up and disappear in the light of a three-quarter moon."

—Live broadcast from a London rooftop during the Blitz, September 21, 1940

Another favorite is radio correspondent Edward R. Murrow. He brings the sounds of war into home-front living rooms.

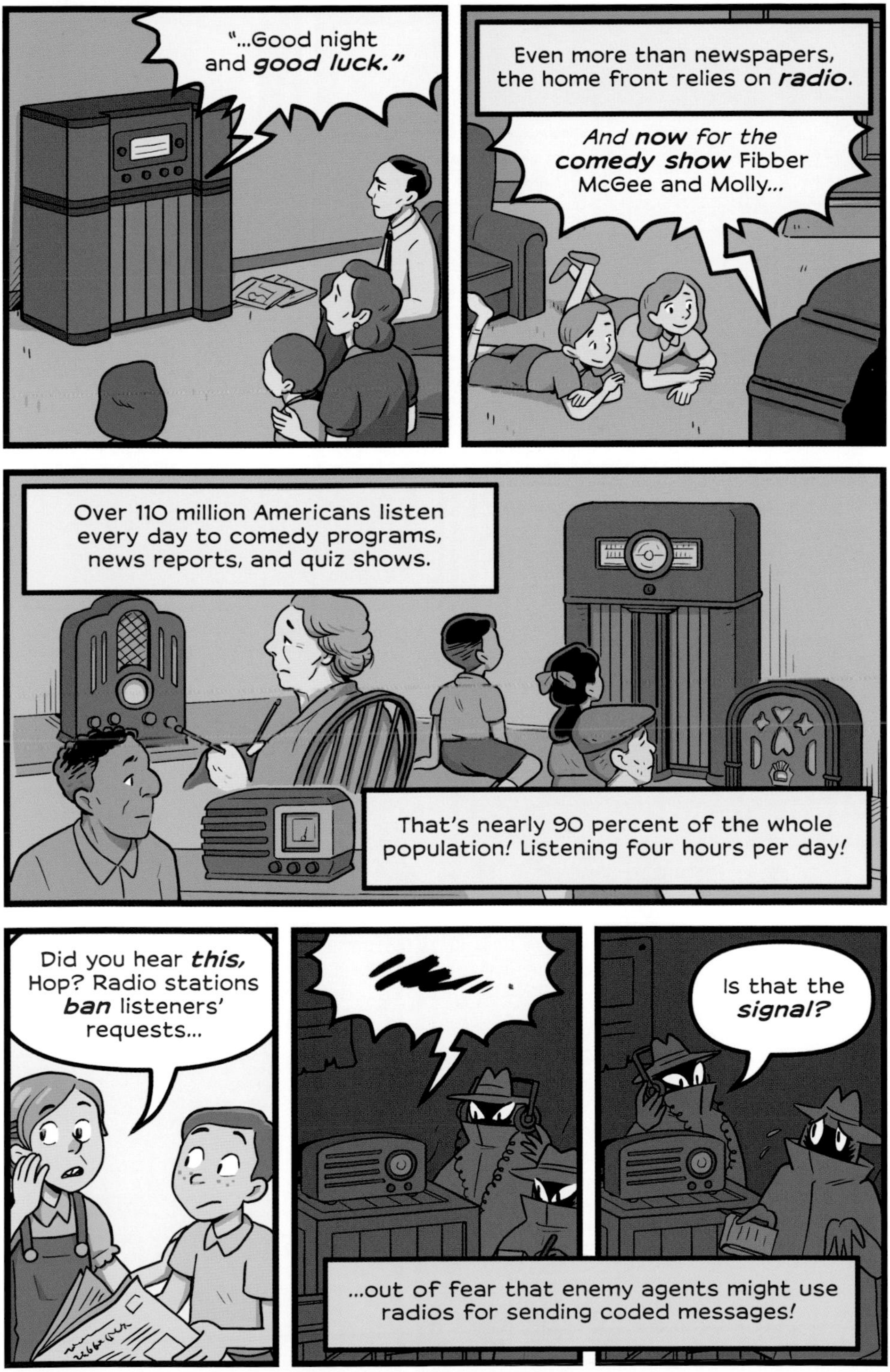
"...Good night and good luck."
Even more than newspapers, the home front relies on radio.
And now for the comedy show Fibber McGee and Molly...
Over 110 million Americans listen every day to comedy programs, news reports, and quiz shows.
That's nearly 90 percent of the whole population! Listening four hours per day!
Did you hear this, Hop? Radio stations ban listeners' requests...
Is that the signal?
...out of fear that enemy agents might use radios for sending coded messages!

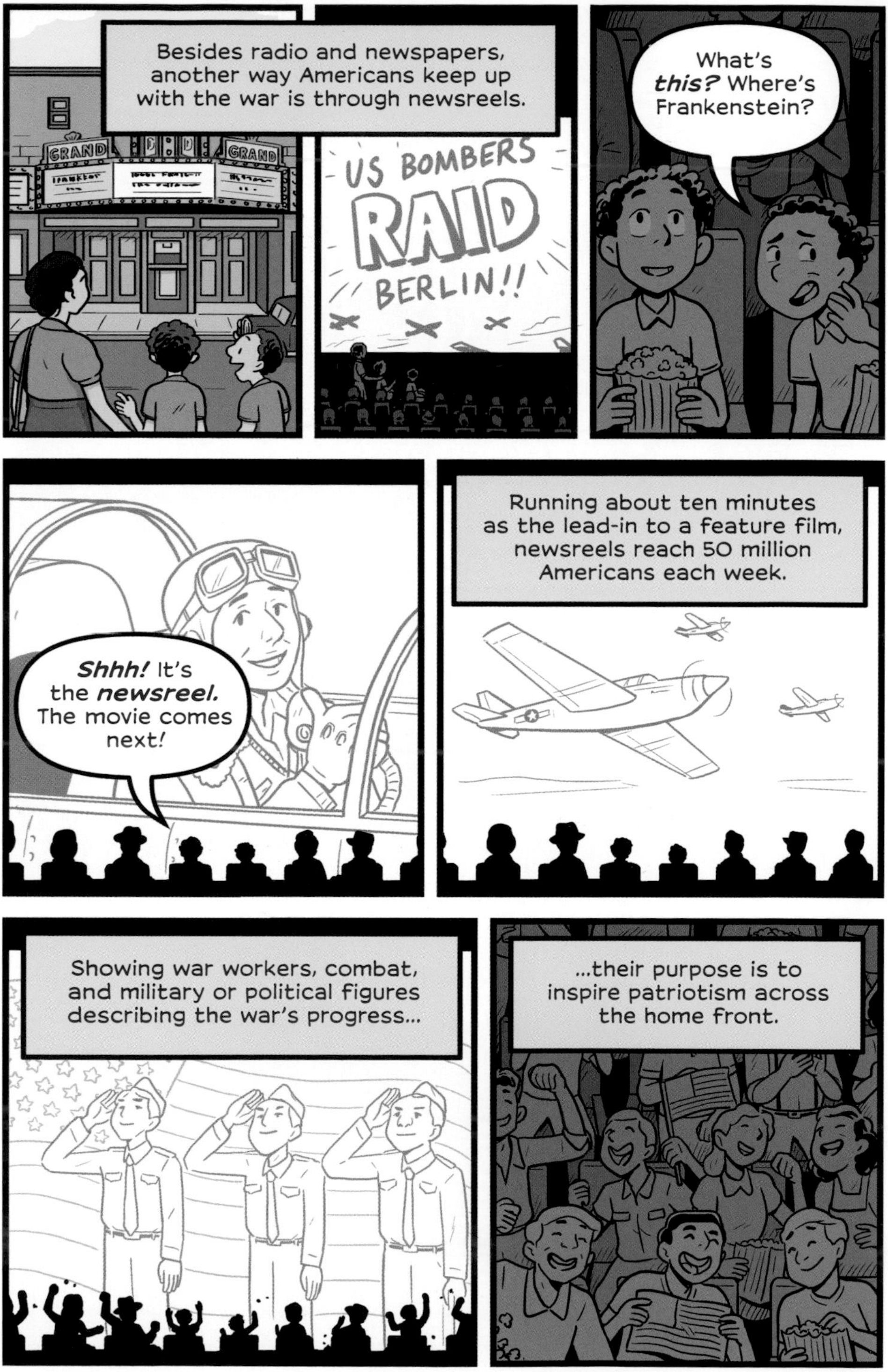
Besides radio and newspapers, another way Americans keep up with the war is through newsreels.
GRAND
GRAND
US BOMBERS RAID BERLIN!!
What's *this?* Where's Frankenstein?
Shhh! It's the *newsreel.* The movie comes next!
Running about ten minutes as the lead-in to a feature film, newsreels reach 50 million Americans each week.
Showing war workers, combat, and military or political figures describing the war's progress...
...their purpose is to inspire patriotism across the home front.

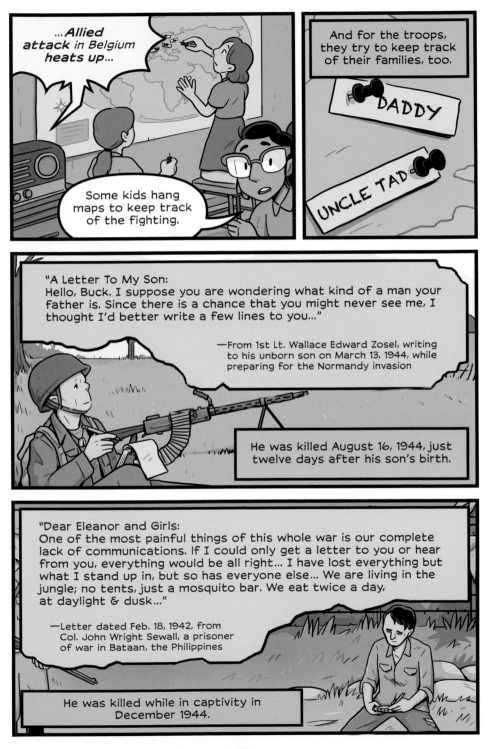

...*Allied attack* in Belgium *heats up...*

Some kids hang maps to keep track of the fighting.

And for the troops, they try to keep track of their families, too.

DADDY

UNCLE TAD

"A Letter To My Son:
Hello, Buck. I suppose you are wondering what kind of a man your father is. Since there is a chance that you might never see me, I thought I'd better write a few lines to you..."

—From 1st Lt. Wallace Edward Zosel, writing to his unborn son on March 13, 1944, while preparing for the Normandy invasion

He was killed August 16, 1944, just twelve days after his son's birth.

"Dear Eleanor and Girls:
One of the most painful things of this whole war is our complete lack of communications. If I could only get a letter to you or hear from you, everything would be all right... I have lost everything but what I stand up in, but so has everyone else... We are living in the jungle; no tents, just a mosquito bar. We eat twice a day, at daylight & dusk..."

—Letter dated Feb. 18, 1942, from Col. John Wright Sewall, a prisoner of war in Bataan, the Philippines

He was killed while in captivity in December 1944.

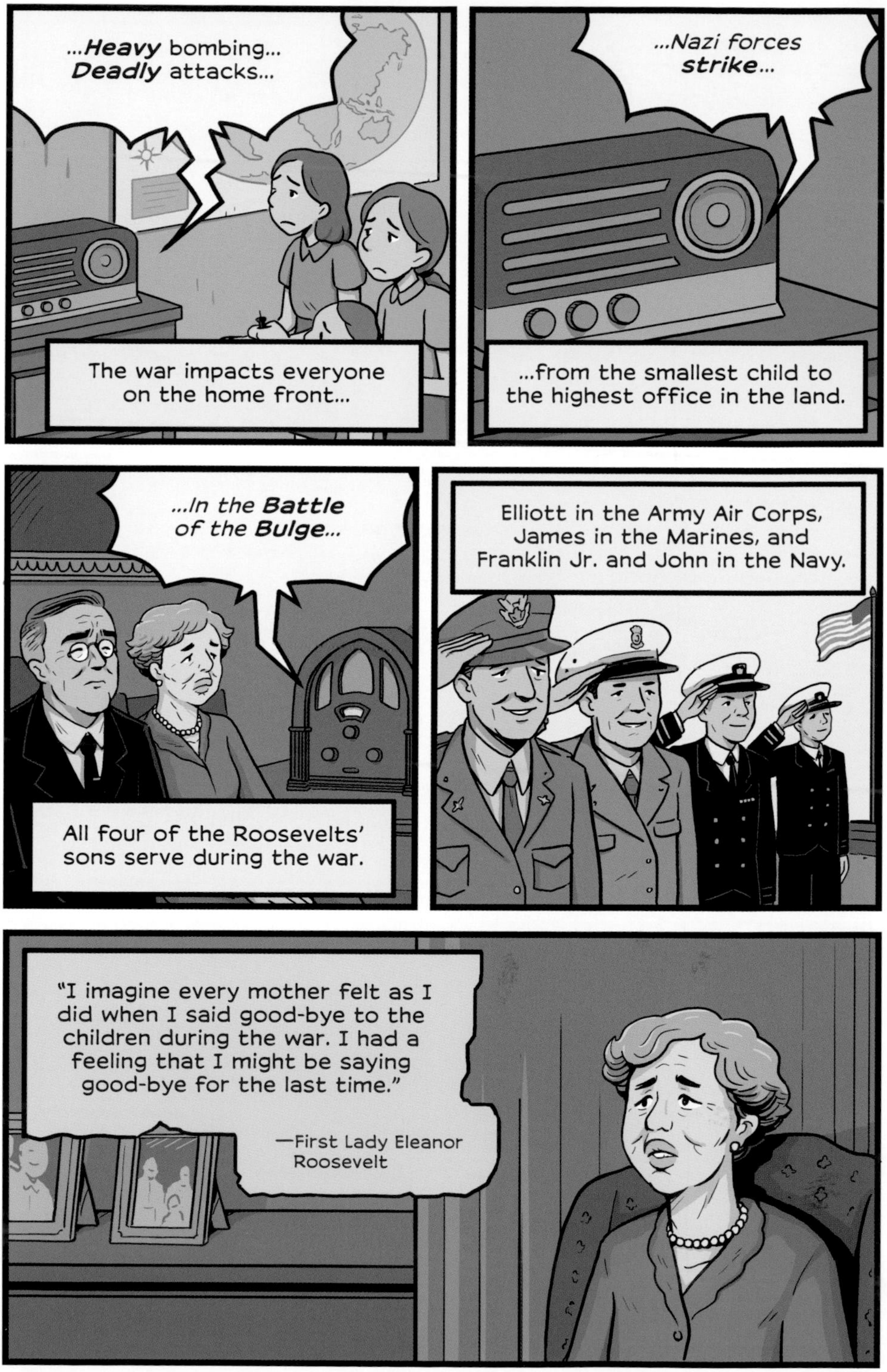
...Heavy bombing... Deadly attacks...
The war impacts everyone on the home front...
...Nazi forces strike...
...from the smallest child to the highest office in the land.
...In the Battle of the Bulge...
All four of the Roosevelts' sons serve during the war.
Elliott in the Army Air Corps, James in the Marines, and Franklin Jr. and John in the Navy.
"I imagine every mother felt as I did when I said good-bye to the children during the war. I had a feeling that I might be saying good-bye for the last time."
—First Lady Eleanor Roosevelt

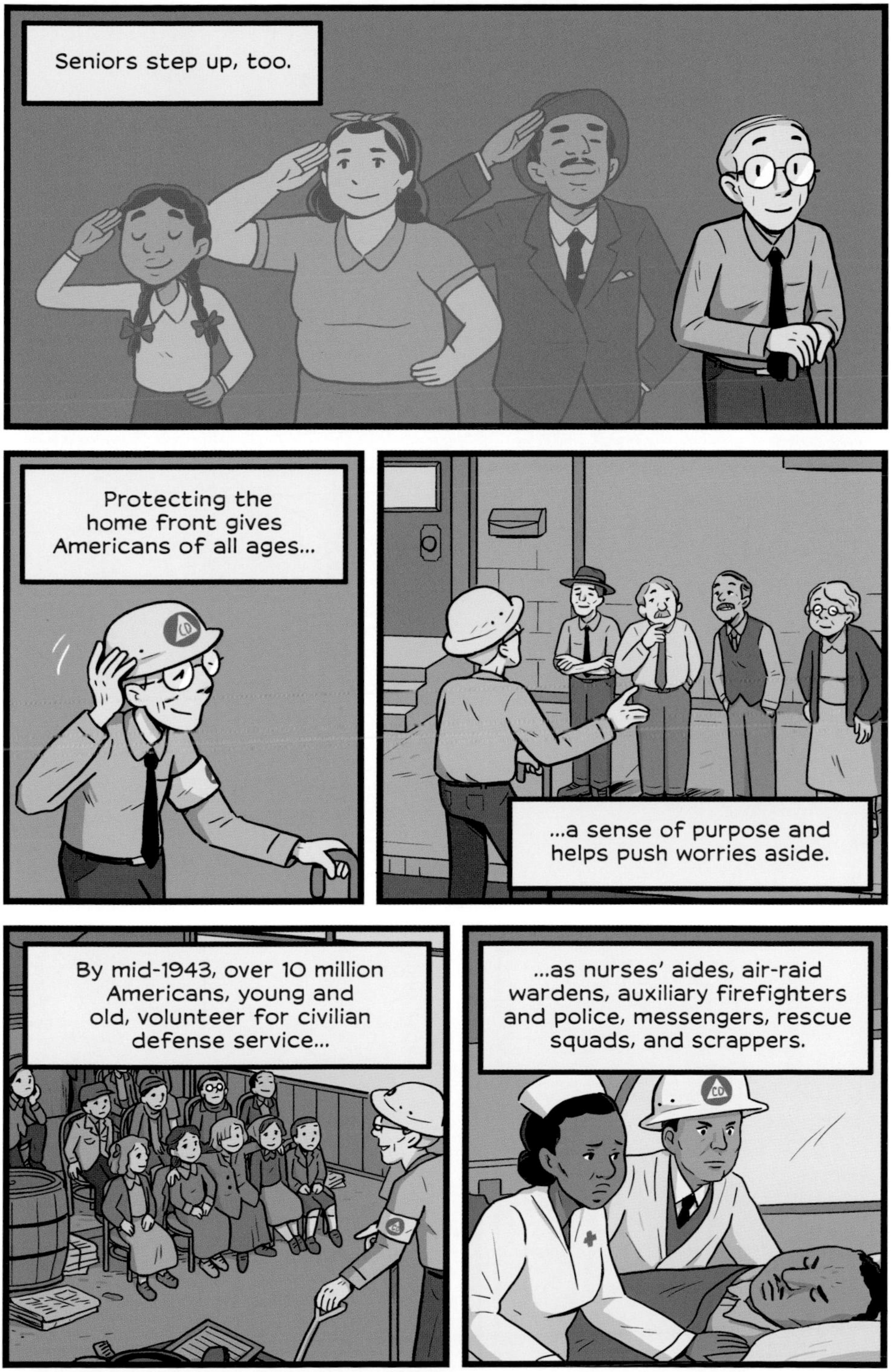
Seniors step up, too.
Protecting the home front gives Americans of all ages...
...a sense of purpose and helps push worries aside.
By mid-1943, over 10 million Americans, young and old, volunteer for civilian defense service...
...as nurses' aides, air-raid wardens, auxiliary firefighters and police, messengers, rescue squads, and scrappers.

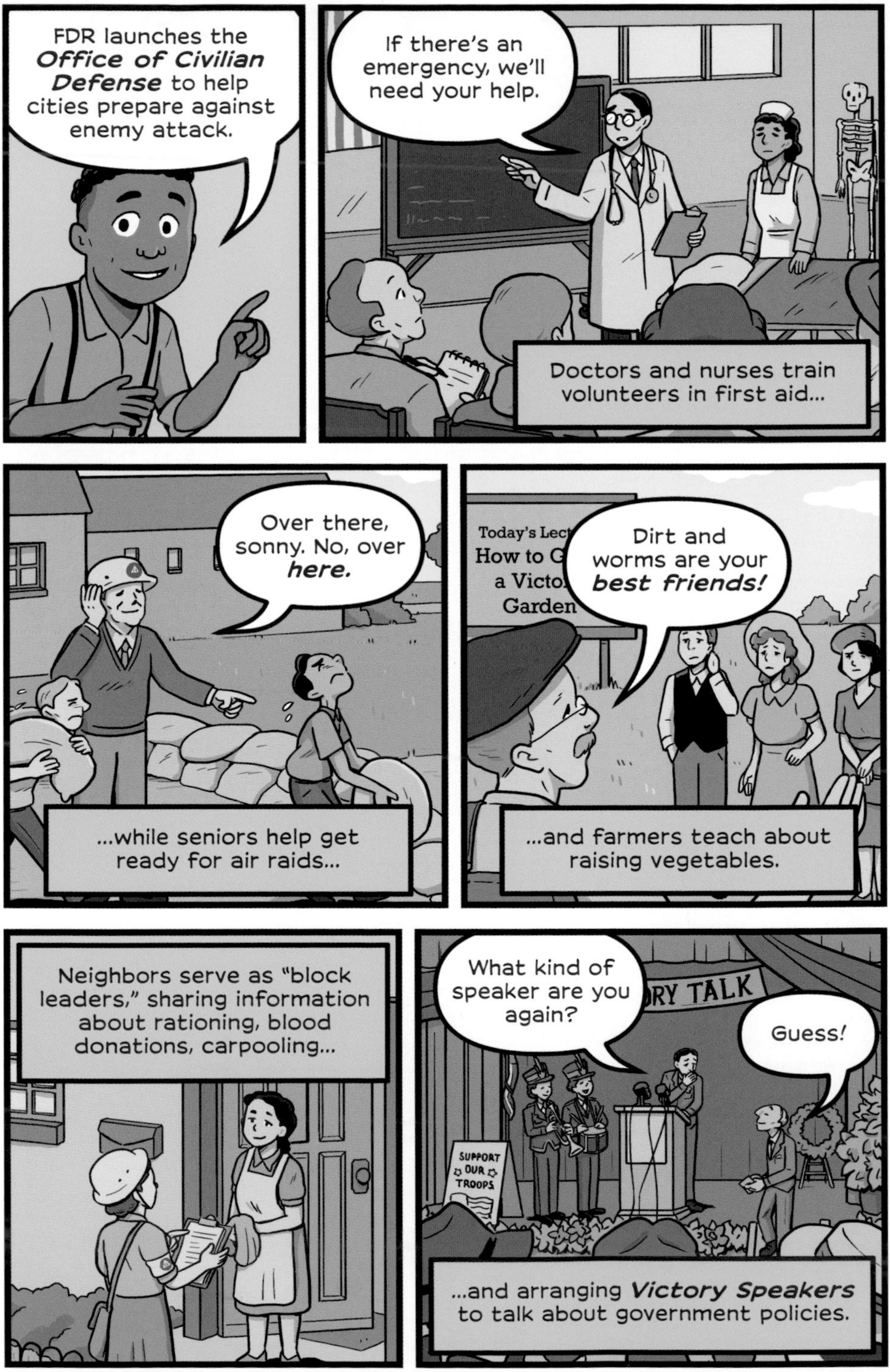
FDR launches the ***Office of Civilian Defense*** to help cities prepare against enemy attack.
If there's an emergency, we'll need your help.
Doctors and nurses train volunteers in first aid...
Over there, sonny. No, over ***here.***
...while seniors help get ready for air raids...
Today's Lect
How to G
a Victo
Garden
Dirt and worms are your ***best friends!***
...and farmers teach about raising vegetables.
Neighbors serve as "block leaders," sharing information about rationing, blood donations, carpooling...
What kind of speaker are you again?
RY TALK
Guess!
SUPPORT OUR TROOPS
...and arranging ***Victory Speakers*** to talk about government policies.

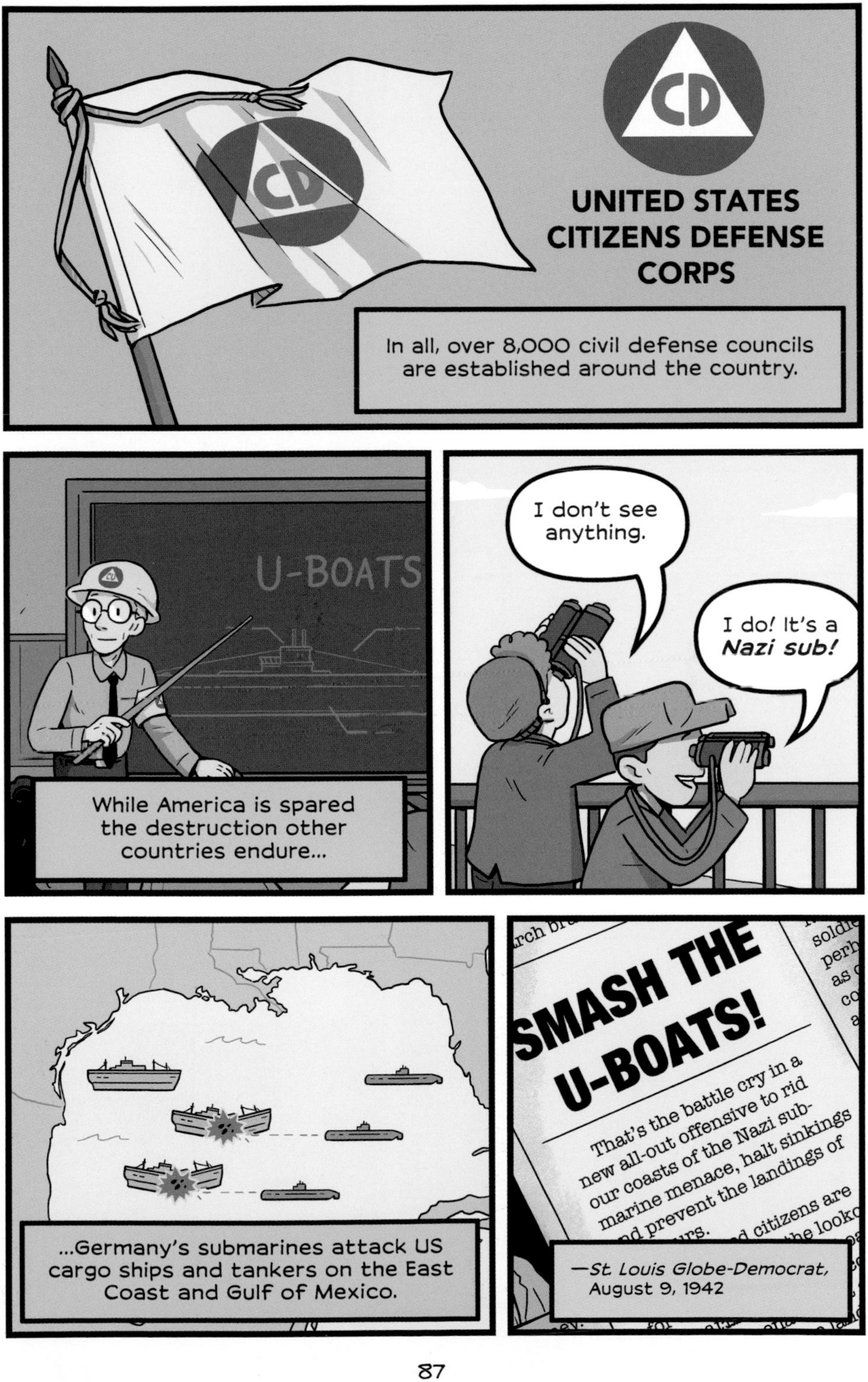

CD
UNITED STATES CITIZENS DEFENSE CORPS
In all, over 8,000 civil defense councils are established around the country.
U-BOATS
While America is spared the destruction other countries endure...
I don't see anything.
I do! It's a *Nazi sub!*
...Germany's submarines attack US cargo ships and tankers on the East Coast and Gulf of Mexico.
SMASH THE U-BOATS!
That's the battle cry in a new all-out offensive to rid our coasts of the Nazi sub- marine menace, halt sinkings
—*St. Louis Globe-Democrat,* August 9, 1942

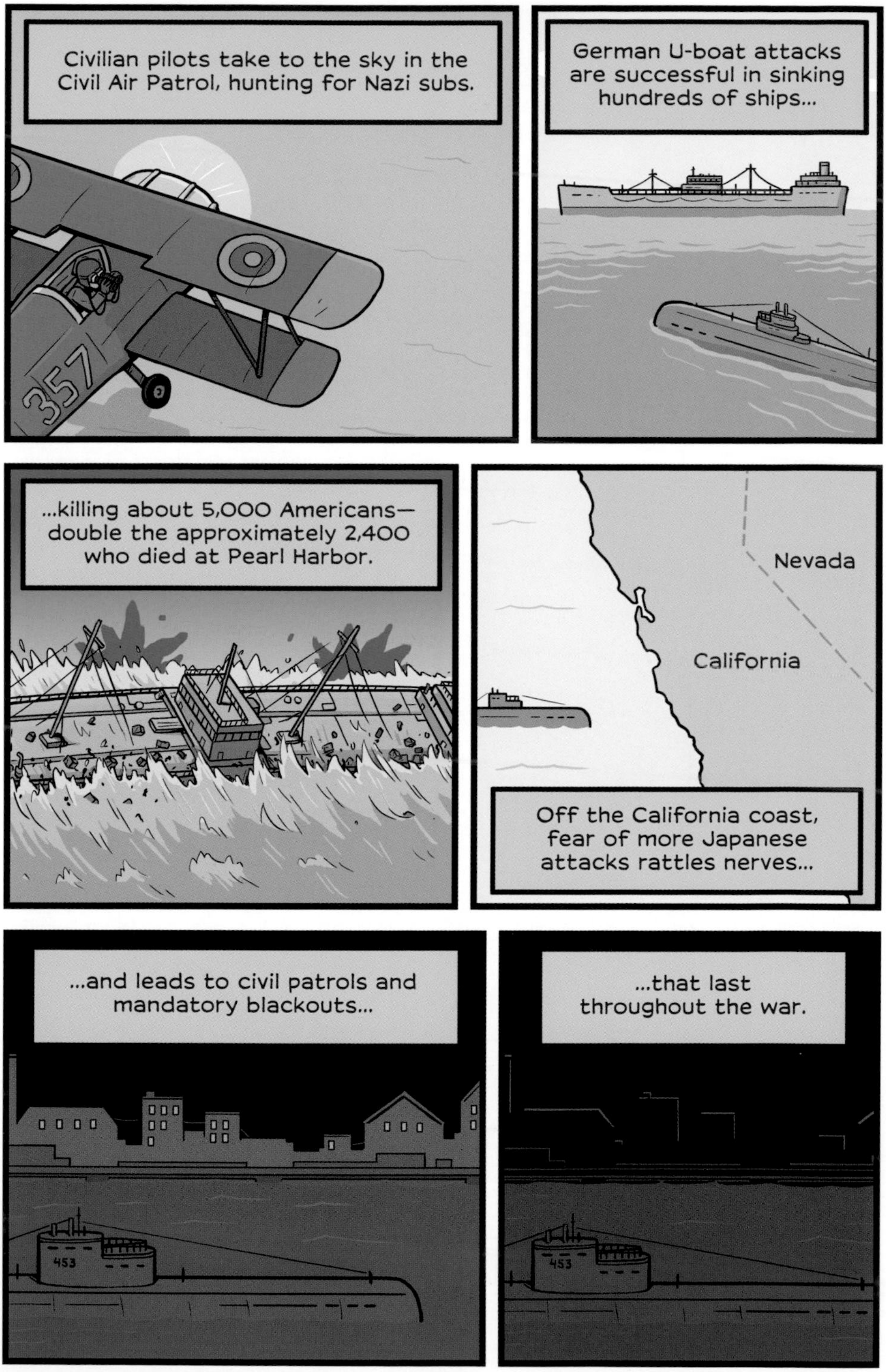
Civilian pilots take to the sky in the Civil Air Patrol, hunting for Nazi subs.
357
German U-boat attacks are successful in sinking hundreds of ships...
...killing about 5,000 Americans—double the approximately 2,400 who died at Pearl Harbor.
Nevada
California
Off the California coast, fear of more Japanese attacks rattles nerves...
...and leads to civil patrols and mandatory blackouts...
453
...that last throughout the war.
453

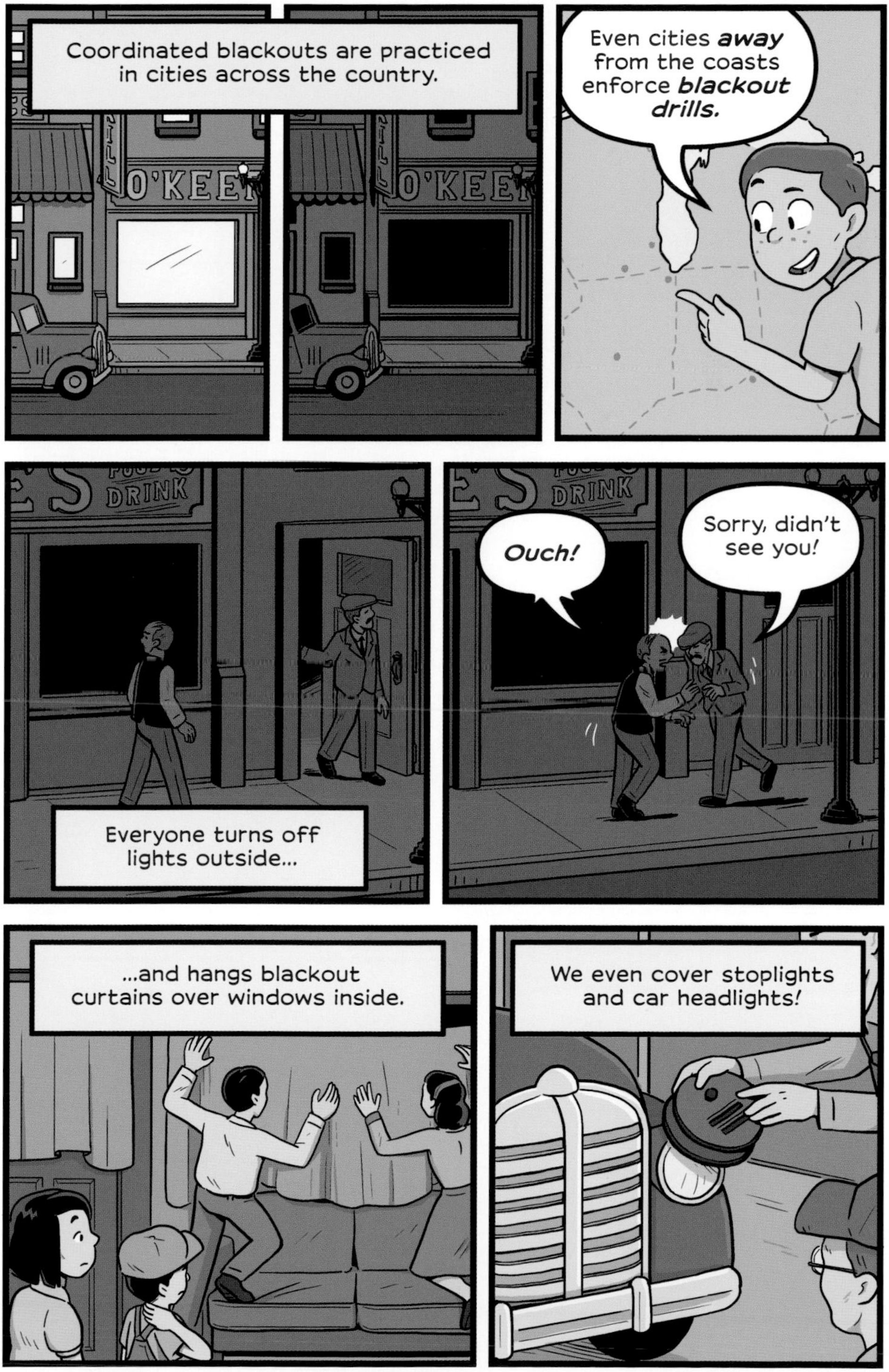
Coordinated blackouts are practiced in cities across the country.
O'KEE
O'KEE
Even cities ***away*** from the coasts enforce ***blackout drills.***
DRINK
Everyone turns off lights outside...
DRINK
Ouch!
Sorry, didn't see you!
...and hangs blackout curtains over windows inside.
We even cover stoplights and car headlights!

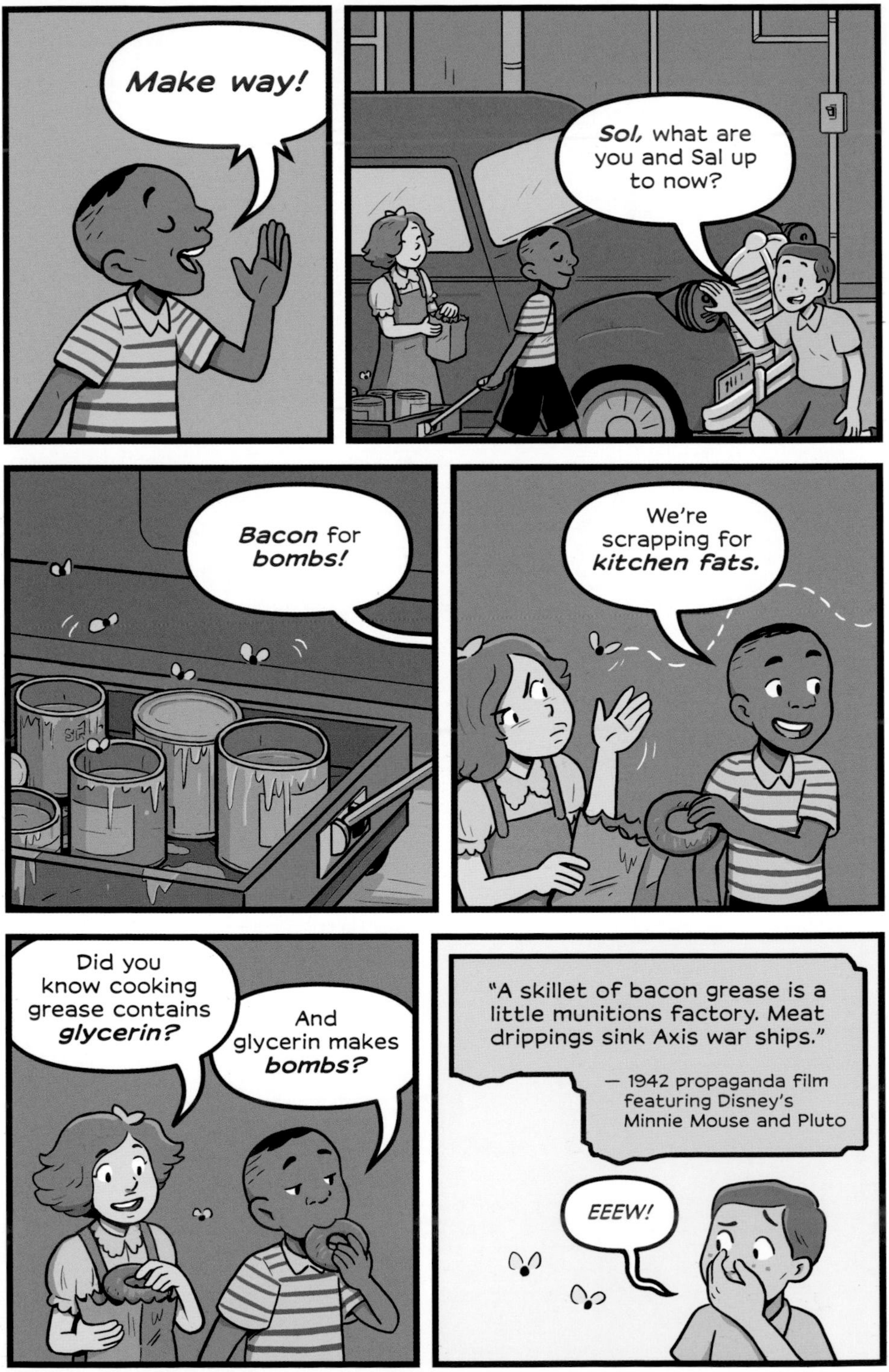

Make way!
Sol, what are you and Sal up to now?
Bacon for bombs!
We're scrapping for kitchen fats.
Did you know cooking grease contains glycerin?
And glycerin makes bombs?
"A skillet of bacon grease is a little munitions factory. Meat drippings sink Axis war ships."
— 1942 propaganda film featuring Disney's Minnie Mouse and Pluto
EEEW!

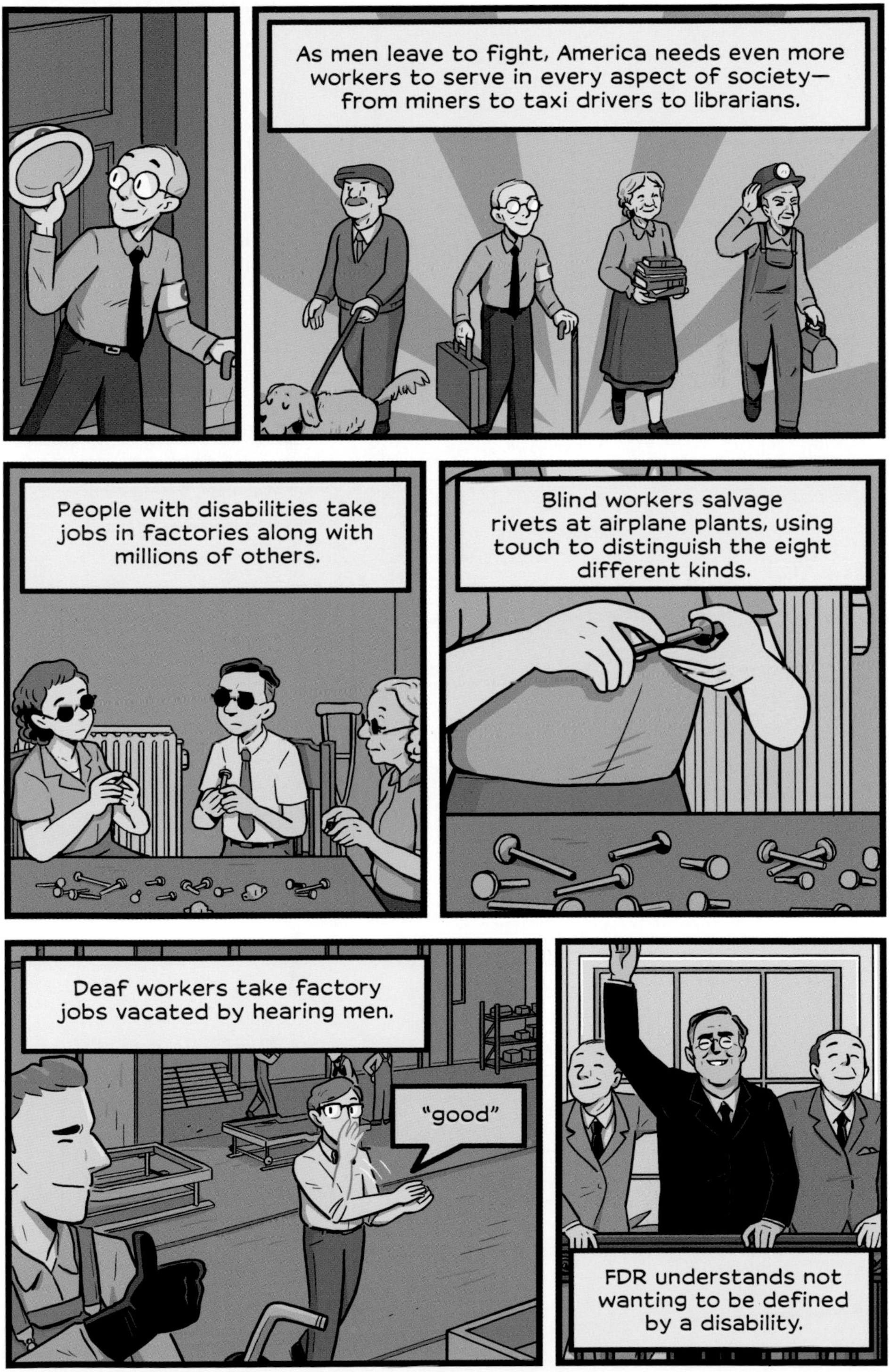
As men leave to fight, America needs even more workers to serve in every aspect of society—from miners to taxi drivers to librarians.
People with disabilities take jobs in factories along with millions of others.
Blind workers salvage rivets at airplane plants, using touch to distinguish the eight different kinds.
Deaf workers take factory jobs vacated by hearing men.
"good"
FDR understands not wanting to be defined by a disability.

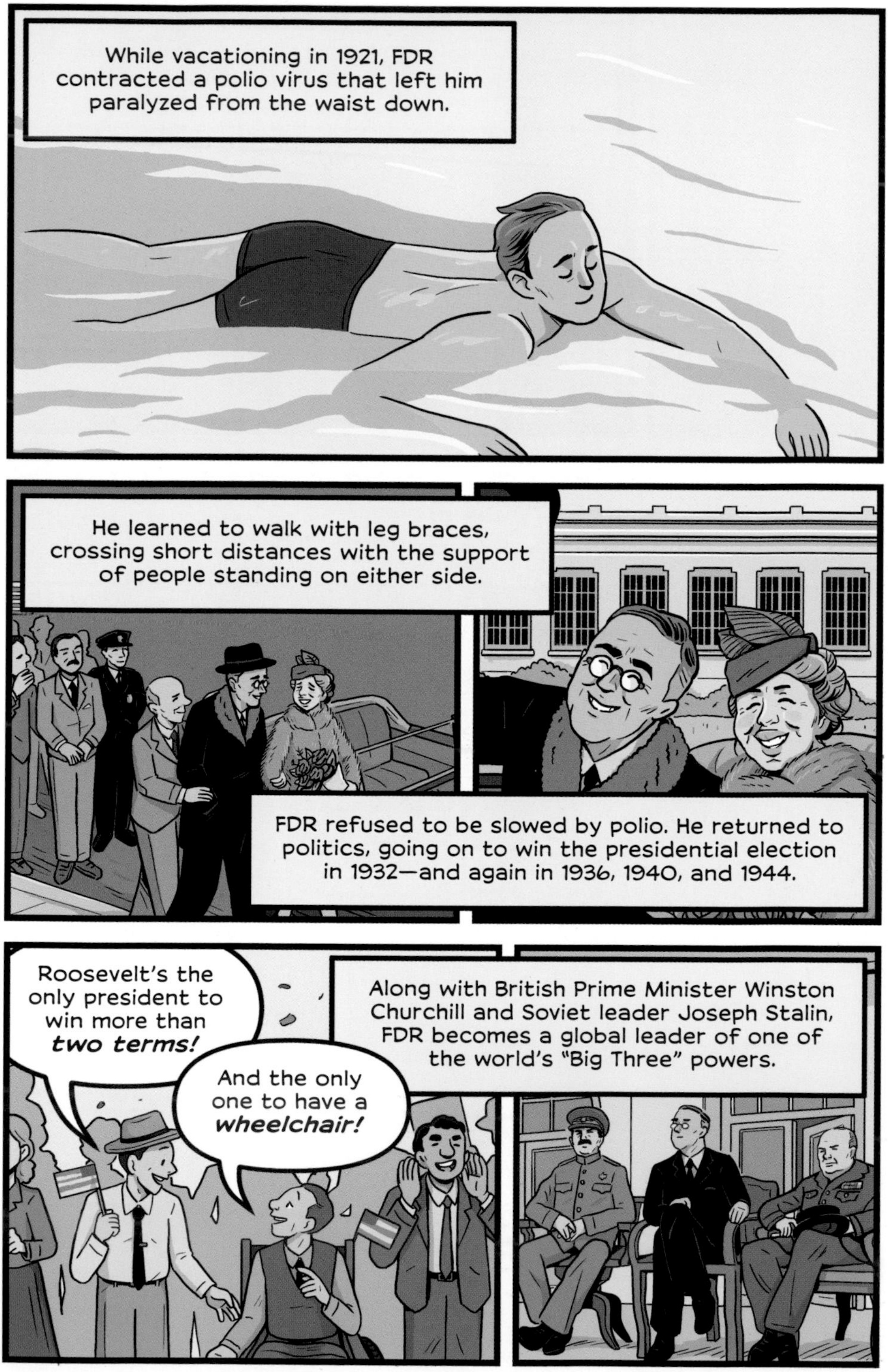
While vacationing in 1921, FDR contracted a polio virus that left him paralyzed from the waist down.
He learned to walk with leg braces, crossing short distances with the support of people standing on either side.
FDR refused to be slowed by polio. He returned to politics, going on to win the presidential election in 1932—and again in 1936, 1940, and 1944.
Roosevelt's the only president to win more than ***two terms!***
And the only one to have a ***wheelchair!***
Along with British Prime Minister Winston Churchill and Soviet leader Joseph Stalin, FDR becomes a global leader of one of the world's "Big Three" powers.

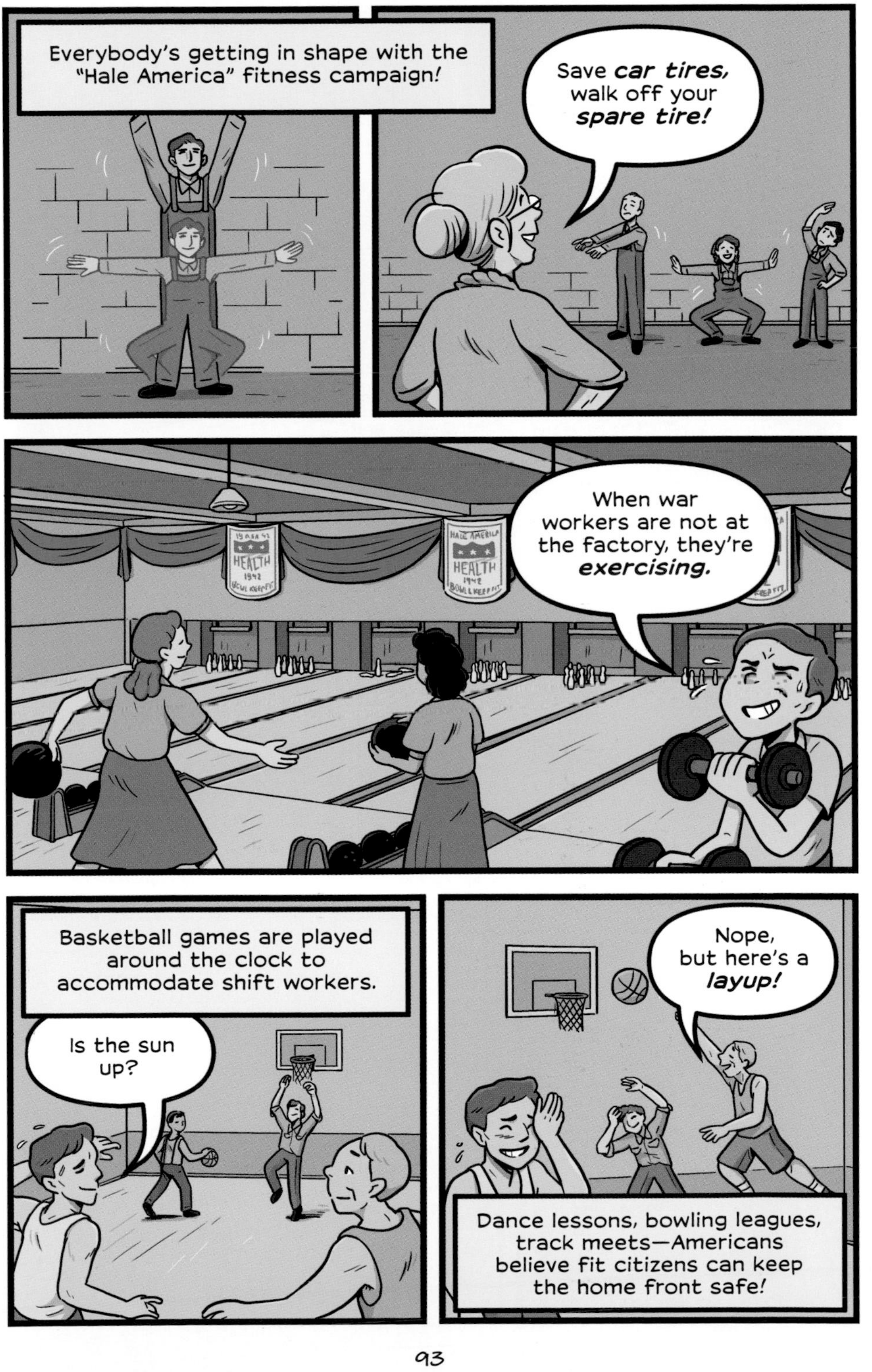
Everybody's getting in shape with the "Hale America" fitness campaign!
Save *car tires,* walk off your *spare tire!*
When war workers are not at the factory, they're *exercising.*
Basketball games are played around the clock to accommodate shift workers.
Is the sun up?
Nope, but here's a *layup!*
Dance lessons, bowling leagues, track meets—Americans believe fit citizens can keep the home front safe!

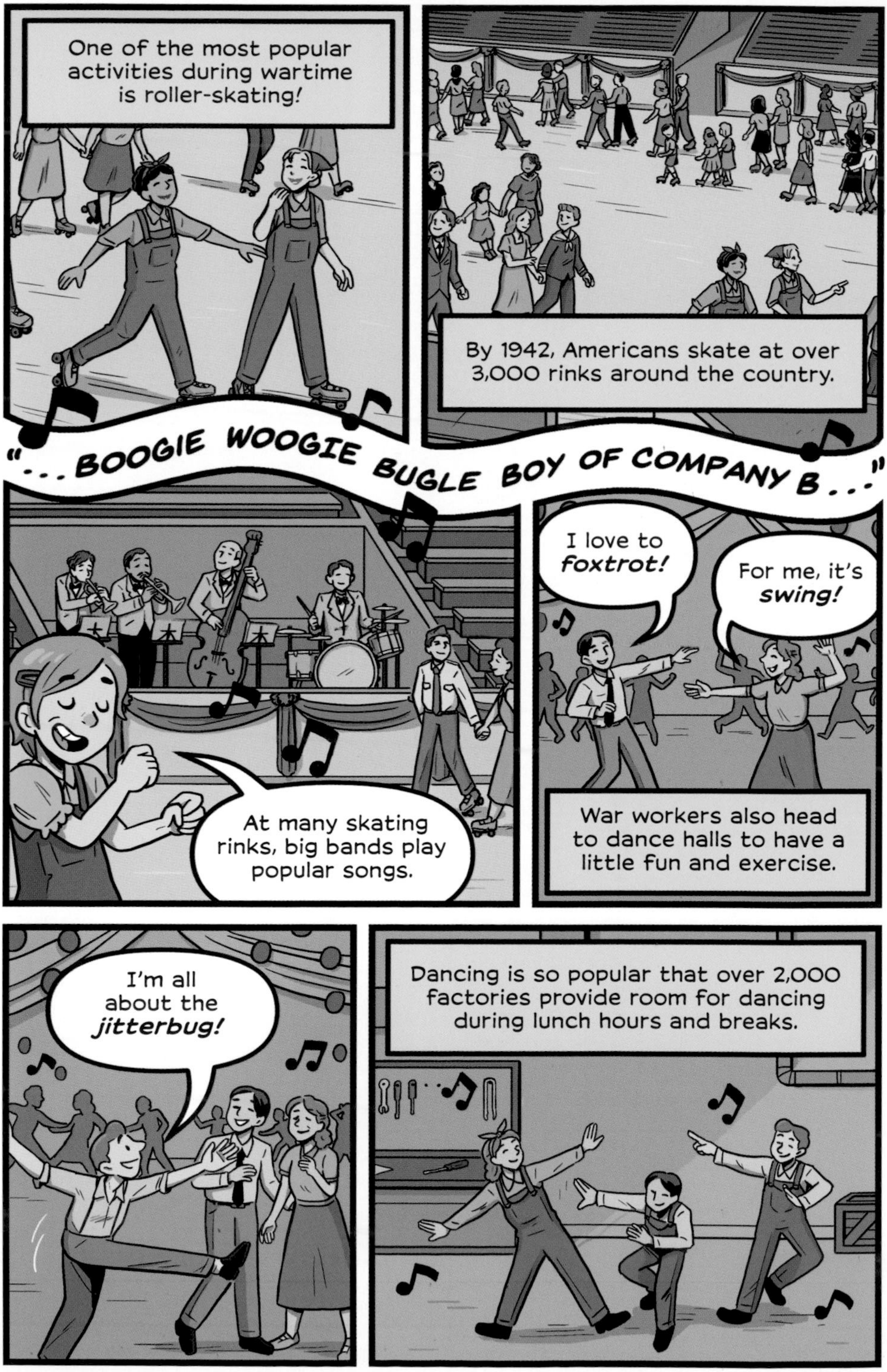
One of the most popular activities during wartime is roller-skating!
By 1942, Americans skate at over 3,000 rinks around the country.
"...BOOGIE WOOGIE BUGLE BOY OF COMPANY B..."
At many skating rinks, big bands play popular songs.
I love to *foxtrot!*
For me, it's *swing!*
War workers also head to dance halls to have a little fun and exercise.
I'm all about the *jitterbug!*
Dancing is so popular that over 2,000 factories provide room for dancing during lunch hours and breaks.

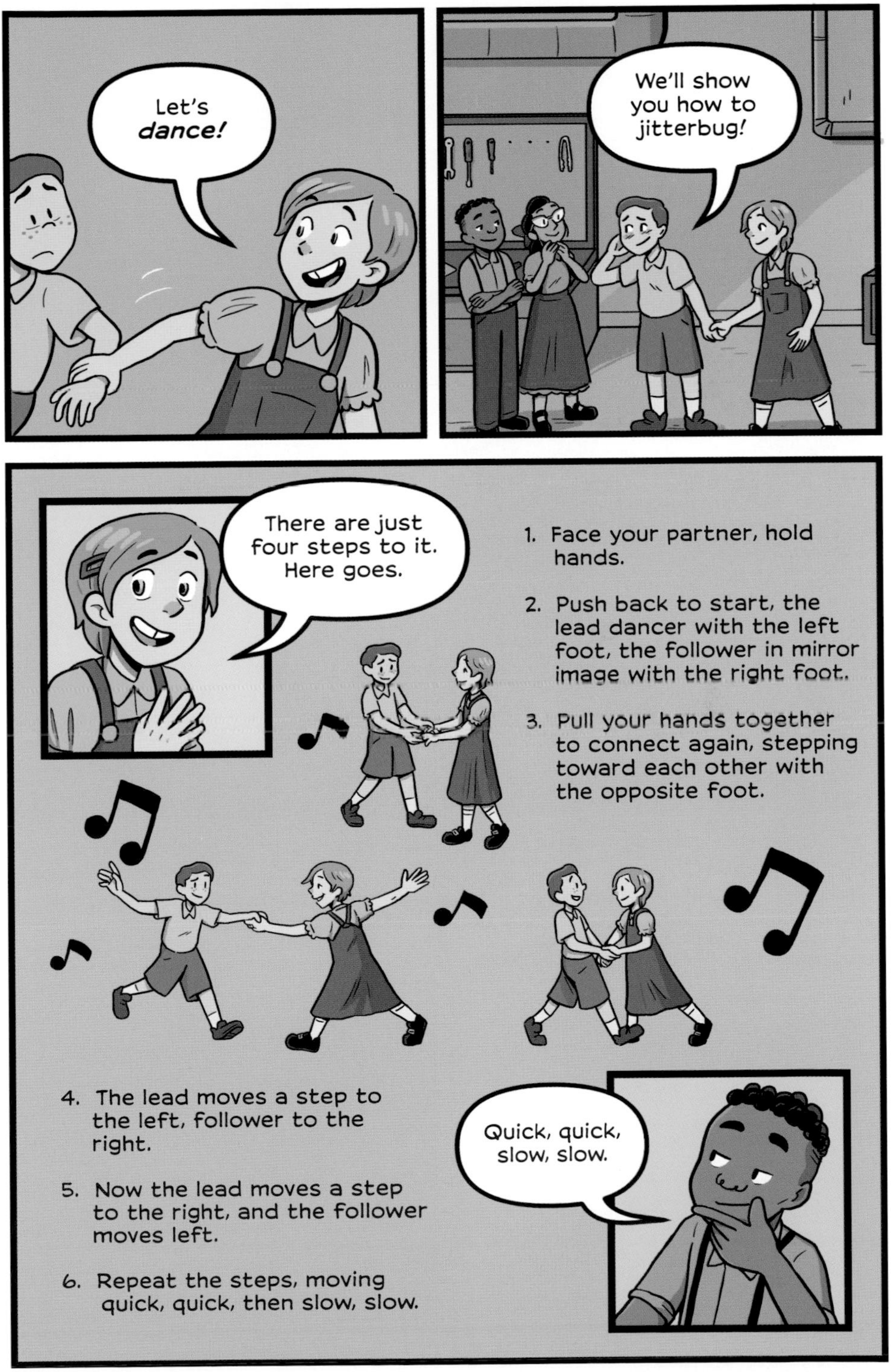
Let's *dance!*
We'll show you how to jitterbug!
There are just four steps to it. Here goes.
1. Face your partner, hold hands.
2. Push back to start, the lead dancer with the left foot, the follower in mirror image with the right foot.
3. Pull your hands together to connect again, stepping toward each other with the opposite foot.
4. The lead moves a step to the left, follower to the right.
5. Now the lead moves a step to the right, and the follower moves left.
6. Repeat the steps, moving quick, quick, then slow, slow.
Quick, quick, slow, slow.

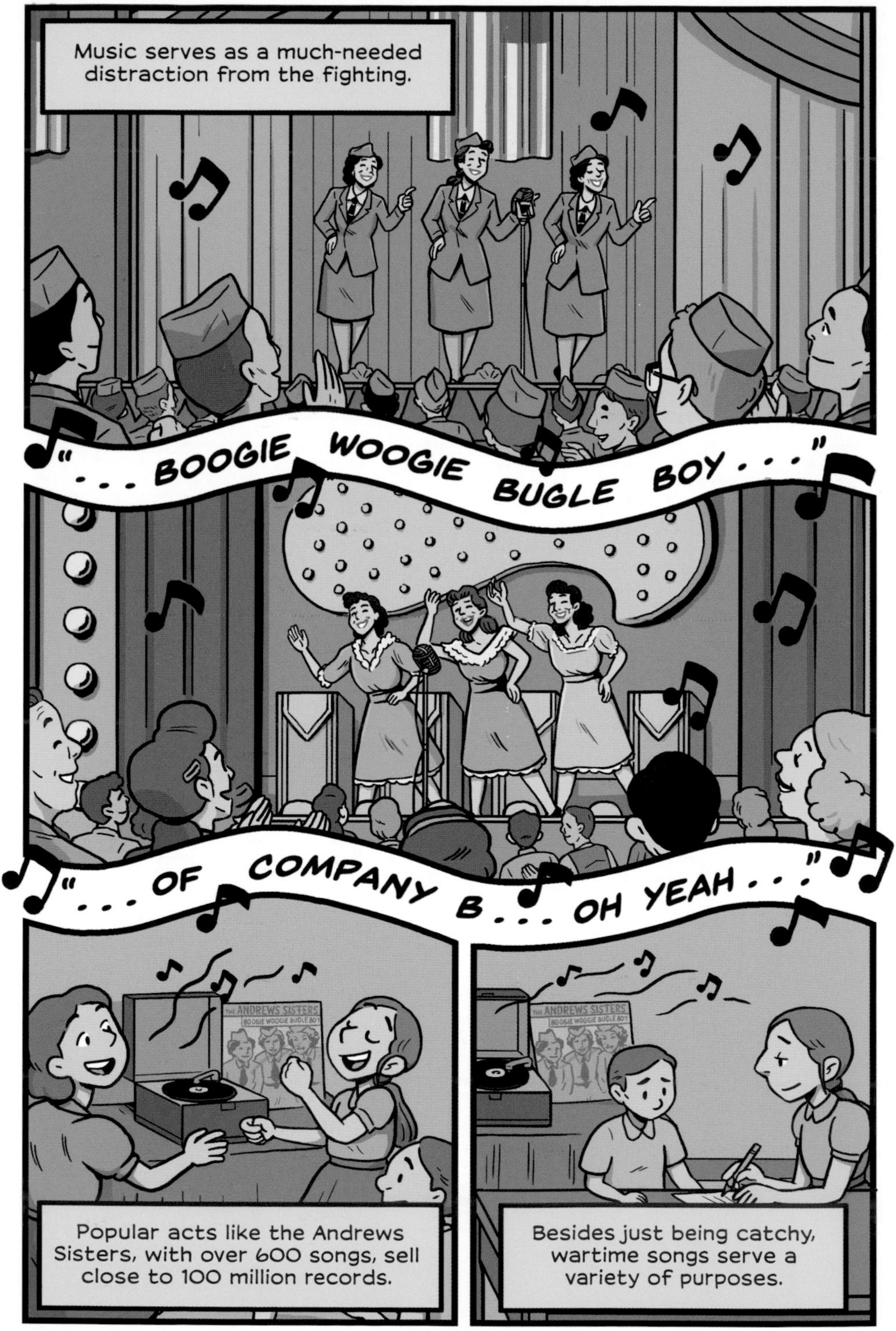

Music serves as a much-needed distraction from the fighting.
". . . BOOGIE WOOGIE BUGLE BOY . . ."
". . . OF COMPANY B . . . OH YEAH . . ."
THE ANDREWS SISTERS
BOOGIE WOOGIE BUGLE BOY
Popular acts like the Andrews Sisters, with over 600 songs, sell close to 100 million records.
THE ANDREWS SISTERS
BOOGIE WOOGIE BUGLE BOY
Besides just being catchy, wartime songs serve a variety of purposes.

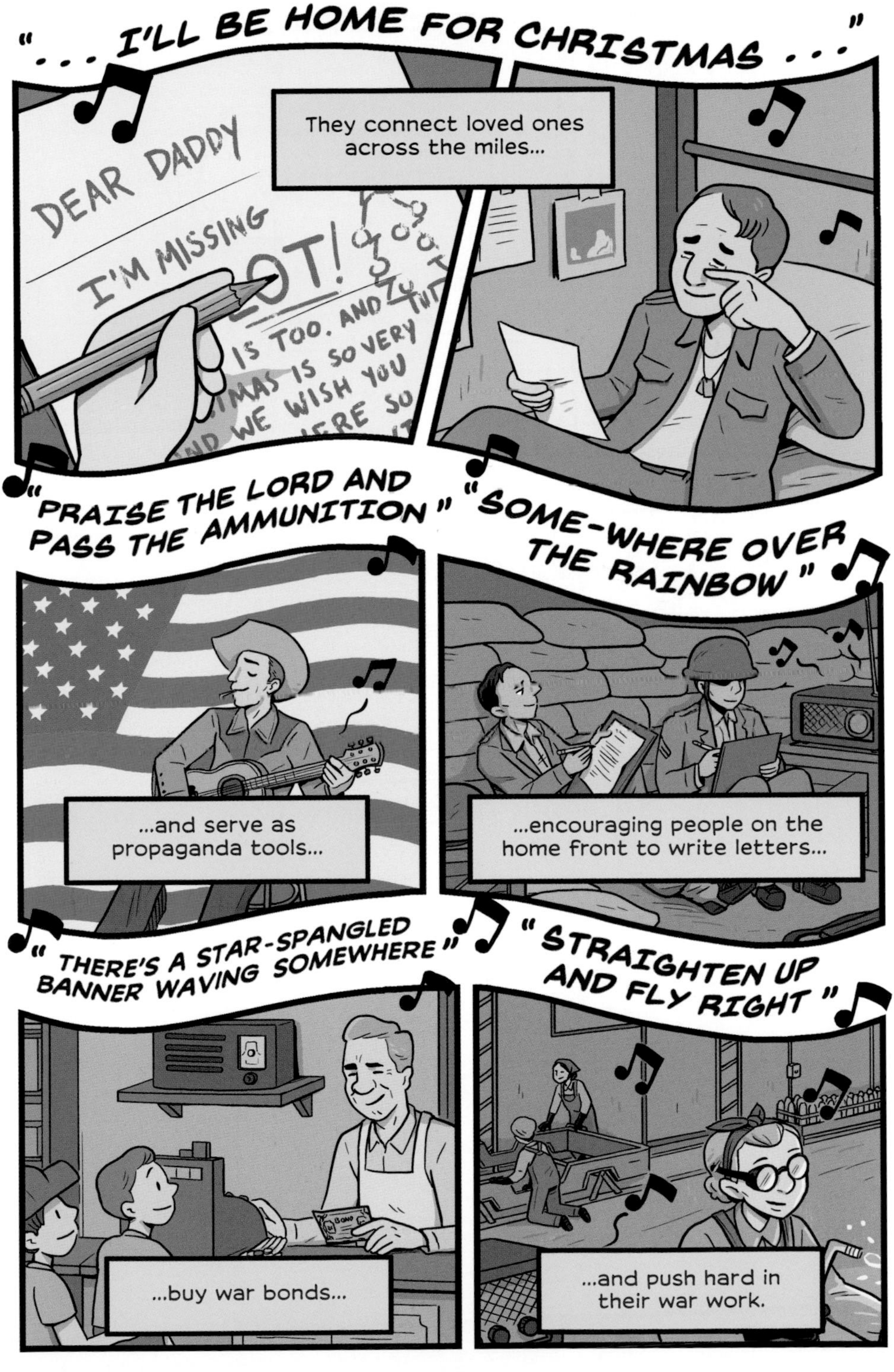
"... I'LL BE HOME FOR CHRISTMAS ..."
DEAR DADDY
I'M MISSING
IS TOO. AND
IS SO VERY
WE WISH YOU
They connect loved ones across the miles...
"PRAISE THE LORD AND PASS THE AMMUNITION"
...and serve as propaganda tools...
"SOME-WHERE OVER THE RAINBOW"
...encouraging people on the home front to write letters...
"THERE'S A STAR-SPANGLED BANNER WAVING SOMEWHERE"
...buy war bonds...
"STRAIGHTEN UP AND FLY RIGHT"
...and push hard in their war work.

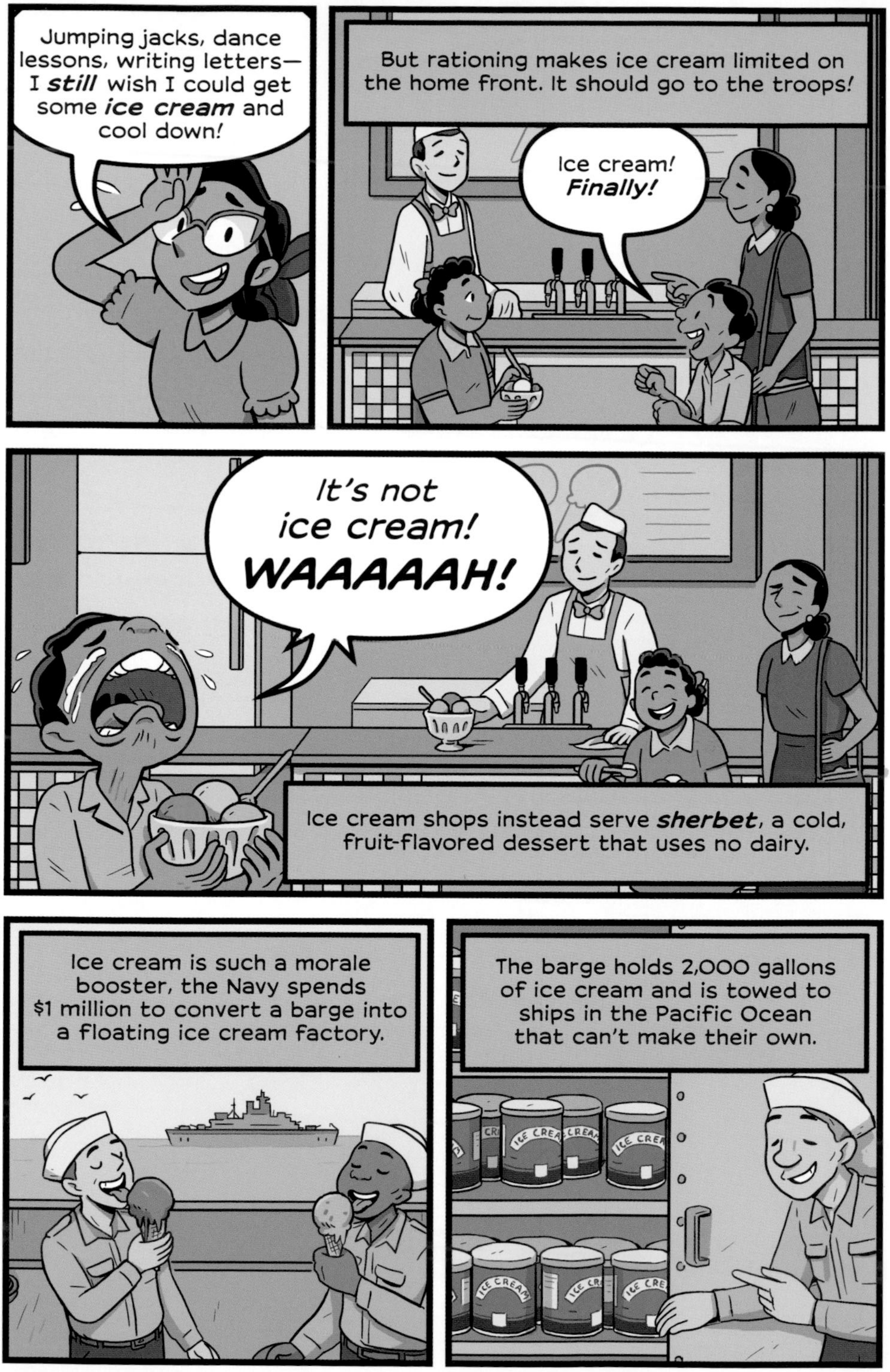
Jumping jacks, dance lessons, writing letters—I *still* wish I could get some *ice cream* and cool down!
But rationing makes ice cream limited on the home front. It should go to the troops!
Ice cream! *Finally!*
It's not ice cream! **WAAAAAH!**
Ice cream shops instead serve ***sherbet***, a cold, fruit-flavored dessert that uses no dairy.
Ice cream is such a morale booster, the Navy spends $1 million to convert a barge into a floating ice cream factory.
The barge holds 2,000 gallons of ice cream and is towed to ships in the Pacific Ocean that can't make their own.
ICE CREAM

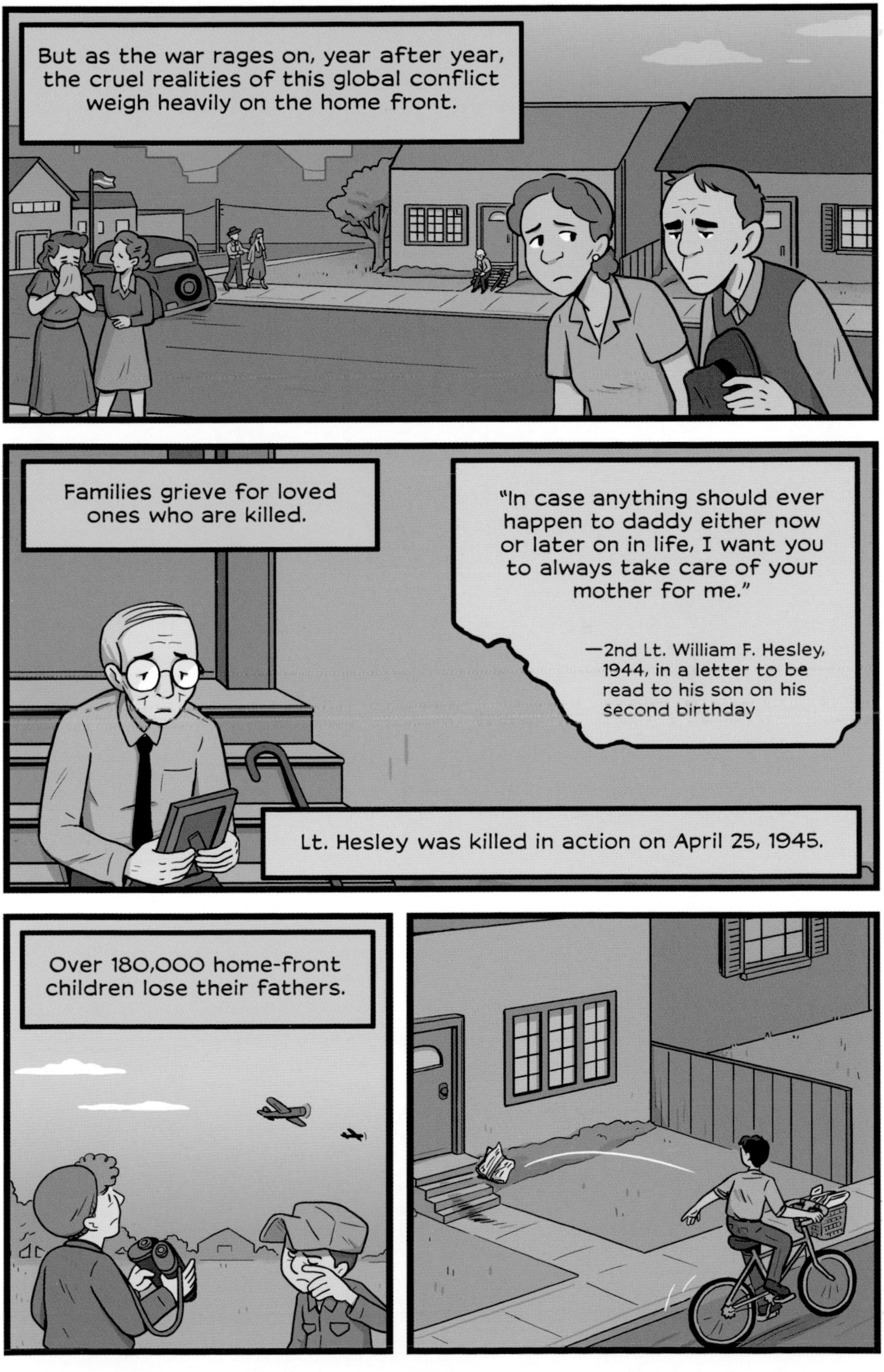
But as the war rages on, year after year, the cruel realities of this global conflict weigh heavily on the home front.
Families grieve for loved ones who are killed.
"In case anything should ever happen to daddy either now or later on in life, I want you to always take care of your mother for me."
—2nd Lt. William F. Hesley, 1944, in a letter to be read to his son on his second birthday
Lt. Hesley was killed in action on April 25, 1945.
Over 180,000 home-front children lose their fathers.

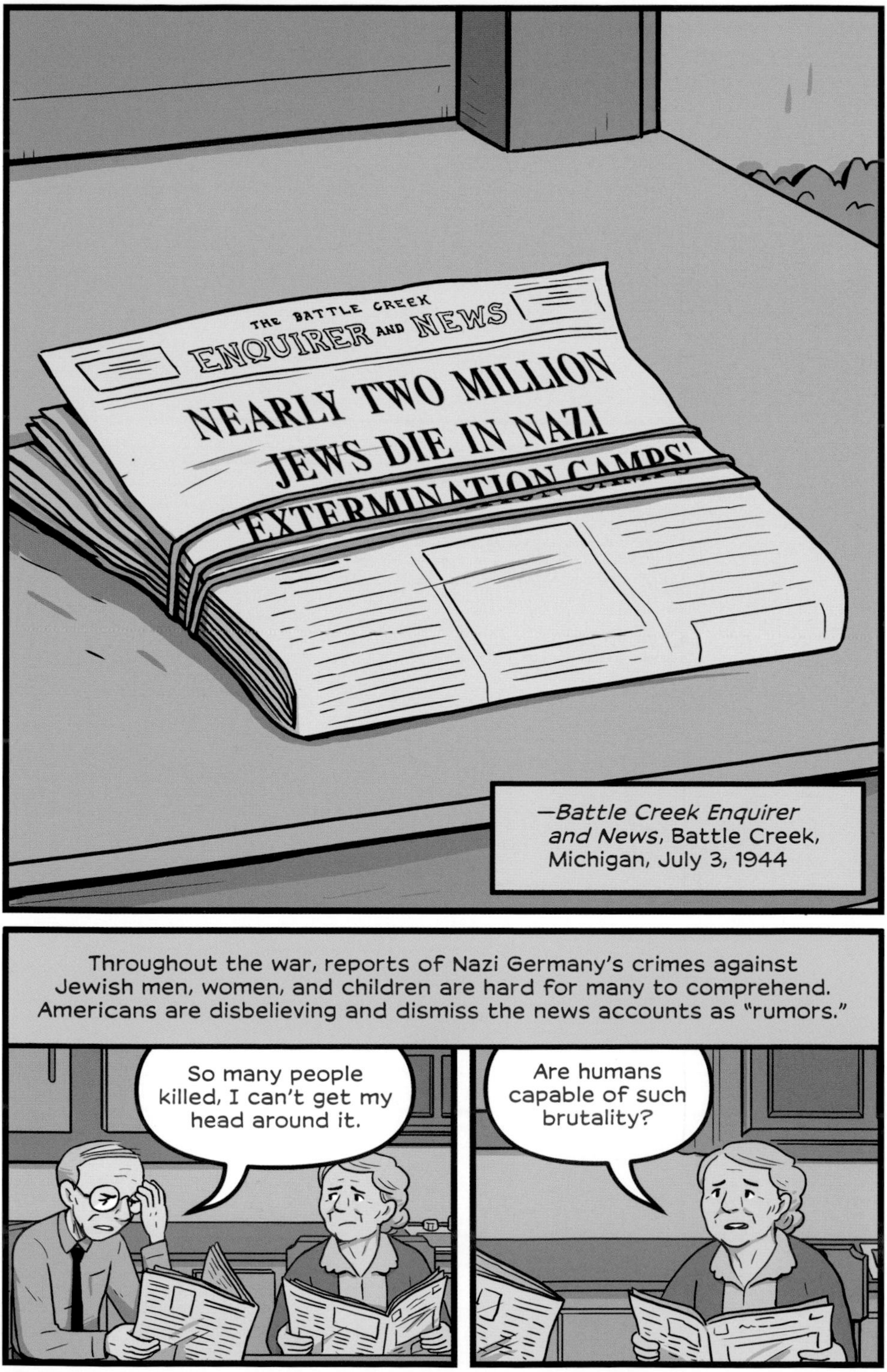

THE BATTLE CREEK
ENQUIRER AND NEWS
NEARLY TWO MILLION JEWS DIE IN NAZI EXTERMINATION CAMPS!
—*Battle Creek Enquirer and News*, Battle Creek, Michigan, July 3, 1944
Throughout the war, reports of Nazi Germany's crimes against Jewish men, women, and children are hard for many to comprehend. Americans are disbelieving and dismiss the news accounts as "rumors."
So many people killed, I can't get my head around it.
Are humans capable of such brutality?

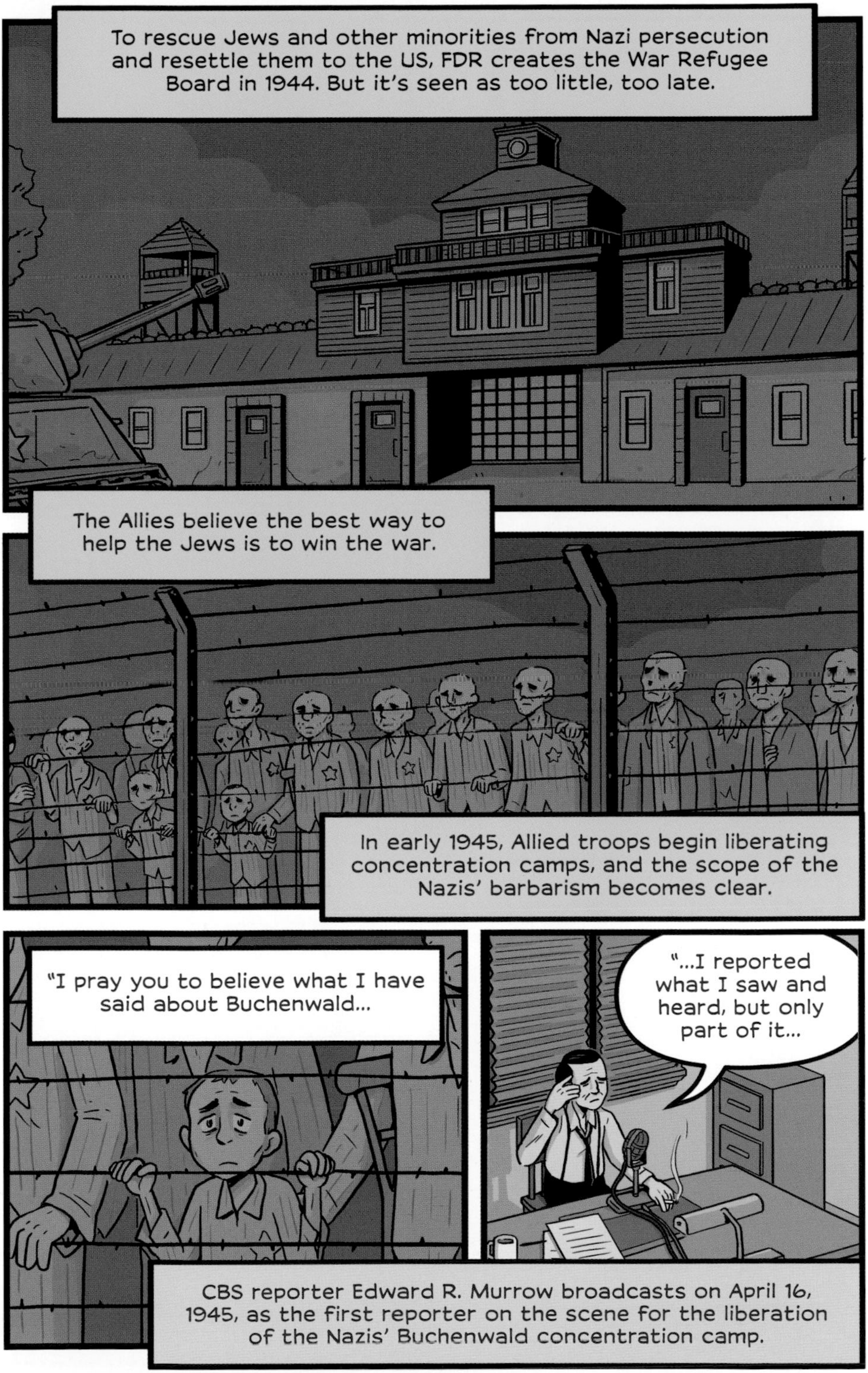
To rescue Jews and other minorities from Nazi persecution and resettle them to the US, FDR creates the War Refugee Board in 1944. But it's seen as too little, too late.
The Allies believe the best way to help the Jews is to win the war.
In early 1945, Allied troops begin liberating concentration camps, and the scope of the Nazis' barbarism becomes clear.
"I pray you to believe what I have said about Buchenwald...
"...I reported what I saw and heard, but only part of it...
CBS reporter Edward R. Murrow broadcasts on April 16, 1945, as the first reporter on the scene for the liberation of the Nazis' Buchenwald concentration camp.

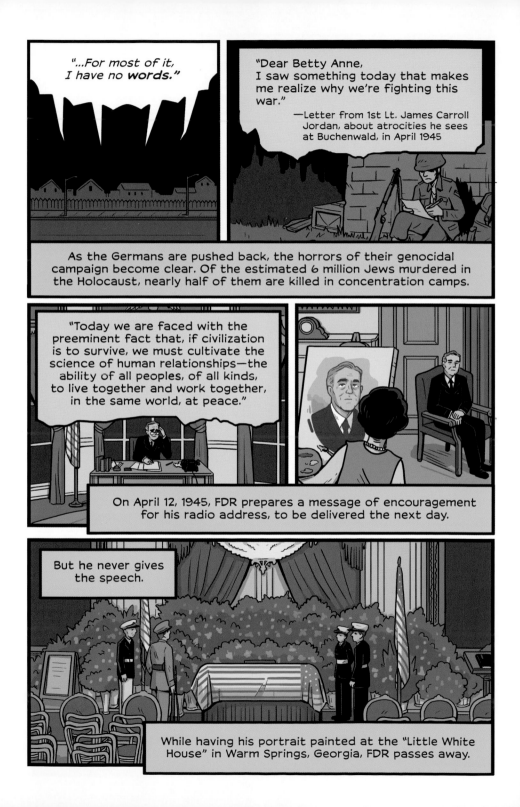

"...For most of it, I have no **words.**"

"Dear Betty Anne, I saw something today that makes me realize why we're fighting this war."

—Letter from 1st Lt. James Carroll Jordan, about atrocities he sees at Buchenwald, in April 1945

As the Germans are pushed back, the horrors of their genocidal campaign become clear. Of the estimated 6 million Jews murdered in the Holocaust, nearly half of them are killed in concentration camps.

"Today we are faced with the preeminent fact that, if civilization is to survive, we must cultivate the science of human relationships—the ability of all peoples, of all kinds, to live together and work together, in the same world, at peace."

On April 12, 1945, FDR prepares a message of encouragement for his radio address, to be delivered the next day.

But he never gives the speech.

While having his portrait painted at the "Little White House" in Warm Springs, Georgia, FDR passes away.

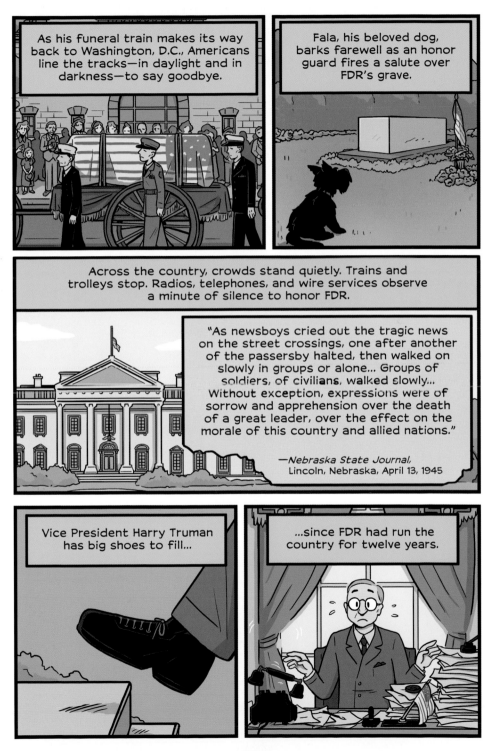

As his funeral train makes its way back to Washington, D.C., Americans line the tracks—in daylight and in darkness—to say goodbye.

Fala, his beloved dog, barks farewell as an honor guard fires a salute over FDR's grave.

Across the country, crowds stand quietly. Trains and trolleys stop. Radios, telephones, and wire services observe a minute of silence to honor FDR.

"As newsboys cried out the tragic news on the street crossings, one after another of the passersby halted, then walked on slowly in groups or alone... Groups of soldiers, of civilians, walked slowly... Without exception, expressions were of sorrow and apprehension over the death of a great leader, over the effect on the morale of this country and allied nations."

—*Nebraska State Journal,*
Lincoln, Nebraska, April 13, 1945

Vice President Harry Truman has big shoes to fill...

...since FDR had run the country for twelve years.

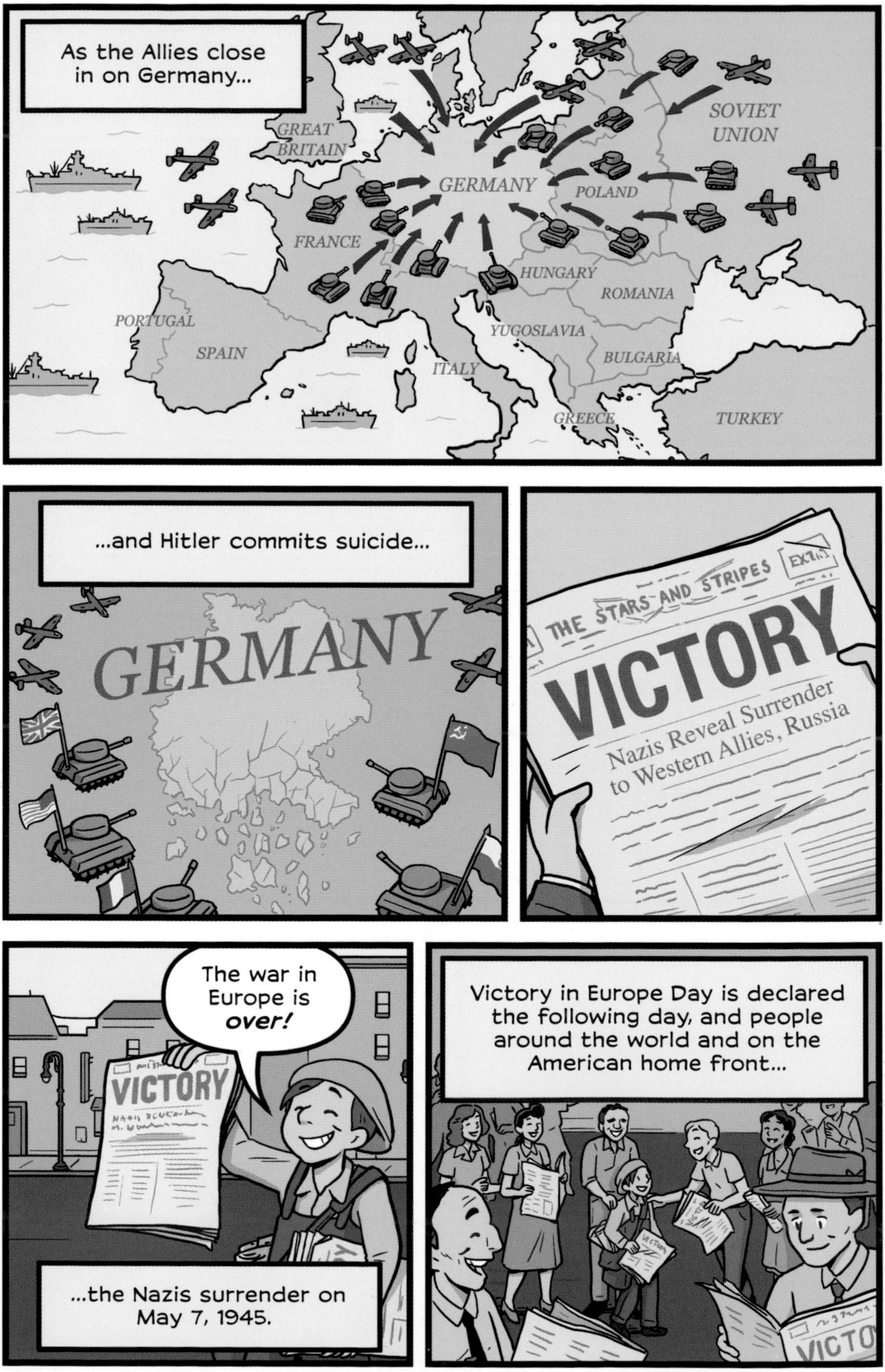

As the Allies close in on Germany...
GREAT BRITAIN
SOVIET UNION
GERMANY
POLAND
FRANCE
HUNGARY
ROMANIA
PORTUGAL
SPAIN
YUGOSLAVIA
BULGARIA
ITALY
GREECE
TURKEY
...and Hitler commits suicide...
GERMANY
THE STARS AND STRIPES
VICTORY
Nazis Reveal Surrender to Western Allies, Russia
The war in Europe is *over!*
VICTORY
...the Nazis surrender on May 7, 1945.
Victory in Europe Day is declared the following day, and people around the world and on the American home front...

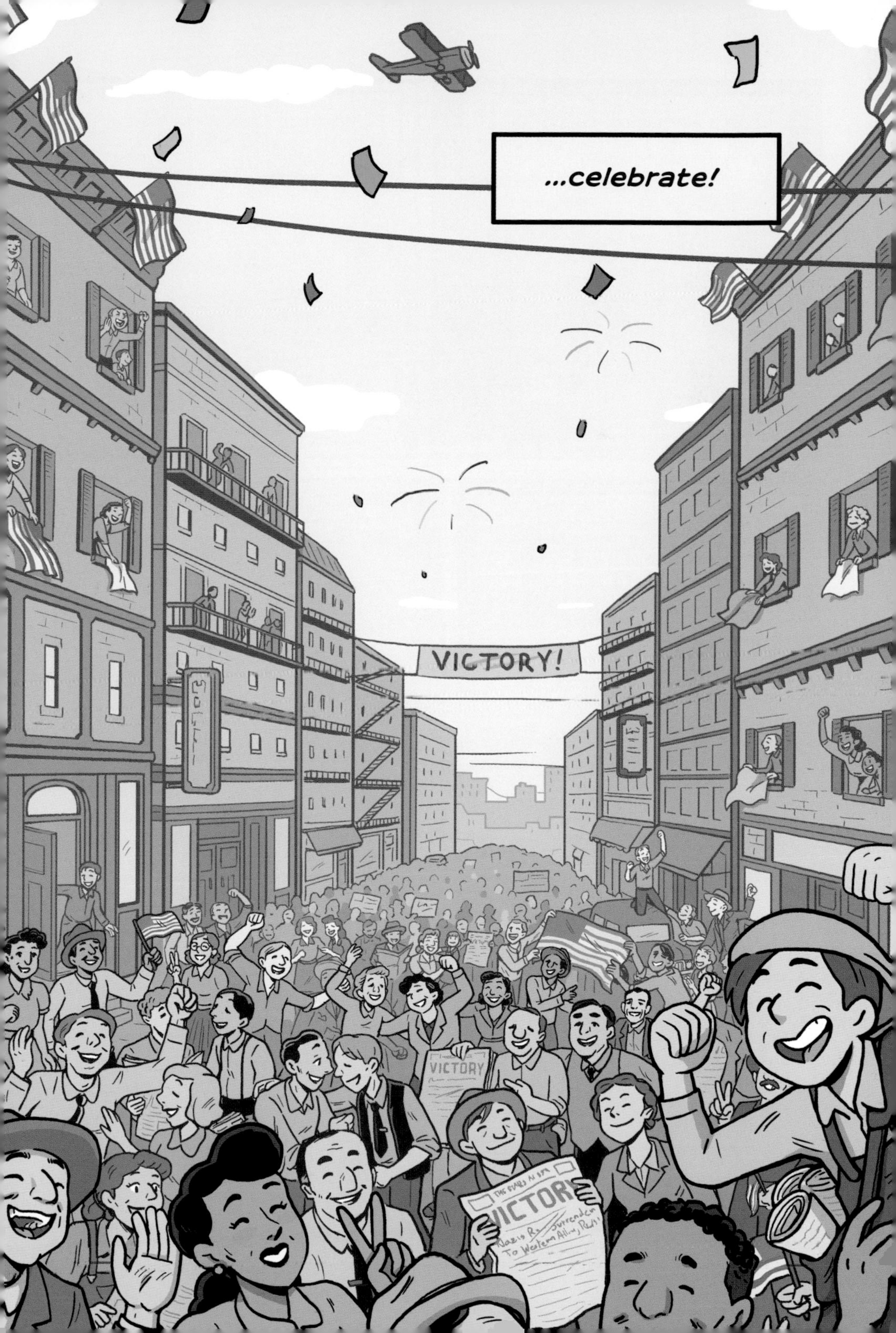

...celebrate!
VICTORY!
VICTORY

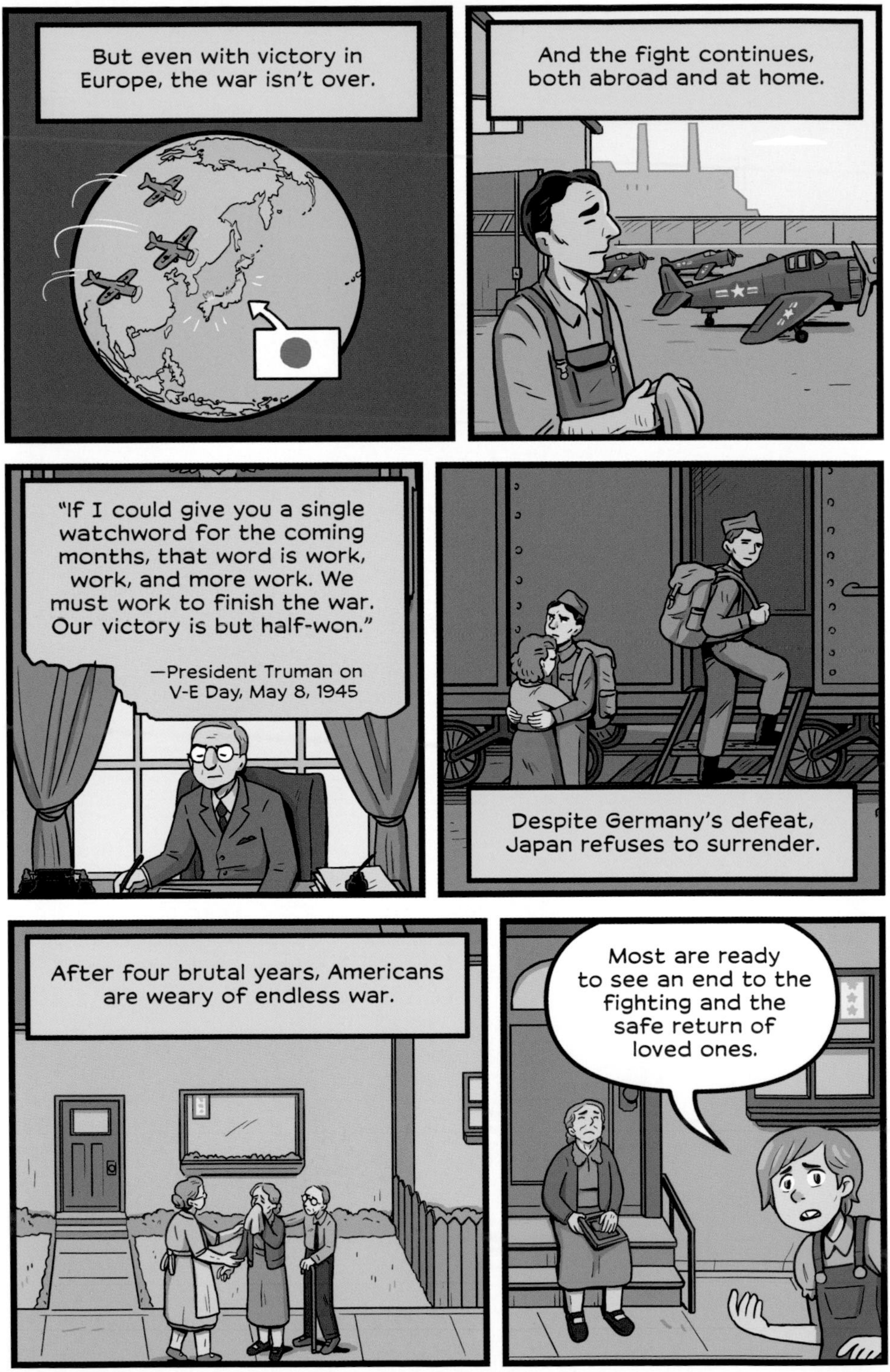
But even with victory in Europe, the war isn't over.
And the fight continues, both abroad and at home.
"If I could give you a single watchword for the coming months, that word is work, work, and more work. We must work to finish the war. Our victory is but half-won."
—President Truman on V-E Day, May 8, 1945
Despite Germany's defeat, Japan refuses to surrender.
After four brutal years, Americans are weary of endless war.
Most are ready to see an end to the fighting and the safe return of loved ones.

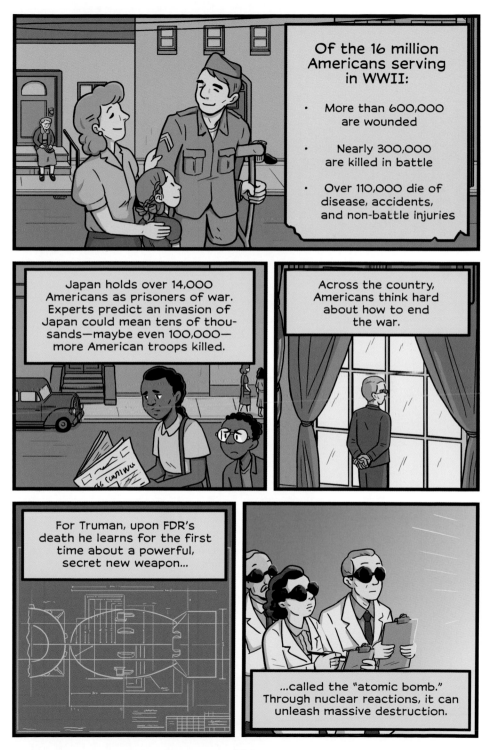

Of the 16 million Americans serving in WWII:

- More than 600,000 are wounded
- Nearly 300,000 are killed in battle
- Over 110,000 die of disease, accidents, and non-battle injuries

Japan holds over 14,000 Americans as prisoners of war. Experts predict an invasion of Japan could mean tens of thousands—maybe even 100,000—more American troops killed.

Across the country, Americans think hard about how to end the war.

For Truman, upon FDR's death he learns for the first time about a powerful, secret new weapon...

...called the "atomic bomb." Through nuclear reactions, it can unleash massive destruction.

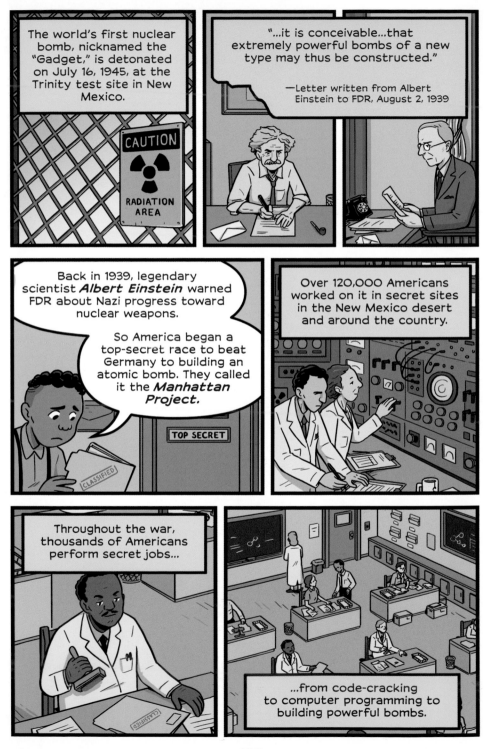

The world's first nuclear bomb, nicknamed the "Gadget," is detonated on July 16, 1945, at the Trinity test site in New Mexico.

CAUTION

RADIATION AREA

"...it is conceivable...that extremely powerful bombs of a new type may thus be constructed."

—Letter written from Albert Einstein to FDR, August 2, 1939

Back in 1939, legendary scientist **Albert Einstein** warned FDR about Nazi progress toward nuclear weapons.

So America began a top-secret race to beat Germany to building an atomic bomb. They called it the **Manhattan Project.**

TOP SECRET

CLASSIFIED

Over 120,000 Americans worked on it in secret sites in the New Mexico desert and around the country.

Throughout the war, thousands of Americans perform secret jobs...

...from code-cracking to computer programming to building powerful bombs.

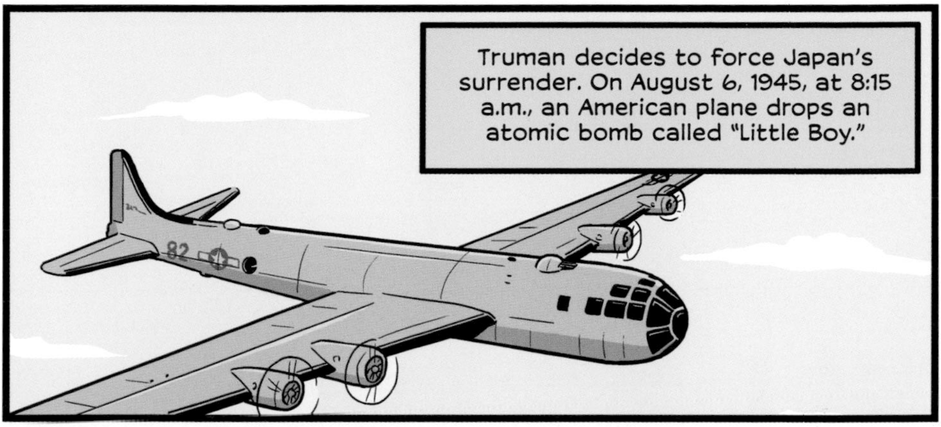
Truman decides to force Japan's surrender. On August 6, 1945, at 8:15 a.m., an American plane drops an atomic bomb called "Little Boy."

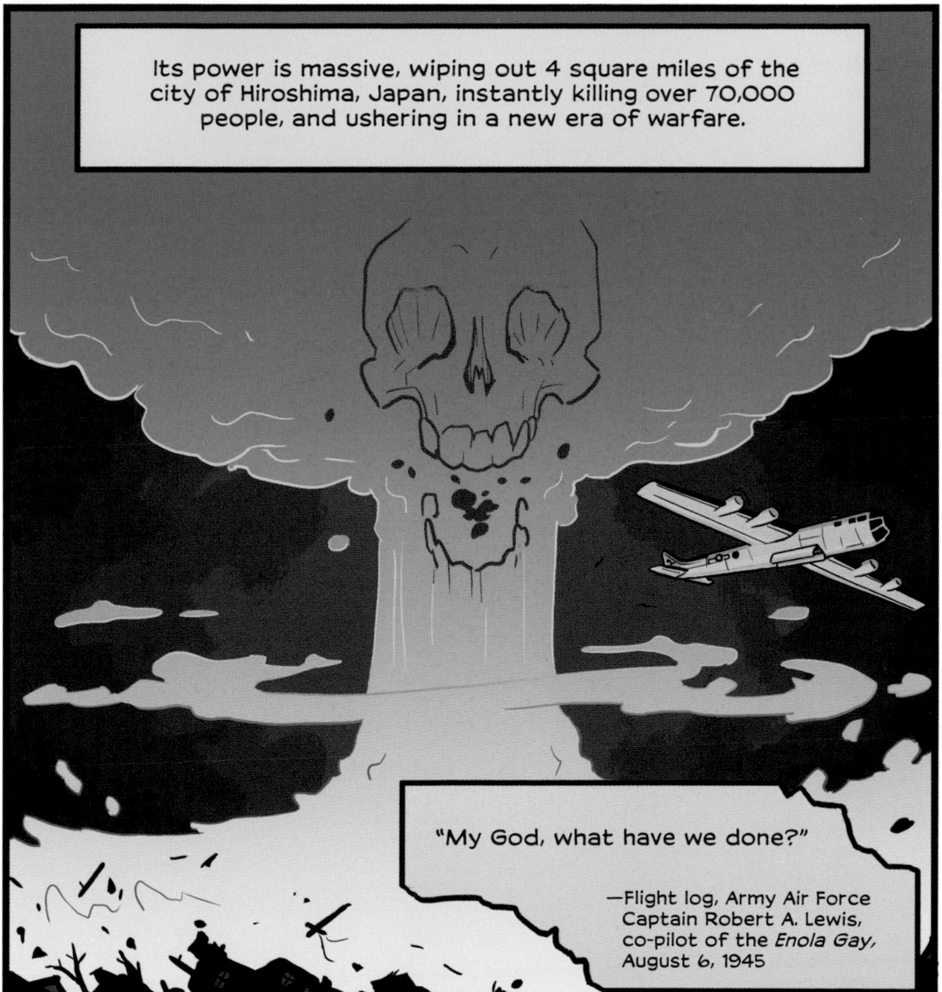
Its power is massive, wiping out 4 square miles of the city of Hiroshima, Japan, instantly killing over 70,000 people, and ushering in a new era of warfare.
"My God, what have we done?"
—Flight log, Army Air Force Captain Robert A. Lewis, co-pilot of the *Enola Gay*, August 6, 1945

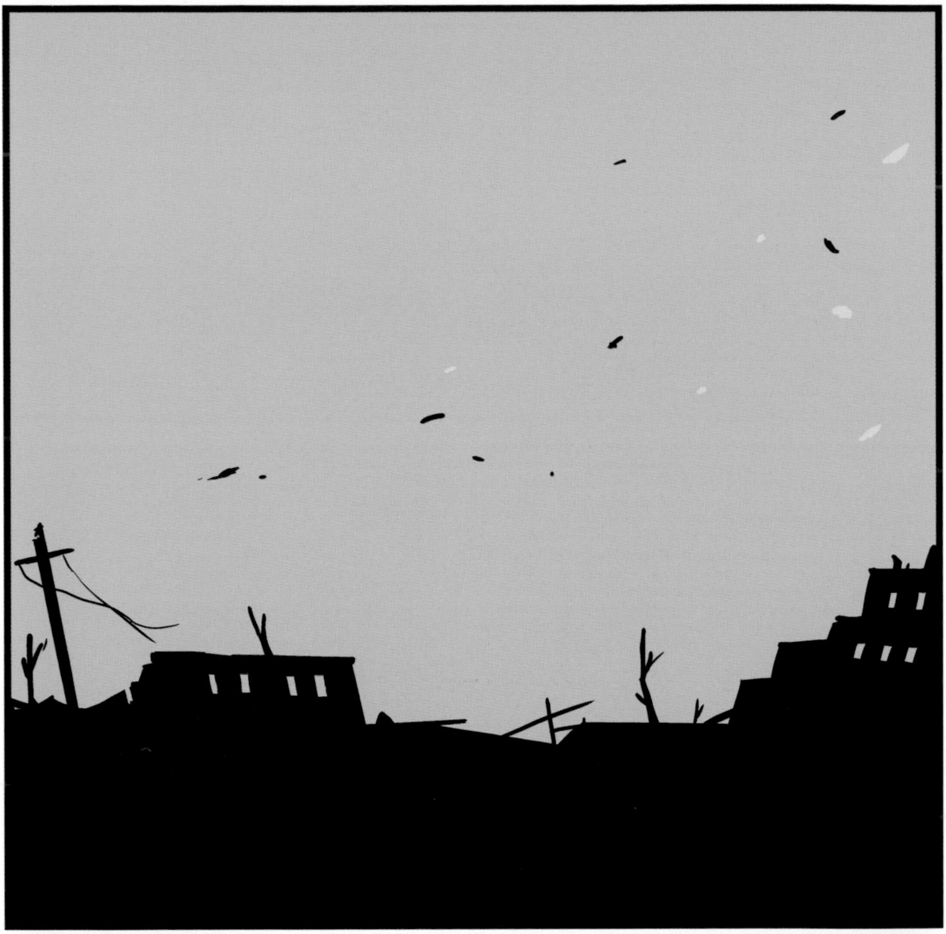

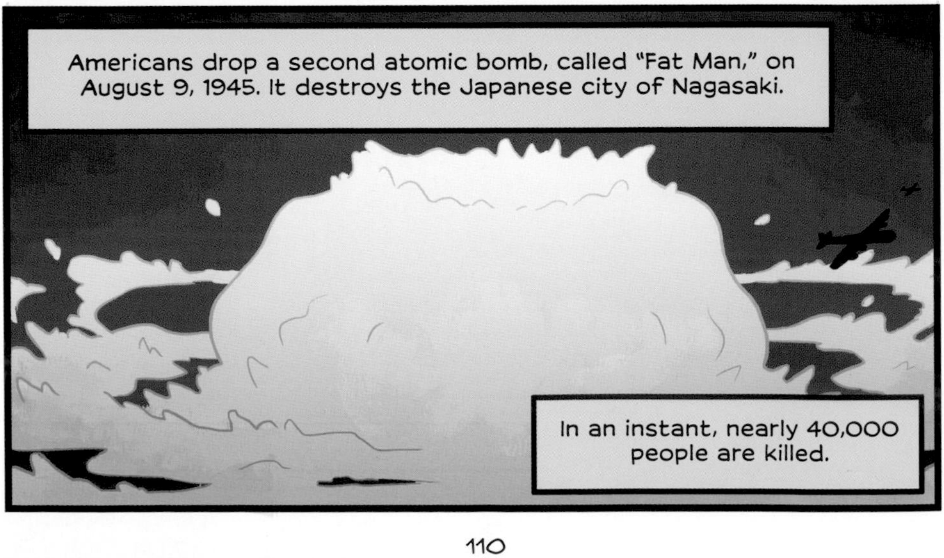
Americans drop a second atomic bomb, called "Fat Man," on August 9, 1945. It destroys the Japanese city of Nagasaki.
In an instant, nearly 40,000 people are killed.

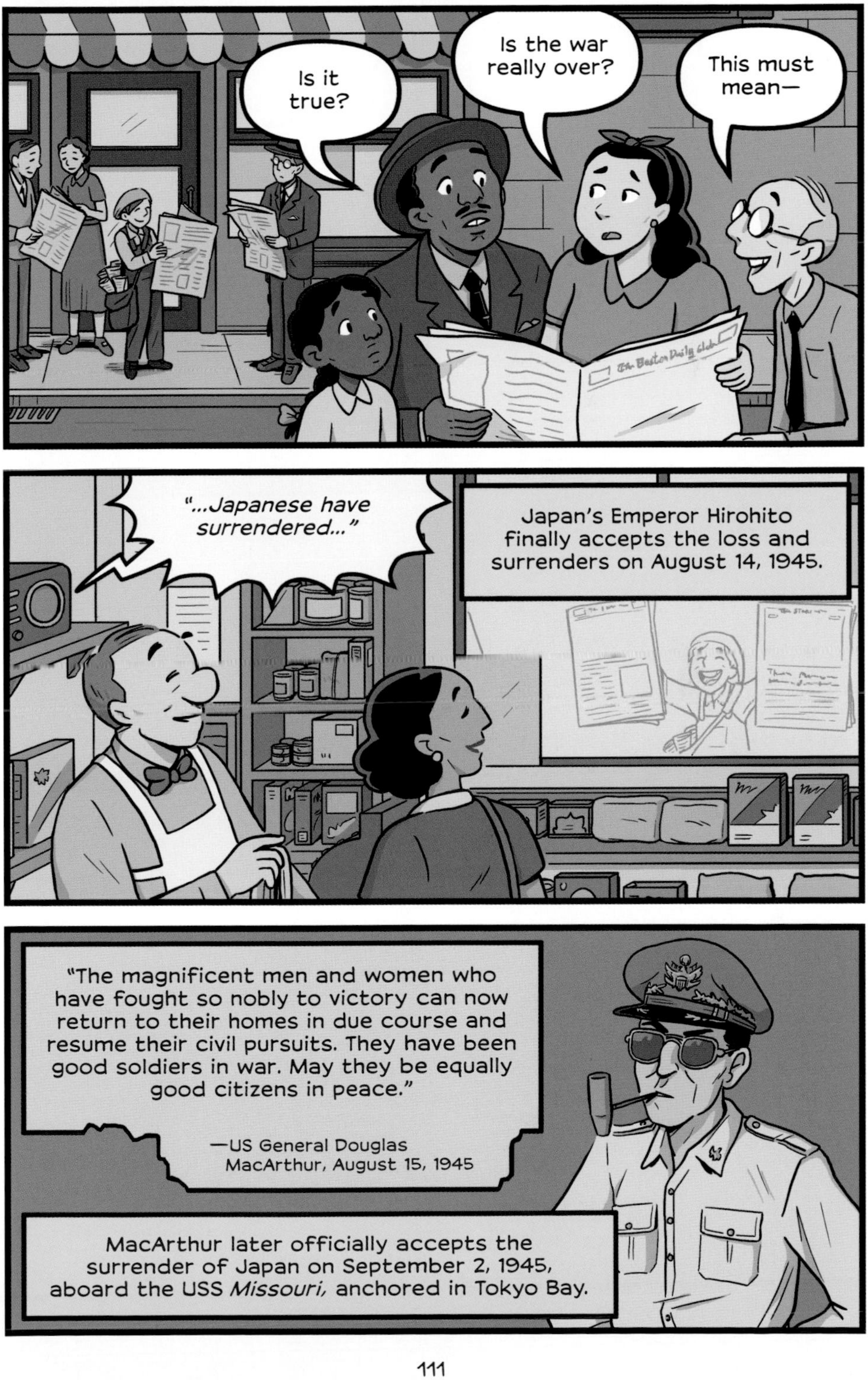
Is it true?
Is the war really over?
This must mean—
"...Japanese have surrendered..."
Japan's Emperor Hirohito finally accepts the loss and surrenders on August 14, 1945.
"The magnificent men and women who have fought so nobly to victory can now return to their homes in due course and resume their civil pursuits. They have been good soldiers in war. May they be equally good citizens in peace."
—US General Douglas MacArthur, August 15, 1945
MacArthur later officially accepts the surrender of Japan on September 2, 1945, aboard the USS *Missouri,* anchored in Tokyo Bay.

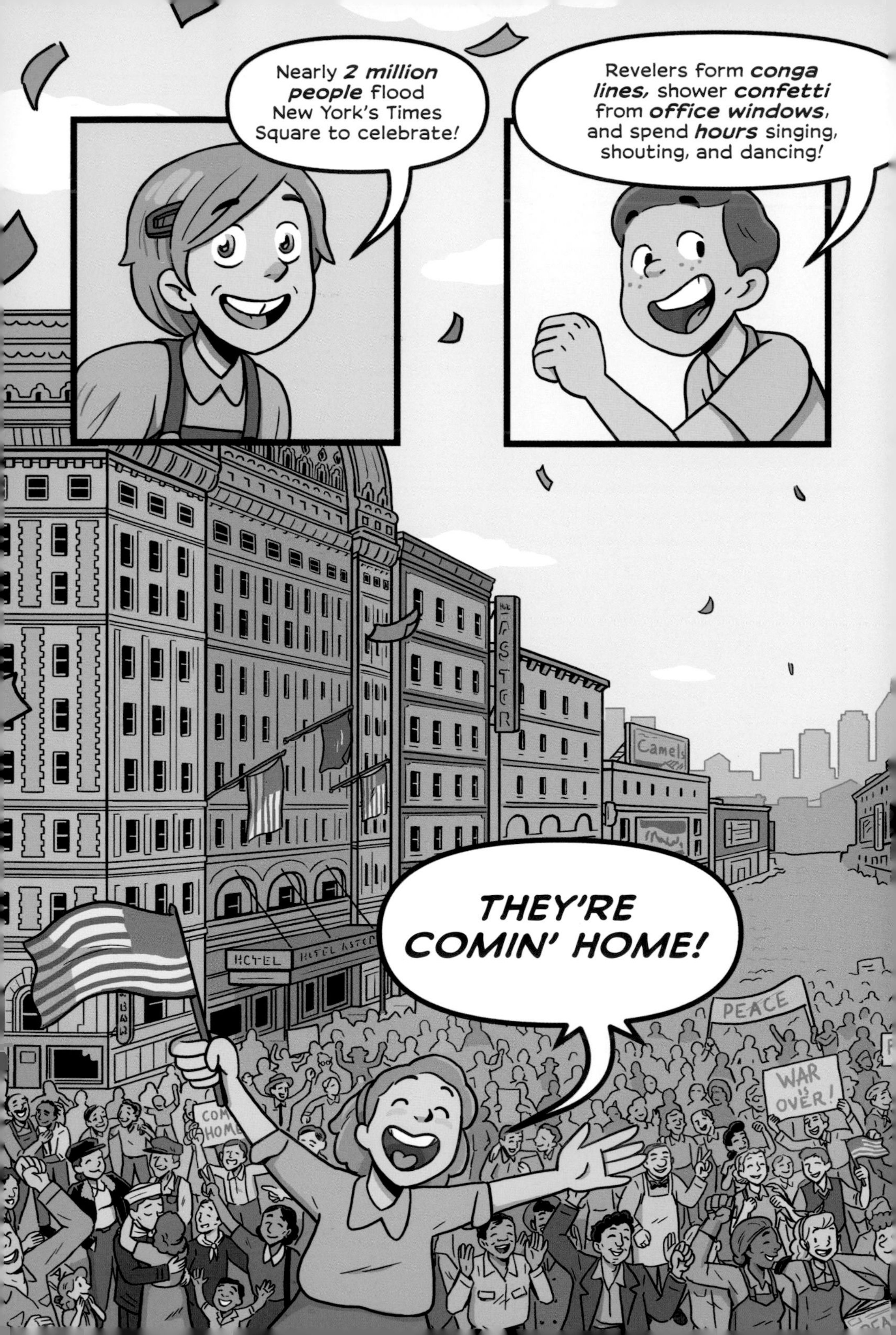
Nearly 2 million people flood New York's Times Square to celebrate!
Revelers form conga lines, shower confetti from office windows, and spend hours singing, shouting, and dancing!
ASTOR
Camels
HOTEL
HOTEL ASTOR
THEY'RE COMIN' HOME!
PEACE
WAR IS OVER!

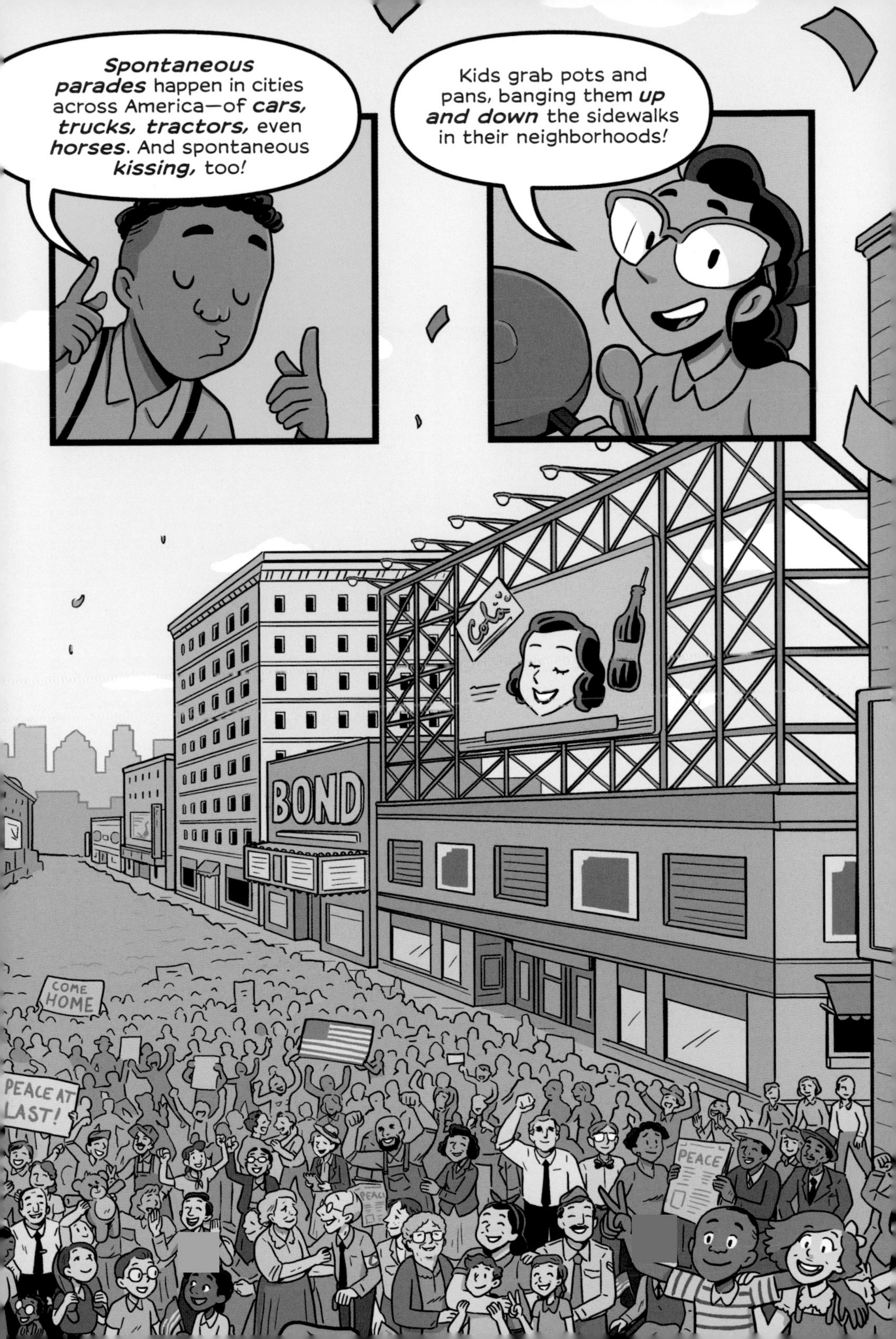
Spontaneous parades happen in cities across America—of ***cars, trucks, tractors,*** even ***horses***. And spontaneous ***kissing,*** too!
Kids grab pots and pans, banging them ***up and down*** the sidewalks in their neighborhoods!
BOND
COME HOME
PEACE AT LAST!
PEACE

HOW WWII CHANGED THE HOME FRONT

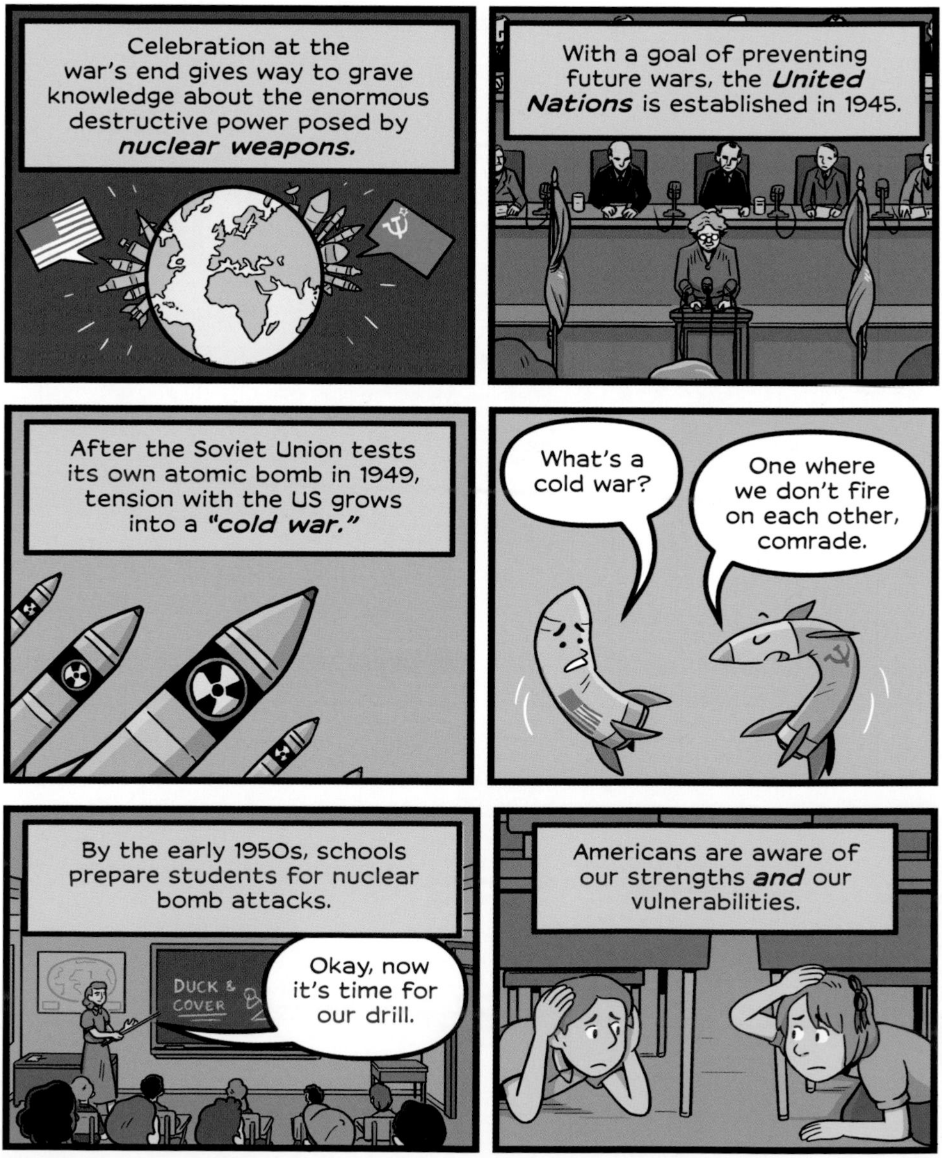
Celebration at the war's end gives way to grave knowledge about the enormous destructive power posed by *nuclear weapons.*
With a goal of preventing future wars, the *United Nations* is established in 1945.
After the Soviet Union tests its own atomic bomb in 1949, tension with the US grows into a *"cold war."*
What's a cold war?
One where we don't fire on each other, comrade.
By the early 1950s, schools prepare students for nuclear bomb attacks.
DUCK & COVER
Okay, now it's time for our drill.
Americans are aware of our strengths *and* our vulnerabilities.

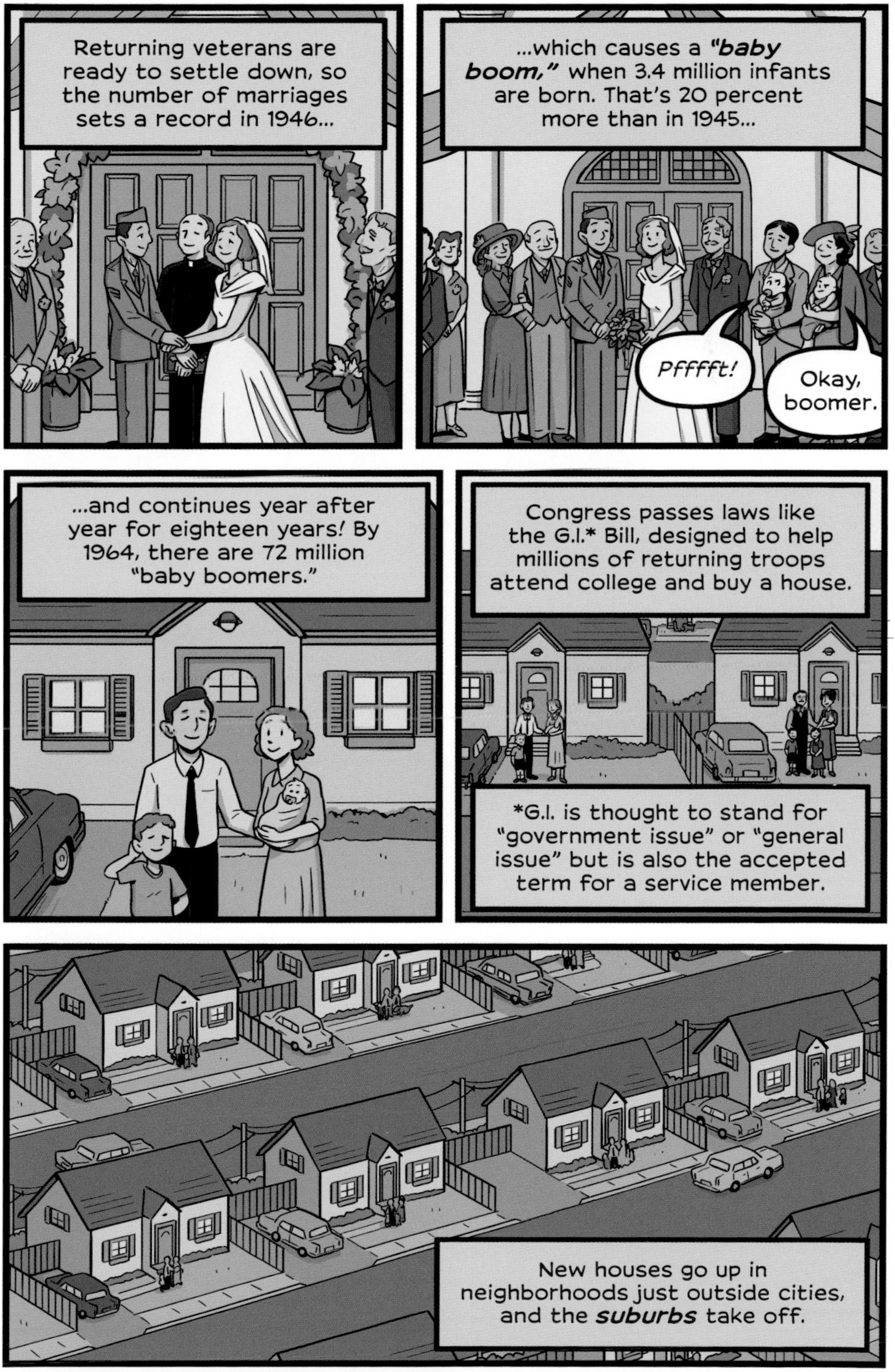
Returning veterans are ready to settle down, so the number of marriages sets a record in 1946...
...which causes a *"baby boom,"* when 3.4 million infants are born. That's 20 percent more than in 1945...
Pfffft!
Okay, boomer.
...and continues year after year for eighteen years! By 1964, there are 72 million "baby boomers."
Congress passes laws like the G.I.* Bill, designed to help millions of returning troops attend college and buy a house.
*G.I. is thought to stand for "government issue" or "general issue" but is also the accepted term for a service member.
New houses go up in neighborhoods just outside cities, and the *suburbs* take off.

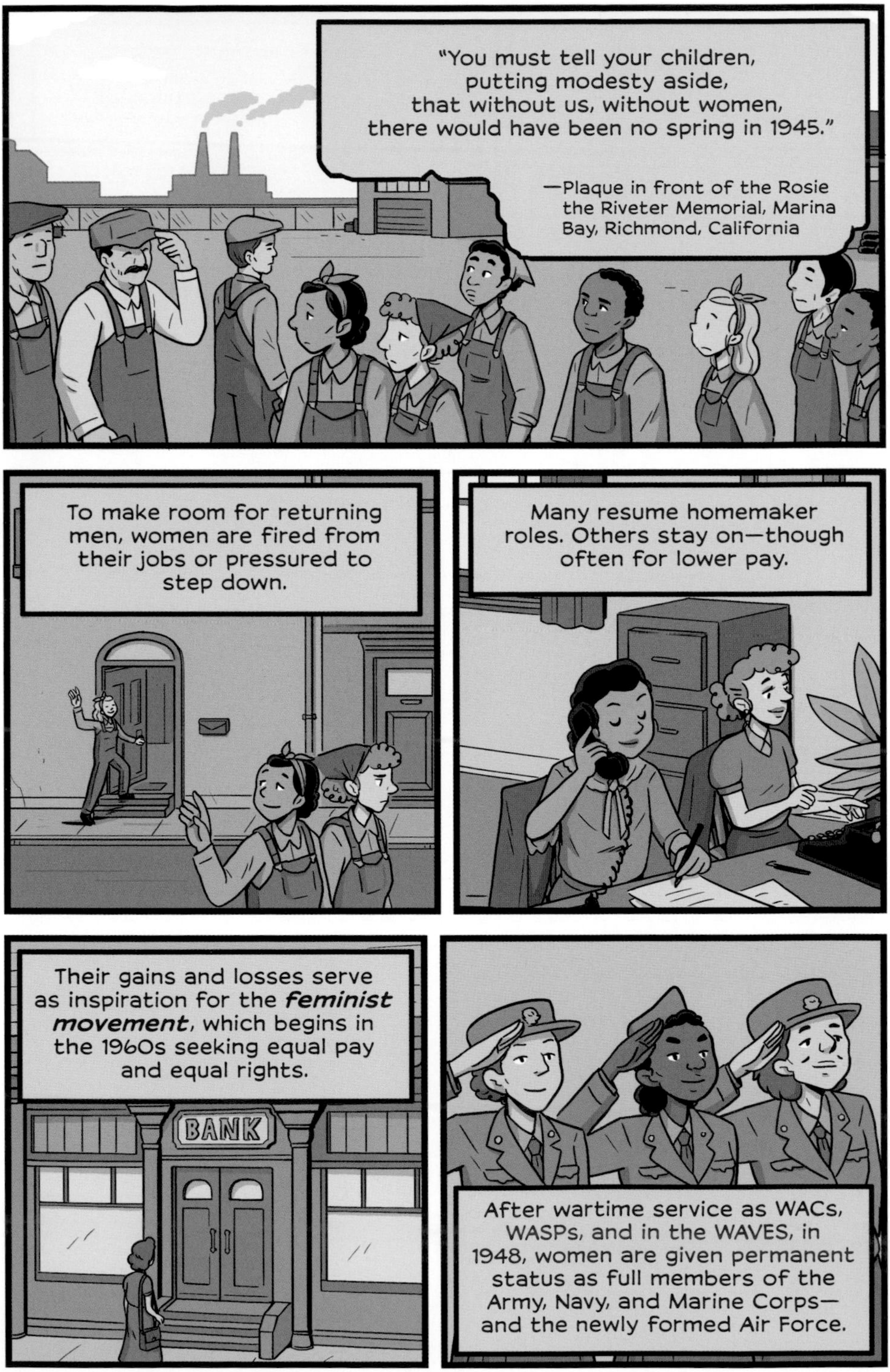
"You must tell your children, putting modesty aside, that without us, without women, there would have been no spring in 1945."
—Plaque in front of the Rosie the Riveter Memorial, Marina Bay, Richmond, California
To make room for returning men, women are fired from their jobs or pressured to step down.
Many resume homemaker roles. Others stay on—though often for lower pay.
Their gains and losses serve as inspiration for the ***feminist movement***, which begins in the 1960s seeking equal pay and equal rights.
BANK
After wartime service as WACs, WASPs, and in the WAVES, in 1948, women are given permanent status as full members of the Army, Navy, and Marine Corps—and the newly formed Air Force.

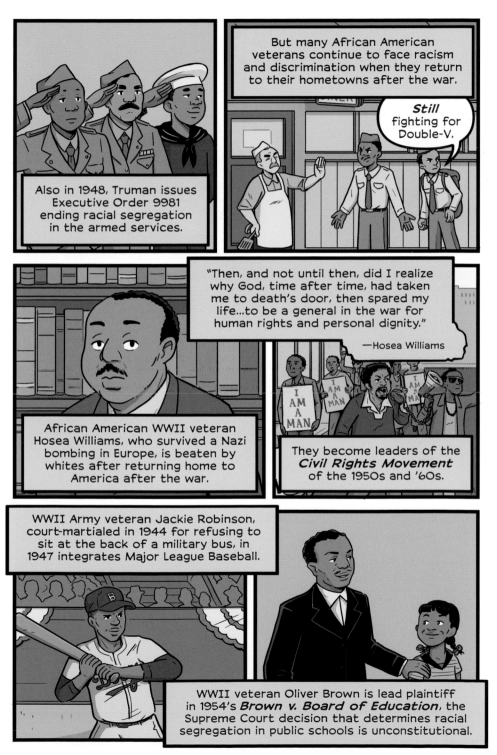

Also in 1948, Truman issues Executive Order 9981 ending racial segregation in the armed services.

But many African American veterans continue to face racism and discrimination when they return to their hometowns after the war.

Still fighting for Double-V.

"Then, and not until then, did I realize why God, time after time, had taken me to death's door, then spared my life...to be a general in the war for human rights and personal dignity."

—Hosea Williams

African American WWII veteran Hosea Williams, who survived a Nazi bombing in Europe, is beaten by whites after returning home to America after the war.

I AM A MAN

They become leaders of the *Civil Rights Movement* of the 1950s and '60s.

WWII Army veteran Jackie Robinson, court-martialed in 1944 for refusing to sit at the back of a military bus, in 1947 integrates Major League Baseball.

WWII veteran Oliver Brown is lead plaintiff in 1954's *Brown v. Board of Education*, the Supreme Court decision that determines racial segregation in public schools is unconstitutional.

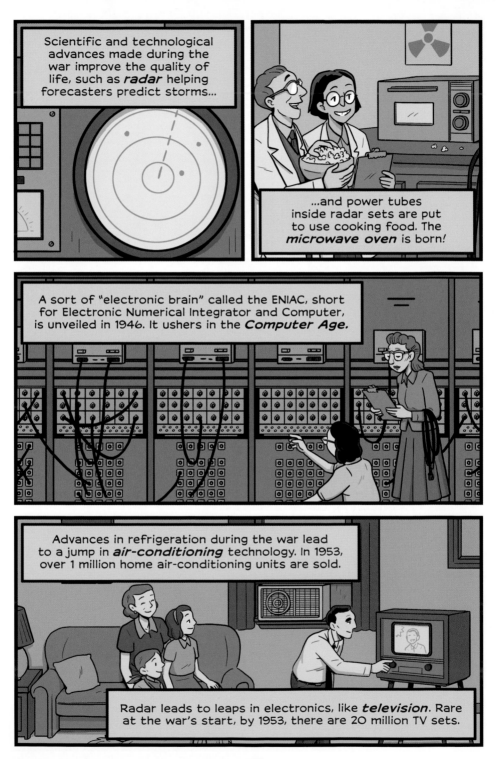

Scientific and technological advances made during the war improve the quality of life, such as *radar* helping forecasters predict storms...

...and power tubes inside radar sets are put to use cooking food. The *microwave oven* is born!

A sort of "electronic brain" called the ENIAC, short for Electronic Numerical Integrator and Computer, is unveiled in 1946. It ushers in the *Computer Age.*

Advances in refrigeration during the war lead to a jump in *air-conditioning* technology. In 1953, over 1 million home air-conditioning units are sold.

Radar leads to leaps in electronics, like *television*. Rare at the war's start, by 1953, there are 20 million TV sets.

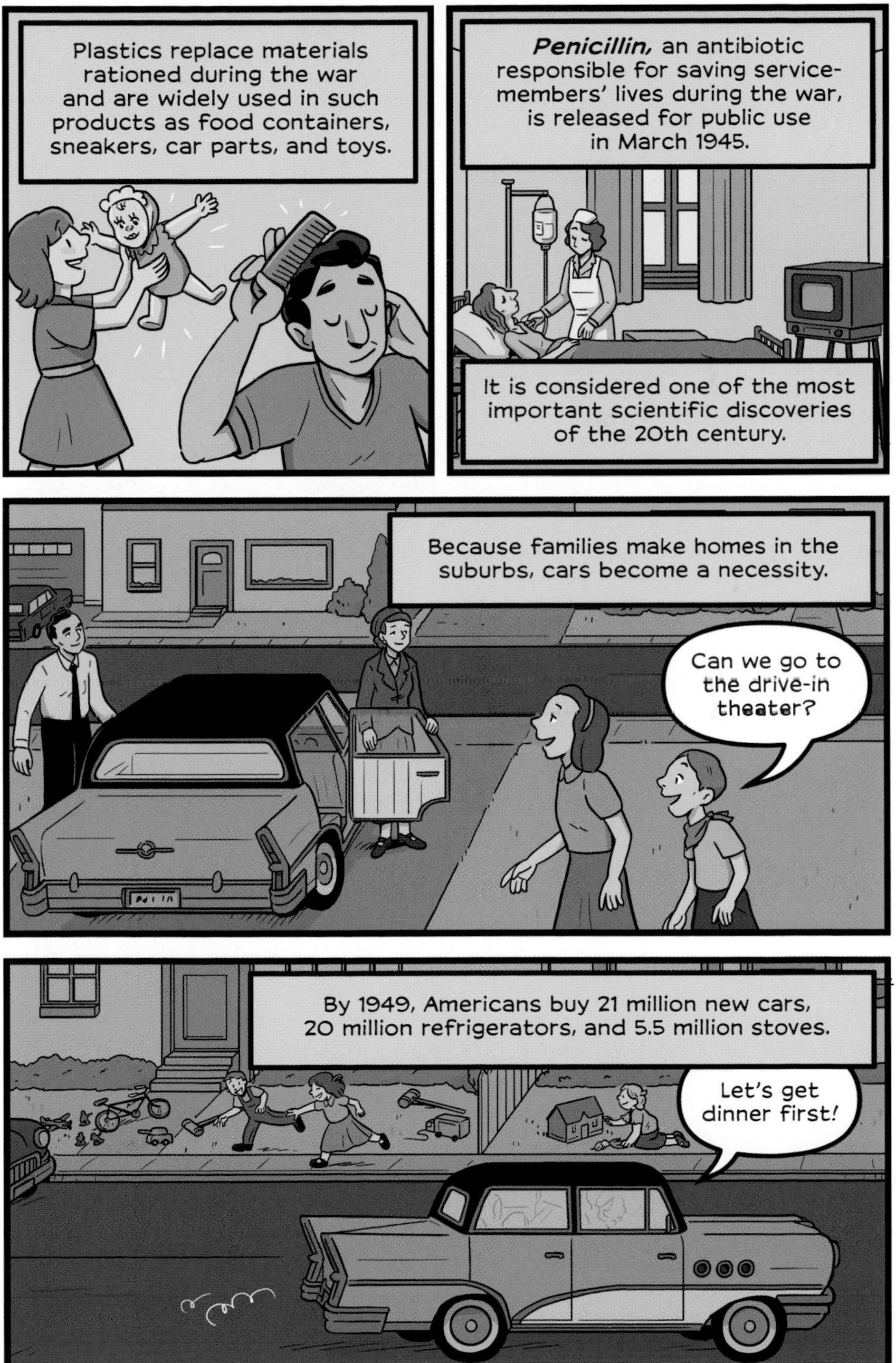
Plastics replace materials rationed during the war and are widely used in such products as food containers, sneakers, car parts, and toys.
Penicillin, an antibiotic responsible for saving service-members' lives during the war, is released for public use in March 1945.
It is considered one of the most important scientific discoveries of the 20th century.
Because families make homes in the suburbs, cars become a necessity.
Can we go to the drive-in theater?
By 1949, Americans buy 21 million new cars, 20 million refrigerators, and 5.5 million stoves.
Let's get dinner first!

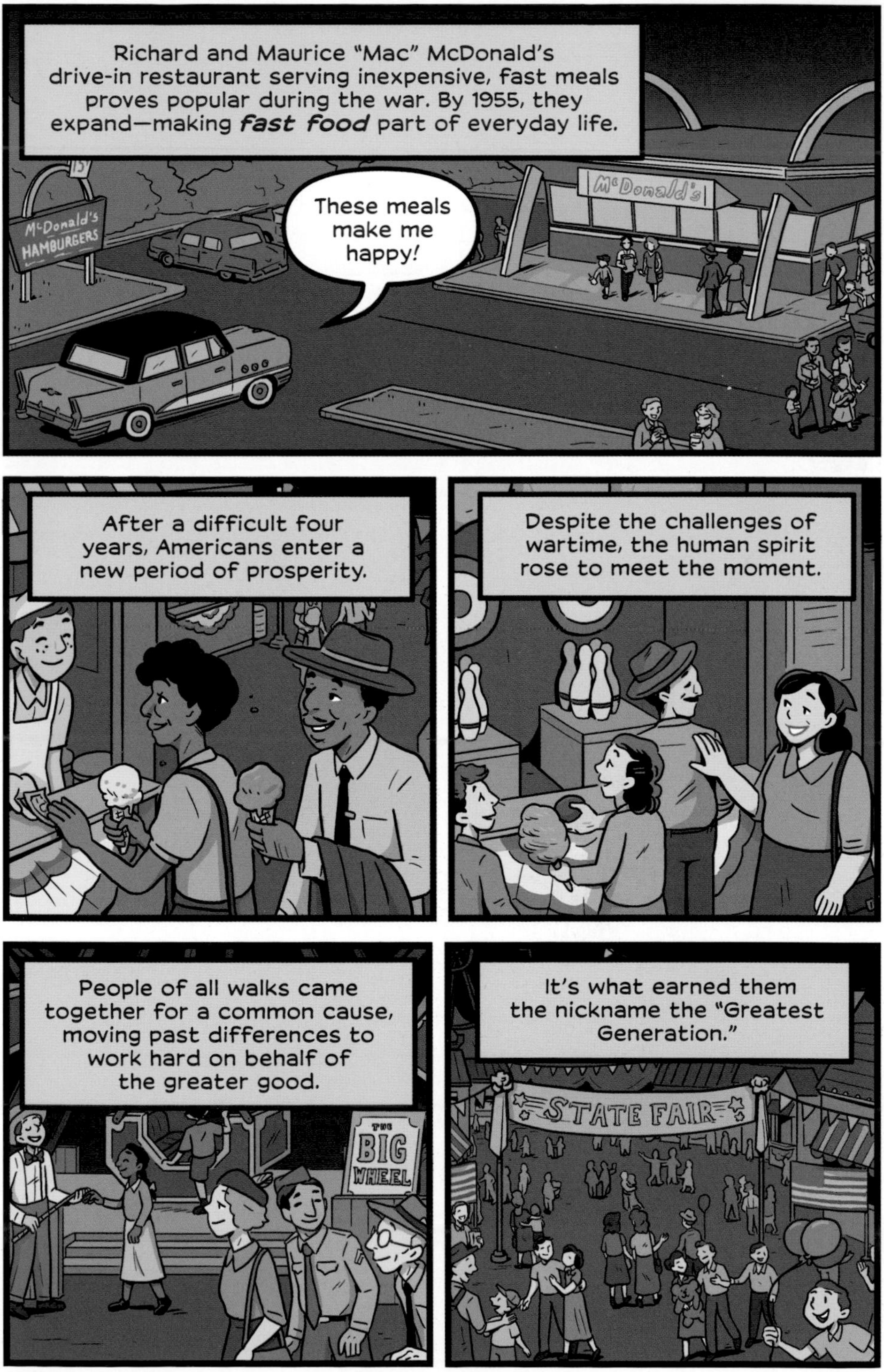
Richard and Maurice "Mac" McDonald's drive-in restaurant serving inexpensive, fast meals proves popular during the war. By 1955, they expand—making ***fast food*** part of everyday life.
McDonald's
HAMBURGERS
McDonald's
These meals make me happy!
After a difficult four years, Americans enter a new period of prosperity.
Despite the challenges of wartime, the human spirit rose to meet the moment.
People of all walks came together for a common cause, moving past differences to work hard on behalf of the greater good.
THE BIG WHEEL
It's what earned them the nickname the "Greatest Generation."
STATE FAIR

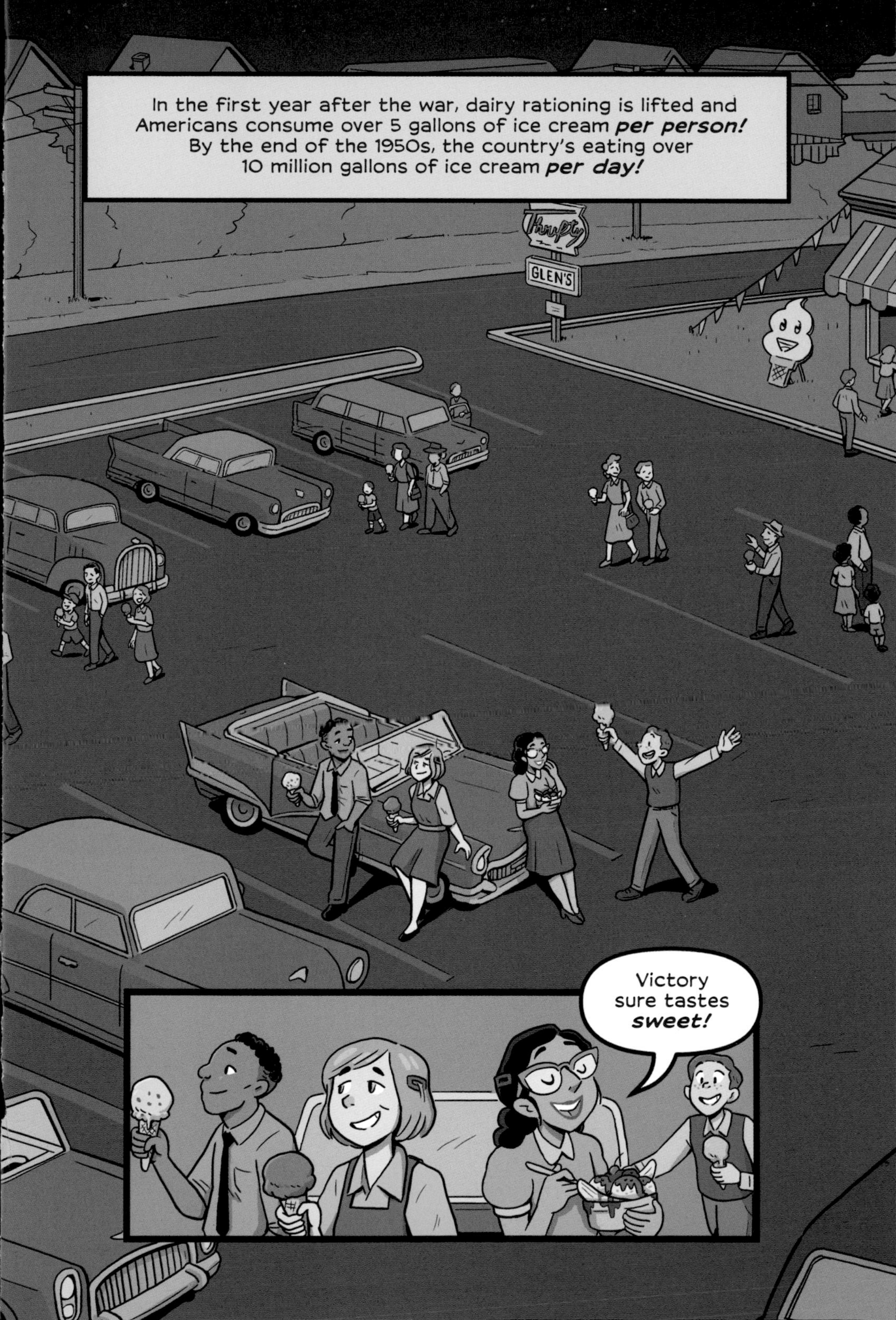
In the first year after the war, dairy rationing is lifted and Americans consume over 5 gallons of ice cream ***per person!*** By the end of the 1950s, the country's eating over 10 million gallons of ice cream ***per day!***
Thrifty
GLEN'S
Victory sure tastes ***sweet!***

WHERE YOU CAN LEARN MORE

Here is a partial list of resources used and where you can go to learn more about World War II on the home front.

BOOKS

The African American Experience During World War II, by Neil A. Wynn (Rowman & Littlefield, 2010; Lanham, Maryland)

Americans Remember the Home Front: An Oral Narrative of the World War II Years in America, by Roy Hoopes (Berkley Publishing Group, 1977; New York)

Daddy's Gone to War: The Second World War in the Lives of America's Children, by William M. Tuttle Jr. (Oxford University Press, 1993; New York)

The Darkest Year: The American Home Front 1941–1942, by William K. Klingaman (St. Martin's Press, 2019; New York)

Don't You Know There's a War On?: The American Home Front 1941–1945, by Richard R. Lingeman (G. P. Putnam's Sons, 1970; New York)

Double Victory: A Multicultural History of America in World War II, by Ronald Takaki (Little, Brown, 2000; Boston)

The Forgotten Generation: American Children and World War II, by Lisa L. Ossian (University of Missouri Press, 2011; Columbia)

Home Front: A Memoir from WWII, by C.D. Peterson (Self Reliance Press, 2017; Brookfield, Connecticut)

The Home Front and Beyond: American Women in the 1940s, by Susan M. Hartmann (G. K. Hall & Co., 1982; Boston)

One Woman's Army: A Black Officer Remembers the WAC, by Charity Adams Earley (Texas A&M University Press, 1989; College Station)

Since You Went Away: World War II Letters from American Women on the Home Front, by Judy Barrett Litoff and David C. Smith (Oxford University Press, 1991; New York)

Spam: A Biography, the Amazing True Story of America's "Miracle Meat," by Carolyn Wyman (Harcourt Brace, 1999; San Diego)

Tuskegee Love Letters, by Kim Russell (702 Entertainment LLC, 2012; Las Vegas)

War Letters: Extraordinary Correspondence from American Wars, edited by Andrew Carroll (Scribner, 2001; New York)

Wartime America: The World War II Home Front, by John W. Jeffries (Ivan R. Dee, 1996; Chicago)

Women at War: The Women of World War II — At Home, at Work, on the Front Line, by Brenda Ralph Lewis (Reader's Digest, 2002; New York)

World War II, Letters edited by Bill Adler (St. Martin's Press, 2002; New York)

You Learn by Living, by Eleanor Roosevelt (Westminster John Knox Press, 1960; Kentucky)

WEBSITES

American Red Cross at RedCross.org

Department of Veterans Affairs at VA.gov

Library of Congress at LOC.gov

National Archives at Archives.gov

National Park Service at NPS.gov

Naval History and Heritage Command at History.Navy.mil

New England Historical Society at NewEnglandHistoricalSociety.com

Oregon Secretary of State at SOS.Oregon.gov

Pew Research Center at Journalism.org

U.S. Army Center of Military History at History.Army.mil

U.S. Bureau of Labor Statistics at BLS.gov

U.S. Census Bureau at Census.gov

U.S. Department of Defense at Defense.gov

U.S. Government Office of War Information at Guides.LOC.gov